POLITICS AND STATE IN THE THIRD WORLD

Macmillan International College Editions (MICE) will bring to university, college, professional and school students in developing countries low cost but authoritative books covering the history and cultures of the Third World, and the special aspects of its scientific, technical, social and economic development. In other parts of the world MICE will satisfy the growing demand for information about the developing countries. The MICE programme contains many distinguished series in a wide range of disciplines, some titles being regionally biassed, others being more international. Library editions will usually be published simultaneously with the low cost paperback editions. For full details of the MICE list, please contact the publishers.

POLITICS AND STATE
IN THE
THIRD WORLD

edited by

HARRY GOULBOURNE

First published 1979 by
THE MACMILLAN PRESS LTD
London and Basingstoke
Associated companies in Delhi Dublin
Hong Kong Johannesburg Lagos Melbourne

Printed in Hong Kong

British Library Cataloguing in Publication Data

Politics and state in the third world.
1. Underdeveloped areas – Politics and government –
Addresses, essays, lectures
I. Goulbourne, Harry
320.9′172′4   JF60

ISBN 0–333–26422–3
ISBN 0–333–26423–1 Pbk

Contents

Preface

Although a growing body of radical and marxist literature on the third world is becoming available to students and the interested public it is still the case that some of the most interesting and insightful papers on developments in these areas are usually to be found in specialised and academic journals which are not always easily available. It is also the case that many of the collections in circulation are too often of a general nature. With regards to politics and the state in third-world countries, far too frequently they are treated just as aspects of other, albeit interesting, developments. One result of this is the blurring of the importance of the state and politics in these formations in the collections that exist. Of course, this situation reflects, to a large degree, the fact that there is relatively little theorisation of politics and the state in these societies. Part of the aim of the book, therefore, is to make available some of the more important radical and marxist speeches and writings on the third world which will reflect both the strengths and the weaknesses of the present state of analysis of developments in these formations.

The general aim of the book, however, is to expose students to an initial radical and marxist orientation towards the study of politics and state in the third world. The papers included were written in a polemical vein and should therefore, hopefully, stimulate further discussion and interest in the subjects treated. An 'orientation' may denote certain agreements but these do not negate or limit disagreements as the pieces themselves demonstrate. The extracts are rather lengthy because it is the view that this is more satisfying for those who wish to understand the issues involved, than short, although plentiful, extracts would be. For those who wish to follow through certain points which may be treated inadequately in the extracts, it is hoped that the bibliography at the end of the text will be useful.

The effort does not represent, then, an exhaustive treatment of politics and state in third-world countries. In the first place the selection is not representative of the whole of the region commonly designated the 'third world'. Although there are pieces on Asia, Latin America and the Caribbean, the emphasis is on the African experience. Also there is a bias towards those third-world countries which are not orientated towards revolutionary socialism. For example, there is nothing specifically on the newly liberated countries of Mozambique, Angola, Guinea-Bissau in Africa or on Cuba and Indo-China, all of which are important parts of the third world and regard themselves as such. Rather, the bias is towards the 'backward' or 'underdeveloped' capitalist formations in the third world which are intricately woven into the world capitalist system of production and exchange.

These are states which have had their political independence for some time and where definite structures have emerged and are well established. To have included pieces on other sections of the third world would have involved a much longer book and the pieces themselves would have been quite different since the directions in which some of these states are going are not yet clear. Such inclusion would pose more difficult questions about politics and state, modes of production and the problems of transition from one mode to another, than this modest selection is capable of handling.

Although the contents of the pieces are very closely interrelated it has been convenient, from an organisational point of view, to establish somewhat arbitrary distinctions between them. These distinctions serve another purpose also: the four sections into which the text is divided help to emphasise the different aspects of political patterns and developments in the countries under consideration.

To be more precise: the papers in Section 2 are concerned with the problem of characterising the state in particular third-world countries; Section 3 contains papers which attempt to specify some of the structures in, and relationships between, the state and society—thus embracing class struggle and the institutions and activities of the state. The final Section is markedly different from the rest, because it deals with some general problems of the third world, in the words of some of the most outspoken leaders of the third world itself. These problems arise out of the contradictions inherent in the world capitalist system and are of particular concern to capitalist third-world countries because of the subordinate role they are forced to play in the international division of labour. These sections are preceded by short introductory notes to the essays and therefore it is not necessary to say any more about them here.

Section 1 however, is not preceded by an introductory note since it is itself the Introduction to the selection as a whole. A word about the pieces in this Section is necessary therefore because they are not obvious. The first reading is a brief excerpt from Marx's well-known 'Preface' to *A Contribution to the Critique of Political Economy* (1859), which focusses sharply on the nature of the relationship between the economic 'base' of society and the political and ideological 'superstructure' which arises out of the former. This is followed by a more lengthy extract from a letter from Engels to Schmidt (1890) in which Engels attempts to elucidate and elaborate upon some of the problems involved in the metaphor 'base'/'superstructure'. Given the brevity and terseness of these passages, their insertion is liable to cause some confusion for the newcomer to Marx. For example, at a first reading Marx would appear to be saying that it is the contradictions inherent in the forces of production (implements of labour, technology) which provide the impetus for social change. Yet, a second and more careful reading of Marx—which involves more than this short extract—reveals that for him it is the contradictions in the relations of production (the capital–labour relation in capitalist society) which provide this impetus. This risk, however, of an oversimplified understanding of Marx from these brief extracts serves to emphasise the introductory nature of the book as a whole.

With respect to the specificity of politics and the state, the extracts do highlight the relationship, in general terms, between 'base' and 'superstructure' in a manner that is very suggestive and provocative when applied to third-world contexts. In particular, the stress that Engels places on the possible effects of the political 'superstructure' upon the economic 'base' reveals not only a dialectical relationship between 'economic' forms and ideological and political ones, but also the fact that the state in capitalist society must be understood as deriving its forms and functions from the contradictions at the level of the economic 'base'.

Too often unfortunately a statement of this kind is made as mere lip-service to a fundamental marxist tenet. Quite clearly, it is to be regarded only as a starting-point towards specifying the nature of the relationship that obtains in different socio-historical contexts—precisely the point that Engels felt bound to make repeatedly to young marxists in the 1890s. However, and this is unfortunate, the introductory nature of the book does not permit the inclusion of some of the really excellent work being done on the specificities of economic forms in third-world countries and the ways in which these are linked to the dominant world capitalist system of production and exchange. Dissatisfaction with the rather too simplistic 'centre'/'periphery' model of Gundar Frank is leading to a number of attempts to outline more clearly the forms that capitalism has taken in the third world. While for some writers the economies in these countries are rampantly capitalist, for others there are any number of modes of production co-existing or being held together by a predominant capitalist system. Thus, the terms such as 'merchant capital', 'dependent capital', 'peripheral capitalism', etc., contain arguments around the important question of how to characterise modes of production that are found in the third world and how these come to form part(s) of a world system. (A good critical description of the various attempts to grapple with this problem is to be found in a recent article by A. Foster-Carter in *New Left Review*, January/February 1978.) The fact that the book does not take explicit account of these debates does not mean that there is a lack of awareness of the problem with which they are concerned. The point of the selection is not to provide an all-embracing text in the fashion of the class textbook, but to focus upon a specific aspect of a greater whole.

The third piece, 'Some Problems of Analysis of the Political in Backward Capitalist Social Formations', attempts to depict the nature of the literature on the specificity of politics and state in the third world and to link this to the current debate around the state in advanced capitalism. The intention is that it should serve to introduce some of the problems dealt with in more detail in the sections that follow.

Finally, a word of warning: the terms 'the third world', 'the underdeveloped countries', 'the backward areas', 'transitional societies'; 'the post-colonial state', 'the neo-colonial state', etc., are used very loosely and are largely ideological in their usage and therefore can be taken to express attitudes of one kind or another rather than having any precise analytical value. In

various parts of the book these terms may be used interchange-
ably and therefore cannot be taken to describe adequately the
current world situation. This does not mean, fortunately, that
this situation will remain unchanged, particularly in view of the
current general and theoretical interest in the developments
taking place in the 'third world'.

Acknowledgements

The author and publishers wish to thank the following who have kindly given permission for the use of copyright material:

African Business, for articles 'The New International Economic Order' in *African Development*, Vol. 1, No. 1, 1976 and 'Ideology and Development in Guinea' in *African Development*, Vol. 11, No. 1, 1977;

Andre Deutsch Ltd. and Howard University Press for a chapter from *The Politics of Change: A Jamaican Testament*;

Heinemann Educational Books Ltd. and Monthly Review Press for an extract from *Politics and Class Formation in Uganda* by Mamood Mamdani;

Jamaica Publishing House Ltd. for the article by Donald J. Harris in *Essays on Power and Change in Jamaica* by Dr. Carl Stone and Dr. Aggrey Brown;

Lawrence & Wishart Ltd. for extracts from *Selected Works* (1969) and *Selected Correspondence* (1975) by K. Marx and F. Engels;

Longman Group Ltd. for an extract from *The Development of an African Working Class: Studies in Class Formation and Action* by R. Sandbrook and R. Cohen;

The Merlin Press Ltd. for an article in *The Socialist Register 1974* by R. Miliband and J. Saville;

J. K. Nyerere for an extract from his speech at Ibadan University November 1976;

Tanzania Publishing House for an extract 'The Post-Mwongozo Proletarian Struggles in Tanzania' from *The Class Struggles in Tanzania* (1975) by Issa G. Shivji;

United Nations for an extract from an Address to a Conference by Samora Machel later published in *Decolonization*, No. 8, July 1977.

Every effort has been made to trace all the copyright holders but if any have been inadvertently overlooked the publishers will be pleased to make the necessary arrangement at the first opportunity.

ONE:

Introduction

1 KARL MARX

The relationship between the economic base and the political and ideological superstructures[†]

. . . . My investigation [into 'politico–economic' questions–ed.] led to the result that legal relations as well as forms of state are to be grasped neither from themselves nor from the so-called general development of the human mind, but rather have their roots in the material conditions of life, the sum total of which Hegel, following the example of the Englishmen and Frenchmen of the eighteenth century, combines under the name of 'civil society', that, however, the anatomy of civil society is to be sought in political economy. . . . The general result at which I arrived and which, once won, served as a guiding thread for my studies, can be briefly formulated as follows: In the social production of their life, men enter into definite relations that are indispensable and independent of their will, relations of production which correspond to a definite stage of development of their material productive forces. The sum total of these relations of production constitutes the economic structure of society, the real foundation, on which rises a legal and political superstructure and to which correspond definite forms of social consciousness. The mode of production of material life conditions the social, political and intellectual life process in general. It is not the consciousness of men that determines their being, but, on the contrary, their social being that determines their consciousness. At a certain stage of their development, the material productive forces of society come in conflict with the existing relations of production, or—what is but a legal expression for the same thing—with the property

† Extract from 'Preface', *A Contribution to the Critique of Political Economy*, in K. Marx and F. Engels, *Selected Works* (Progress Publishers, 1969), vol. I, pp. 503–4—ed.

relations within which they have been at work hitherto. From forms of development of the productive forces these relations turn into their fetters. Then begins an epoch of social revolution. With the change of the economic foundation the entire immense superstructure is more or less rapidly transformed. In considering such transformations a distinction should always be made between the material transformation of the economic conditions of production, which can be determined with the precision of natural science, and the legal, political, religious, aesthetic or philosophic—in short, ideological forms in which men become conscious of this conflict and fight it out. Just as our opinion of an individual is not based on what he thinks of himself, so can we not judge of such a period of transformation by its own consciousness; on the contrary, this consciousness must be explained rather from the contradictions of material life, from the existing conflict between the social productive forces and the relations of production. No social order ever perishes before all the productive forces for which there is room in it have developed; and new, higher relations of production never appear before the material conditions of their existence have matured in the womb of the old society itself. Therefore mankind always sets itself only such tasks as it can solve; since, looking at the matter more closely, it will always be found that the task itself arises only when the material conditions for its solution already exist or are at least in the process of formation. In broad outlines Asiatic, ancient, feudal, and modern bourgeois modes of production can be designated as progressive epochs in the economic formation of society. The bourgeois relations of production are the last antagonistic form of the social process of production— antagonistic not in the sense of individual antagonism, but one arising from the social conditions of life of the individuals; at the same time the productive forces developing in the womb of bourgeois society create the material conditions for the solution of that antagonism. This social formation brings, therefore, the prehistory of human society to a close.

2 F. ENGELS

Some problems of the relationship between 'base' and 'superstructure'[†]

Dear Schmidt,

. . . . Economic, political and other reflections are just like [reflections] in the human eye: they pass through a convex lens and therefore appear upside down, standing on their heads. But the nervous apparatus to put them on their feet again in our imagination is lacking. The money market man sees the movement of industry and of the world market only in the inverted reflection of the money and stock market and thus effect becomes cause to him. I noticed that already in the forties in Manchester: the London stock exchange reports were utterly useless for understanding the course of industry and its periodical maxima and minima because these gentlemen tried to explain everything by crises on the money market, which were after all usually only symptoms. . . .

Where there is division of labour on a social scale the separate labour processes become independent of each other. In the last instance production is the decisive factor. But as soon as trade in products becomes independent of production proper, it has a movement of its own, which, although by and large governed by that of production, nevertheless in particulars and within this general dependence again follows laws of its own inherent in the nature of this new factor; this movement has phases of its own and in its turn reacts on the movement of production. . . .

So it is, too, with the money market. As soon as trade in money becomes separate from trade in commodities it has—under

[†] Extract from letter to Conrad Schmidt in K. Marx and F. Engels, *Selected Correspondence*.

definite conditions determined by production and commodity trade and within these limits—a development of its own, specific laws determined by its own nature and distinct phases. Add to this the fact that money trade, developing further, comes to include trade in securities and that these securities are not only government papers but also industrial and transport stocks, consequently money trade gains direct control over a portion of the production by which it is on the whole itself controlled, thus the repercussions of money trading on production become still stronger and more complicated. The money-dealers become owners of railways, mines, iron works, etc. These means of production take on a double aspect: their operation is governed sometimes by the interests of direct production, sometimes however also by the requirements of the shareholders, in so far as they are money-dealers. . . .

With these few indications of my conception of the relation of production to commodity trade and of both to money trade, I have actually answered your questions about 'historical materialism' generally. The thing is easiest to grasp from the point of view of the division of labour. Society gives rise to certain common functions which it cannot dispense with. The persons appointed for this purpose form a new branch of the division of labour *within society*. This gives them particular interests, distinct, too, from the interests of their mandators; they make themselves independent of the latter and—the state is in being. And now things proceed in a way similar to that in commodity trade and later in money trade: the new independent power, while having in the main to follow the movement of production, reacts in its turn, by virtue of its inherent relative independence—that is, the relative independence once transferred to it and gradually further developed—upon the conditions and course of production. It is the interaction of two unequal forces: on the one hand, the economic movement, on the other, the new political power, which strives for as much independence as possible, and which, having once been set up, is endowed with a movement of its own. On the whole, the economic movement prevails, but it has also to endure reactions from the political movement which it itself set up and endowed with relative independence, from the movement of the state power, on the one hand, and of the opposition simultaneously engendered, on the other. Just as the movement of the industrial market is, in the main and with the reservations already indicated, reflected in the money market and, of course, in *inverted* form, so the struggle between the classes already existing and fighting with one another is reflected in the struggle between government and opposition, but likewise in inverted form, no longer directly but indirectly, not as a class struggle but as a fight for political principles, and it is so distorted that it has taken us thousands of years to get to the bottom of it.

The retroaction of the state power upon economic development can be of three kinds: it can proceed in the same direction, and then things move more rapidly; it can move in the opposite direction, in which case nowadays it [the state] will go to pieces in the long run in every great people; or it can prevent the economic development from proceeding along certain lines, and prescribe other lines. This case ultimately reduces itself to one of the two previous ones. But it is obvious that in cases two·and three the political power can do great damage to the economic development and cause extensive waste of energy and material.

Then there is also the case of the conquest and brutal destruction of economic resources, as a result of which, in certain circumstances, the entire economic development in a particular locality or in a country could be ruined in former times. Nowadays such a case usually has the opposite effect, at least with great peoples: in the long run the vanquished often gains more economically, politically and morally than the victor.

Similarly with law. As soon as the new division of labour which creates professional lawyers becomes necessary, another new and independent sphere is opened up which, for all its general dependence on production and trade, has also a specific capacity for reacting upon these spheres. In a modern state, law must not only correspond to the general economic condition and be its expression, but must also be an *internally coherent* expression which does not, owing to internal conflicts, contradict itself. And in order to achieve this, the faithful reflection of economic conditions suffers increasingly. All the more so the more rarely it happens that a code of law is the blunt, unmitigated, unadulterated expression of the domination of a class—this in itself would offend the 'conception of right'. Even in the *Code Napoléon* the pure, consistent conception of right held by the revolutionary bourgeoisie of 1792–96 is already adulterated in many ways, and, in so far as it is embodied in the Code, has daily to undergo all sorts of attenuations owing to the rising power of the proletariat. This does not prevent the *Code Napoléon* from being the statute book which serves as the basis of every new code of law in every part of the world. Thus to a great extent the course of the 'development of law' simply consists in first attempting to eliminate contradictions which arise from the direct translation of economic relations into legal principles, and to establish a harmonious system of law, and then in the repeated breaches made in this system by the influence and compulsion of further economic development, which involves it in further contradictions. (I am speaking here for the moment only of civil law.)

The reflection of economic relations in the form of legal principles is likewise bound to be inverted: it goes on without the person who is acting being conscious of it; the jurist imagines he is operating with *a priori* propositions, whereas they are really only economic reflections; everything is therefore upside down. And it seems to me obvious that this inversion, which, so long as it remains unrecognised, forms what we call *ideological outlook*, influences in its turn the economic basis and may, within certain limits, modify it. The basis of the right of inheritance is an economic one, provided the level of development of the family is the same. It would, nevertheless, be difficult to prove, for instance, that the absolute liberty of the testator in England and the severe and very detailed restrictions imposed upon him in France are due to economic causes alone. But in their turn they exert a very considerable effect on the economic sphere, because they influence the distribution of property.

As to the realms of ideology which soar still higher in the air—religion, philosophy, etc.—these have a prehistoric stock, found already in existence by and taken over in the historical period, of what we should today call nonsense. These various false conceptions of nature, of man's own being, of spirits, magic forces, etc., have for the most part only a negative economic factor as their basis; the low economic development of the prehistoric period is supplemented and also partially conditioned and even caused by the false conceptions of nature. And even though economic necessity was the main driving force of the increasing knowledge of nature and has become ever more so, yet it would be pedantic to try and find economic causes for all this primitive nonsense. The history of science is the history of the gradual clearing away of this nonsense or rather of its replacement by fresh but less absurd nonsense. The people who attend to this belong in their turn to special spheres in the division of labour and they think that they are working in an independent field. And to the extent that they form an independent group within the social division of labour, their output, including their errors, exerts in its turn an effect upon the whole development of society, and even on its economic development. But all the same they themselves are in turn under the predominant influence of economic development. In philosophy, for instance, this can be most readily proved true for the bourgeois period. Hobbes was the first modern materialist (in the sense of the eighteenth century) but he was an absolutist at a time when absolute monarchy was in its heyday throughout Europe and began the battle against the people in England. Locke was in religion and in politics the child of the class compromise of 1688. The English deists and their consistent followers, the French materialists, were the true philosophers of the bourgeoisie, the French even of the bourgeois revolution. The German philistinism runs through German philosophy from Kant to Hegel, sometimes in a positive and sometimes negative way. But the precondition of the philosophy of each epoch regarded as a distinct sphere in the division of labour is a definite body of thought which is handed down to it by its predecessors, and which is also its starting point. And that is why economically backward countries can still play first fiddle in philosophy: France in the eighteenth century as compared with England, on whose philosophy the French based themselves, and later Germany as compared with both. But both in France and in Germany philosophy and the general blossoming of literature at that time were the result of an economic revival. The ultimate supremacy of economic development is for me an established fact in these spheres too, but it operates within the terms laid down by the particular sphere itself: in philosophy, for instance, by the action of economic influences (which in their turn generally operate only in their political, etc., make-up) upon the existing philosophic material which has been handed down by predecessors. Here economy creates nothing anew, but it determines the way in which the body of thought found in existence is altered and further developed, and that too for the most part indirectly, for it is the political, legal and moral reflexes which exert the greatest direct influence on philosophy. . . .

Hence if Barth* alleges that we altogether deny that the political, etc., reflections of the economic movement in their turn exert any effect upon the movement itself, he is simply tilting at windmills. He should only look at Marx's *Eighteenth Brumaire*, which deals almost exclusively with the *particular* part played by political struggles and events, of course within their *general* dependence upon economic conditions. Or *Kapital*, the section on the working day, for instance, where legislation, which is surely a political act, has such a drastic effect. Or the section on the history of the bourgeoisie. And why do we fight for the political dictatorship of the proletariat if political power is economically impotent? Force (that is, state power) is also an economic power!

---

* Reference to the opponent of Marxism, P. Barth.—ed.

3 HARRY GOULBOURNE

Some problems of analysis of the political in backward capitalist social formations

Introduction

There is currently a very lively and serious discussion over the question of the development of the 'backward' (variously referred to as the 'developing' or 'underdeveloped') areas of Latin America, Asia and Africa.[1] Central to this discussion is whether the increasing penetration by the capitalist mode of production is such that these areas may become industrialised so as to be regarded as 'developed' or whether the presence of foreign capital in these countries simply perpetuates an abiding underdevelopment. This question is often considered in terms of the capability or incapability of capitalism to transform these formations from their backwardness. Considerable emphasis is also placed upon the degree of autonomy, or expressed another way, the degree of dependence that the capitalist or dominant classes indigenous to the backward areas, enjoy or suffer from in their relationship with international capital. There is a recognition of the importance of the state and politics in these processes and although the issues often lead to a discussion of aspects of these factors, there is still no systematic theoretical discussion of the specificity of the political (politics and state) in these formations. In the Introduction to a book of this kind it may therefore be useful to indicate some of the problems involved in the important undertaking of elaborating a theory of Politics and State—an undertaking which will have to be tackled more seriously than hitherto.

The problem of conceptualisation

Of course, the discussion regarding development is not new. What is new and refreshing is that there is an attempt underway to transcend the analytical frameworks of both the orthodox 'development' school and that of the 'underdevelopment' school whose thrust constituted a radical critique of the former. It is not the aim here to follow through this discussion partly because the question of development has recently received more competent treatment[2] than could possibly be done here and partly because it is not necessary for the purpose at hand. It is nonetheless useful to indicate the problem involved in conceptualising the notion of development.

Although there have been many theories of development there are a number of factors which are common to all of them. Of crucial importance to behavioural social scientists is the distinction that they have made between the 'traditional' and the 'modern': in one form or another they have tended to see development in terms of the movement of socio–economic and political changes from 'traditional' to 'modern' structures.[3] Stages of 'growth', or 'modernisation' or 'development' could therefore be pin-pointed and compared. Some analysts therefore spoke of 'transitional' societies rather than about 'development'.[4]

For some of the more perceptive of this school the movement from the 'traditional' to the 'modern' is not necessarily an uninterrupted march. There are likely to be 'break-downs' or 'decay'.[4] Perhaps the most thoughtful of these analysts, however, were those who recognised that in most cases both the 'traditional' and the 'modern' exist in 'mixed' forms. Perhaps the best example of this is Riggs's 'prismatic' society in which both 'traditionality' and 'modernity' are said to be integrated.[5] Nonetheless, generally speaking, the concept of development has been defined by this school in terms of the increasing differentiation and integration of structures, functions and roles.[6]

A crucial assumption in this type of analysis has been the view that the backward areas have remained in this condition because they have failed to move from this state of backwardness, from which the developed world has moved towards modernity. There is a tautology in the argument which of course explains nothing—these areas are backward because they are backward—and the tautology is avoided only by identifying tradition as the fount of backwardness. For development to occur therefore it is important to identify specific aspects of tradition-alism and tradition which act as so many obstacles to change.[7] Moreover, these obstacles have not been removed so far because of a profound absence of contact between 'modern' and 'tradi-tional' societies. In this view of development, subsequently, there is seen to exist an essential dualism—between the 'modern' and the 'traditional'—which expresses itself at the social, political and economic levels.

It was precisely these assumptions that the underdevelopment 'theories' took to task. The protagonists led by A. G. Frank in Latin America (where this school developed) and Samir Amin in Africa (where the theory probably has been most widely and seriously treated) contended that far from there being an absence of contact between the 'developed' and the 'underdeveloped' worlds, it has been, on the contrary, the very close contacts between them that has led to the 'development of underdevelop-ment' in these areas.[8] Developed capitalist structures, or 'centres' and underdeveloped 'satellites' or 'peripheries' are therefore two sides of the same coin: the one could not exist without the other; they are complementary pieces of a whole structure. The notion of movement from the 'traditional' to the 'modern' runs counter to the essential question. Far from there being patterns or 'stages' of development there are only patterns of 'underdevelopment', or at best, the 'development of underdevelopment'.

The relationship that is perceived to exist between 'centre' and 'periphery' (and which was wholly lacking in the development thesis) is that of nations 'exploiting' each other and therefore a condition of domination and subordination or dependence obtains.[9] The development of some countries has been at the expense of others and this has taken and is taking place through the mechanisms of unequal exchange in trading of primary and manufactured goods.[10] The concept of development for this school can have no meaning because the underdeveloped countries cannot hope to reverse the process by themselves becoming developed—meaning, economically independent and self-sustaining—within the capitalist mode of production. Socialism—broadly and variously defined—is then offered by some theorists as the only way out of the dependence[11] whilst at least one prominent underdevelopment theorist has suggested that neither socialism nor any of the various 'isms' which he identifies with Europe and North America or the socialist countries, can pull those areas out of their persistent poverty and therefore calls for a new and relevant 'ism' (ideology).[12]

The current debate over development takes as its point of departure the fact that underdevelopment 'theory' has also failed to explain a persistent but not unchanging condition which it has itself gone a considerable way in describing. The *ideological* posture adopted by underdevelopment theorists that the backward areas cannot hope to become developed, is itself confining and limiting on attempts to explain changes that have occurred in these areas over the last two decades or so, or longer in the case of Latin America. The root of the problem may well lie in the very understanding of the concept of 'development' itself as Phillips in a recent paper has ably argued.[13] Development has not been defined in a way that may be empirically or theoretically challenged: that is, 'development' is understood as being the already known changes which capitalism has undergone and which are then taken as given, as constituting the 'real', 'meaningful' development. This, of course, amounts to a very uncritical acceptance of the cruder presentation of the movement of changes in the development argument. In other words, contradictions internal to capitalism and its disjunctions are not taken into account so as to recognise that there is 'no correct form of the development of the productive forces'.[14]

In a general sense then, development is best approached in terms of posing questions regarding the degree of the establishment of the capitalist mode of production, or attempts to transform modes of production, paying attention not only to the productive forces but more importantly to the relations of production. This obviously constitutes only a starting point but it is important to be clear about starting points if only to avoid incorporating assumptions from differing modes of thinking. With regard to 'political development' or 'political change' this is important, particularly since underdevelopment theory hardly concerned itself with the specificity of the political while orthodox development theory presented a much more thoughtful but over-politicised view of the political. Moreover it still remains for contemporary Marxism to develop a general theory of the capitalist state capable of explaining both developed as well as backward capitalist states.

The problem of specifying the political

The general crisis of capital which has the effect of calling the state more directly into the production process in order to guarantee accumulation and thereby strengthen the conditions of the state's own existence, and the corresponding rise in the consciousness of the direct producers are providing new conditions for the development of Marxist political theory. These conditions require that we come to know more clearly the specificity of the capitalist state and the various forms it develops, in correspondence with changes at the economic level in conjunction with its own internal autonomy. In recent years therefore the increasing interest in the capitalist state, particularly in Europe, has made it possible to avoid starting a discussion with the usual comment of not very long ago that apart from the classic works of Marx, Engels, Lenin and Gramsci (who provided only scattered elements for a theory of the state) there is no attempt to fashion a Marxist political theory.

Starting with Nicos Poulantzas's *Pouvoir Politique et Classes Sociales*[15] in 1968 and Miliband's *The State in Capitalist Society*[16] the following year, there ensued a series of exchanges between these writers with others joining in to develop what is now a sizeable body of literature on the state in capitalist formations.[17] This task was well overdue within Marxism and the ongoing work on the state in both developed and backward capitalist formations augers well for the future of a materialist analysis of the political. There are however, some dangers which must be avoided as all who are involved in this enterprise are careful to stress in their own ways, almost as a matter of faith. A Marxist analysis of the political must start in fact, and not merely as a slogan, from the contradictions inherent in capitalist production which provide the conditions for the specificity and forms of the capitalist state. Also, this will enable such an undertaking not only to steer clear of dogmatism within Marxism but also of bourgeois social science, which does not go beyond the appearances of the state in its analysis. In the case of backward capitalist formations the tendency to reduce the political to a mere mechanical response to economic developments is a particular danger because of the often obvious and unconcealed connection between economy and state. The general problem of specifying the political may be elaborated by looking briefly at some of the ways in which politics and the state have been perceived by development and under-development analysts and at the attempt to fashion a Marxist approach to this question.[18]

The Underdevelopment school

The first point to note is that whilst the radical critique of the orthodox development thesis correctly pointed out some of the failings of that school, and most clearly that the condition of 'underdevelopment' is itself a development within the capitalist mode of production, it did not proceed to a delineation of the specificity of the political in any systematic fashion. This has been so despite the fact that underdevelopment theorists nearly always wrote with an implied or explicit political aim in view.[19]

One of the reasons for this failure would appear to be the fact that the radical critique of the development syndrome took place almost entirely upon an economic terrain. Concerned to show that underdevelopment had its roots in capitalist development, underdevelopment theorists (correctly) concentrated on the economic as the best level of a formation to demonstrate their point. It would seem however, that the economic level was so conceived of that the political was perceived as an automatic and therefore unproblematic factor of the economic conditions of underdevelopment. Generally, there was consequently little or no need to hypothesise so as to generate questions about the relationship between the political and the economic levels of backward capitalist formations. Where the question of politics and state was seriously broached in the heyday of underdevelopment theory the problem generally became one of explaining the 'deviation' from a supposedly 'normal' political path, thereby reproducing assumptions of the development school. Thus, although these analysts sought to adopt a political economy approach to the object of their enquiries, the stress was almost entirely on the 'economy' and very little on the 'political', which invariably both reflected and perpetuated a type of economic reductionism.

Examination of the specificity of the political may not have helped directly to show that underdevelopment is the cost of capitalist penetration. Indeed, enquiry into the relative autonomy of the political from the economy and the effects of the political upon the economy in most neo-colonial formations may have had the effect of blunting the thrust of the radical critique of development theory. The probability of this occuring rests upon the contradictory position of the state which is particularly glaring in third-world countries: the capitalist state continues to play its classic role of mediation whilst at the same time becoming more and more involved in the process of production. The changing forms and function of the capitalist state in these conditions tend to make the state the focal point for the expression of the contradictions between conflicting capitals on the one hand, and on the other hand, the contradictions between capital and labour. Analysis of politics and state therefore, may have introduced problems about the wide range of politics and state forms found in the third world and this would have taken underdevelopment theorists beyond their concern with underdevelopment.

There is yet another reason why the political does not receive serious treatment in underdevelopment theory. The radical critique of development theory rests largely upon a moral injunction of capitalism, or, at any rate, the critique levelled at capitalism is a moral one. Consequently, underdevelopment theory in most cases where it addresses itself to the political does so from the perspective of capitalism's supposed failure to develop the backward areas and a humanistic political creed is juxtaposed with the apparently heartless political development thesis. An example of this is Johnson and Ocompo's piece on 'political development' which argues, correctly, on the one hand, that political development must be seen as part of the development of class society and on the other hand argues, erroneously, that political development is about, or ought to be about, the liberation of man.[20]

Thus, a decade or more after the appearance of radical underdevelopment theory there is still no adequate theoretical structure in which analysis of the political in backward or underdeveloped formations may be carried out. As a matter of fact underdevelopment theory did not elaborate a coherent political theory comparable to that postulated by the development theorists let alone pressing beyond the perimeters of that school. There is therefore a need to formulate anew the question of the political in the formations of the so-called third world. First, however, this necessitates a consideration of the relatively coherent presentation of the political in the orthodox development literature.

The Development school

One of the most serious implications of the success of behaviourism in political science has been the loss of the specificity of the political or, what constitutes the legitimate field of political analysis. In Parsonian political sociology what is distinct about the political is lost in the social functions of integration and adaptation of the wider social system. For Lasswell and Kaplan the political is reduced to any act 'performed in power perspective'.[21] In other words the attempt to escape from the Aristotelean definition of the political as being 'the most sovereign and exclusive association' in a given community, has resulted in the widening of the concept of the political so that established political science is presently still at a loss in specifying the object of its investigation.[22] The problem of marking-off the area of the political from other areas of social life became a severe handicap for those who aspired to arrive at 'a common set of categories' with which to compare political systems in the 'developing areas'.

It became necessary therefore for orthodox development theorists to 'experiment with the conceptual vocabulary of political science'[23] as Almond expressed in 1960, in order to overcome both the narrow legal and constitutional mould of the late nineteenth-century political analysts and also the too general and indistinct Parsonian definition. In other words, political analysts concerned with political development became anxious to avoid Weber's influential definition of the political (which involved the state's ability to monopolise force over a given territory) without entirely abandoning it.

To achieve these ends Almond and his colleagues (Powell, Pye, Coleman, Verba, et al) adopted Easton's systems model of the political, a broadened version of Weber's definition of the state and the functionalism of the anthropologists Malinowski and Radcliffe-Brown. The result was the construction of a structural–functionalist model of the political, with the stress being placed very much upon *functions* rather than *structures* in the belief that structures tell very little about actual life situations.

For the purposes at hand what is important is that the functionalists were able to convince themselves and some others that they had arrived at the construction of a 'probabilistic theory of the polity' and moreover, that different political systems could be explained by their 'capacities, conversion functions and systems maintenance and adaptation of functions'.[24] This also defined political development because for them this process entails being able to measure degrees of differentiation (implying specialisation) and secularisation (implying Weber's increasing rationality). Apart from this general approach to the subject these analysts found it of pre-eminent importance also to outline what for them constituted the political.

In the first major attempt to construct a 'common set of categories' necessary for analysing the political in the 'developing areas' Almond's Comparative Politics school at Princeton University defined the political as being the 'legitimate, order–maintaining or transforming system in the society'.[25] In this view the political system is constituted by 'the political' and by 'politics' and it is the use of legitimate force which gives the political system 'its special quality and salience and its coherence as a system'.[26] The political system then is:

that system of interactions to be found in all independent societies which performs the functions of integration and adaptation (both internally and externally vis-a-vis other societies) by means of the employment, or threat of employment, of more or less physical force.[27]

The notion of system explicates certain 'particular set of properties to these interactions'[28] which include 'comprehensiveness', 'interdependence' and the existence of 'boundaries'. The 'inputs' (political socialisation and recruitment, interest articulation and aggregation and political communication) and the 'outputs' (rule–making, rule–application and rule–adjudication) which 'affect the use or the threat of the use of physical coercion',[29] denote the 'comprehensiveness' of the system. Included in these specifications are the juridico–political institutions such as parliament, the executive, the bureaucracy, political parties, etc., and also significantly, *'all the structures in their political aspects'* (emphasis added).[30] Apart from this apparent lapse into generalities a definite view of the political emerges in this formulation.

This allows Almond and his colleagues to reject the usual distinction made by some anthropologists and Marxists between conditions of statelessness and those with state structures.[31] Effects that the sub-systems have on each other reflect an essential interdependence between parts of the whole. The notion of system itself is important in delimiting the area of the political for its existence implies that there are boundaries; that is 'there are points where other systems end and the political system begins',[32] although these boundaries differ from one society to another.

Posing the problem of the political in this manner led this school to believe that they were preparing the ground for 'a unified theory of politics'. More importantly, the formulation enabled these analysts to specify what are for them the functions of the political system in the process of development as well as specifying the terrain of the political. There are then the conversion functions (of interest articulation/aggregation, political communication, rule–making, rule–application and rule–adjudication); the capabilities of the system to cope with 'its environment'; the question of how a system maintains or adapts to 'pressures for change in the long run' (systems maintenance and adaptation of functions). Armed with these theoretical tools the members of the Princeton group felt confident that they could compare and supply some answers to questions from any and all types of political systems, particularly those of the 'developing areas'.

Apart from the criticism of the underdevelopment theorists this formulation has been criticised in terms of the model itself. In spite of its sometimes cautious qualifications (such as 'breakdowns', 'atrophy' and the recognition that problems of development in the newly independent states may have to be tackled cumulatively) its conservatism, its ideological posture, etc., have been attacked and are well documented so that repetition here would border on the banal.[33] It may not be amiss however, to mention two points here.

First, the ahistorical view of change inherent in the formulation constitutes a serious drawback. The notion of politics which informs the whole formulation is that politics is essentially the same in all social formations and what may differ is the degree of accumulated problems or loads that a particular system has to face at definite points. Since the aim is to pin-point features of political life that are common to all societies from the simplest to the most complex forms, the historical dimensions of politics is ignored. There is little appreciation of the periodisation[34] of political development and subsequently a teleological view of the political (whereby the final outcome of a process is seen as a foregone conclusion by virtue of identifying the process itself) is upheld.

Second, changes in society are not related to any concept of modes of production which further accentuates the problem of a lack of periodisation. Although socio–economic changes are recognised as occurring, the relationship between the political and these structures are left vague and unspecified. In Pye's treatment of the question, for example, where there is some sensitivity to the relationship between these factors, only a recognition is registered. 'The argument can be advanced,' Pye willingly admits, 'that it is unnecessary and inappropriate to try to isolate too completely political development from other forms of development.'[35] What this relationship may be however is left to the imagination.

Similarly, there is a conspicuous lack of elaboration regarding the place of social classes in the development process. In the formulation under consideration classes are merely located, along with other important factors as ideology, within the concept of 'political culture'—a concept which covers: 'attitudes, beliefs, values and skills which are current in an entire population as well as those specific propensities and patterns which may be found within separate parts of the population'.[36] Sometimes classes appear alongside religious and ethnic communities, status groups, etc., as a 'sub-culture', thus conflating the question of the relationship between social classes and political power with those of ethnicity, religion, ideology, culture and so forth. The importance of social classes as a crucial factor in development is entirely missed and it is notably not related to political dynamics. Subsequently, politics and the state appear to exist without a socio–economic base thus giving the false impression that the political is independent from these forces. It is at this point that it is important to return to these questions from a materialist perspective.

Marxism and the political

In this regard the work of Nicos Poulantzas is of particular importance for at least two reasons. First, he has attempted to construct a theory of politics and state as a distinct region of a social formation, stressing the independence or relative autonomy of this region from the economic whilst also stressing the crucial links between the two levels. Second, he attempts to situate this within the Marxist classics but develops a rigorous approach to them instead of repeating what had become mere shibboleths from the *Eighteenth Brumaire* or *State and Revolution* or the *Prison Notebooks*, etc. By posing the treatments of politics and the state in classic Marxism as a distinct problem worthy of consideration in its own right rather than simply taking it as a given right, Poulantzas has been able to move beyond a mere empirical reply to behavioural political science. If Marxist political theory is taking the offensive—that rightly belongs to Marxist political theory—against established social science then much of the credit is due to Poulantzas's attempt to mark out the region that constitutes the proper area for political analysis and his attempt to develop concepts appropriate to this task. Despite the weaknesses in the result there is much to gain from this attempt when tackling the problem of how to conceptualise politics and state in backward capitalist social formations.

The political, for Poulantzas, is constituted by the 'juridico–political superstructure of the state' and politics involves 'political class practices' (or the class struggle).[37] There is therefore a general theory of politics to be found, according to Poulantzas, in classic Marxism—a view that some would not readily agree with.

In his view the political occupies a specific place within a social formation, it involves specific social practices which arise from the structures of a social formation. These terms are not applied loosely. 'Specific level' conveys the idea that the political is located at that point where the contradictions of a formation are *reflected* and are *condensed* and it is from an analysis of these that it becomes possible to say that the class struggle°is the vehicle for social change. 'Political practice' denotes that practice which involves, following Althusser, the 'transformation of a definite object' which results 'in the production of something new';[38] that is to say that this type of 'practice' constitutes a 'break' with the elements of the object. The object in this instance involves an understanding of 'the present moment' which is in fact the 'specific object' of politics and constitutes the 'nodal' point where contradictions are condensed. This 'present moment' in turn constitutes the 'conjuncture' which features so prominently in Lenin's political thinking.[39] It is at this point too that the contradictions of a formation are capable of being deciphered. Most crucially, it is at this point that transformation takes place. In this sense therefore the political either transforms or maintains existing structures. Poulantzas recognised too the necessity to specify more clearly the relation between the political and 'political practice' and does so by pointing to the 'institutionalised power of the state' as being the objective of political practice. Central to Marxist political theory therefore is the view that the state constitutes its objective and Marxist political practice aims at its transformation.[40]

It is the functions of the state in a social formation that accounts for this. These may be summarised thus:

(i)   the state, by providing order within the social formation and thereby becoming the 'organisational principle' of the formation, provides the formation with its necessary cohesive factor; the state therefore maintains the unity of the social formation;

(ii) since the state provides the very structures within which the social contradictions are condensed the state is therefore the place where the 'index' of class domination must be deciphered and it is therefore here that transformation of structures takes place.

Poulantzas's work has been the subject of a great deal of discussion and criticism.[41] For some critics it is highly over-politicised, that is, for some his formulation has over-stressed the function of the political within a social formation and for others he has attributed to the political features which do not properly belong to that domain.[42] To some extent Poulantzas's own remarks regarding the 'modalities of the function of the state' would seem to bear out this point:

> Strictly speaking, there are no technico–economic, ideological or 'political' functions of the state: there is a global function of cohesion which is ascribed to it by its place and there are modalities of this function overdetermined by the specifically political modality.[43]

Poulantzas's use of Althusser's notion of the ideological state apparatuses (as distinct from the repressive ones) would appear to lay him bare to the charge of over-politicising the political since the notion of the ideological state apparatuses as first formulated by Althusser, tends to over-politicise the 'specifically political modality'.[44]

There may also be some grounds for giving qualified support to the criticism that Poulantzas does not place sufficient distance between himself and radical structural–functionalism. Certainly, there is a tendency to stress functions whilst only tacking-on rather limply the historical process to his analysis. This does not however provide support for the railing accusation by Clarke that Poulantzas's work amounts to a reproduction of radical bourgeois social science with a Marxist veneer.[45] The more correct point is rather that, as Laclau has argued, Poulantzas has not shown how bourgeois social science is defective and why therefore it should be superseded; his mistake has been to take these as given. Perhaps because of these a number of parallels between structural–functionalism and Poulantzas are evident. The point where this seems most clear is the formal status given the state by structural–functionalism and Poulantzas, but the similarity ends here. For, whereas for Poulantzas transformation or maintenance of structures which are carried out at the level of the state find their source in the class struggle, for Almond et al the notion of class struggle, which rests on the antagonism between capital and labour in capitalist society, is not even implied.

Third, although Poulantzas makes it clear from time to time that he is dealing with the state in capitalist society—a point he returns to repeatedly in his 1976 reply to Miliband and Laclau[46]—there are points in his discussion when it appears that he has in mind not only the capitalist mode of production but others also. This takes him very close to formulating a general theory of the political which may be applied in the same manner as that of the functionalists in any historical period. The point here is not that there are no general statements which may be made about the political irrespective of modes of production but that the specificity of the state in capitalist society (with which Poulantzas is concerned) cannot be elaborated so as to account for the state in all modes. This would be to return to the Hegelian notion of the universal ideal unfolding itself in human history—a notion that Althusser, Poulantzas and others have been concerned to distinguish themselves from.[47]

Yet another point of Poulantzas's formulation that is unsatisfactory is his exposition that the state reflects the unity of the social formation. The point is better made by saying that there is an ambiguity in the treatment of the relations between a 'formation' and the 'state' which is not resolved in his analysis. At times the state is presented as 'reflecting' this unity of the formation and at other times the state appears to 'constitute' this unity. For example, the state is said to maintain the external conditions of production (correctly) but it is not clear whether this role involves a 'constitution of unity' or only a 'reflection' of this unity. If the answer is that it is a 'reflection' then where does the unity of the formation take place? If it constitutes the unity, then there is a need to clarify and elaborate the patterns of this constitution. From the rest of the text it would appear that the state constitutes the unity of the formation rather than merely reflects this (for example, the notion of the power bloc which is used convincingly to explain the relations between social classes and political power) but this is implied, not explicated.

These remarks do not destroy the seminal nature of Poulantzas's work as first presented in his influential *Political Power and Social Classes* and his later essays, particularly the collection entitled *Classes in Contemporary Capitalism*.[48] The failure of the attempt of course must be taken seriously but the important service Poulantzas has served has been principally to reassert in a rigorous way and within a definite theoretical structure the object of Marxist political analysis, namely, politics and the state and the aim which is to transform these. These are not isolated nor are they indistinguishable from the determinant economic 'base' of a formation. Since we are concerned with the question of 'political development' a point of departure in Poulantzas's work may well be the stress he places upon the state as being the point where transformation of structures are effected or maintained depending on the outcome of particular struggles between classes. The paramount importance of transformation is, of course, a crucial question on the political agenda in third-world countries where the progressive forces are making headway. We are thus removed from the orthodox development theorists who can conceive of changes in the political depending on forces external to societies (such as war, etc.) and for whom 'political development' does not entail transformation but maintenance of stability and order. Nor does the objective of transformation entail any notion of the humanist persuasion of the liberation of 'man' in the abstract.

Some features of 'third-world' politics.

Being able to mark-off the region of the political and politics, the role of the state and its pivotal importance in a social formation constitute only the starting point for an understanding of political life, particularly in 'third-world' countries where developments have not followed the course of Europe and North America directly. It is important to apply theoretical insight to the concrete but since this is hardly the place to attempt this suffice it to indicate—implying a necessarily terse treatment of important questions—one or two glaring features of politics and the political in these formations.

Perhaps the most distinct feature of political life in third-world societies is the tendency for the political and politics to merge, or expressed another way, there is a noticeable tendency for the political to become preponderant over politics, thus hiding features of the class struggle, or making it to appear muted. This situation has been variously explained. For Pye there is an 'avoidance' of politics in these formations because of the monolithic demands of nationalism, the need for planned development, etc., which are used to suppress dissent and discussion, thus denying the existence of legitimate competition.[49] For Alavi (see Essay 4) the post-colonial state dispenses with the mediation of politics because the state is 'overdeveloped' and cannot be controlled by the indigenous capitalist class at the point of political independence. This allows aspects of the state itself (the military and/or the bureaucracy) to play the dominant part in the state and above social classes. In the view of some development theorists this situation is an instance of the tendency to drift towards authoritarianism.

It may be suggested, however, that this situation cannot be explained by reference solely to the state but more importantly to the class struggle itself. Implicit throughout has been the view that nearly all third-world countries have been penetrated by the capitalist mode of production. This does not mean that there are no backward features prevalent in these economies. On the contrary, their very backwardness lies partly in the retention of pre-capitalist modes of production by capitalism in a manner subordinate to itself and the fact that the very forms capital has taken in these formations are themselves backward. This condition of many third-world countries springs from their subordinate place in the international division of labour—whereby they produce raw materials (and increasingly manufactured goods in some cases) whilst developed capitalist societies produce industrial goods—in the historical process of finance capital's search for increasing surplus value. This historical condition can be changed and much of the noise by radical third-world leaders (see Section 4) over a new international economic order is geared towards winning changes within the imperialist international system. This organic link of third-world economies to the world capitalist system has far-reaching implications for politics and state in particular countries. One of the most important implications of this is the immediate recognition of the state by all classes as the point where class contradictions must be resolved, since capital has always used the state in these societies as a leeway into production. The immediate reason behind the avoidance of politics would seem to be therefore the necessity to control or do away with all actual or potential sources of power which could possibly serve as a forum for criticism of those whose interests are defended and promoted by the state.

This is usually defended on the grounds that there is only one national interest and a consensus is usually claimed to be in existence. The class struggle is therefore seen as a threat to the security of the state—meaning a threat to the position of the dominant classes. In practice then, the political, the state, predominates over the area of politics that in developed capitalist formations and underdeveloped ones, which have passed through a long period of colonialism and exhibit developed class structures, usually exercise a relative autonomy. In one prominent post-colonial state for example, the functions of the ministry of labour and those of the leadership of the trade union movement are merged so that the same person is both secretary-general of the trade unions and minister of labour. Thus, at the point where the contradiction between labour and capital finds political expression politics is preponderated over by the state. Discussion is not necessarily denied but all disputes must take place within definite bounds set directly by the state and in a manner which ensures ultimate control.

These developments tend to accentuate the 'centrality' of the state in these formations, vis-à-vis the social and the economic structures. The state appears to be omnipotent insofar as it has an omnipresence. To explain this situation it is not enough to assume that this is part of the general behaviour of the state; this cannot be taken as given. There is need to investigate the specificity of particular states and the contradictions in the social formation that gives rise to such a situation. Generally speaking however, there are certain factors prevalent in the economic and social contexts which are forcing these states towards greater and greater 'centrality' within their specific formations. Monopolism and the increasing internationalisation of capital are forcing contemporary capitalist states of all kinds to intervene directly in social and economic arrangements. For example, the recent depression in the capitalist system is having the effect of radicalising some third-world states because their primary products are selling for less and less whilst their manufactured imports are constantly rising in price. The economic nationalism to which this gives rise reinforces the central role of the state in the formations under discussion. The contradictions that emerge between national and foreign capital (where this distinction can be drawn) tends to pull the state more into the economic field, for the capitalist classes in such formations cannot treat with international capital at this juncture directly and resolution must therefore be sought at the level of the political. In some societies too the dominant classes are not necessarily strong economically and in such situations they tend to use the state to strengthen their social and economic bases (see particularly Essay 10).

Another point to note regarding the political in the formations in the underdeveloped areas is that it is not possible to make many useful statements which may be applicable to all. In some former colonies (as parts of Asia and North and West Africa) the imperialists found developed (pre-capitalist) social formations and affected these in a manner that intensified class antagonisms. In other places (as in parts of East and Central Africa) the pre-colonial social formations were so backward that the effects of imperialism may be regarded as being *initially progressive*. But the class antagonisms that imperialism effected remained but embryonic in the pre-independence period. In the New World the colonialism/imperialism of mercantilism and later of monopoly capitalism created and maintained distinct social classes from the very inception of such societies. In these different situations the centrality of the state or the incorporation of politics into the activities of the state, have different meanings because the class struggle expresses itself differently and outcomes are dissimilar. Unfortunately this is not always appreciated in analyses of these formations and too often statements about African experience are made to explain Asian or Latin American situations and vice versa.

This poses an important problem for those interested in the state in capitalist society and especially for those concerned with the post-colonial version(s). In this regard the present theoretical gap lies between what we know about more specific instances of the state in these formations and the over-arching theoretical insights of the capitalist state in general. One of the immediate tasks ahead, however, is a practical one: the debate on the state in post-colonial societies and that being carried out in Europe over the developed forms of the capitalist state must come closer together.

NOTES

1. See *Review of African Political Economy*, no. 8, January–April 1977, which concentrates on the question of Capitalism in Africa and contains some excellent papers. See also C. Leys, *Underdevelopment in Kenya: The Political Economy of Neo-Colonialism, 1964–71*, (Heinemann, 1975), and his 'Underdevelopment and Dependency: Critical Notes', *Journal of Contemporary Asia*, vol. 7, no. 1, 1977; G. Kay, *Development and Underdevelopment: A Marxist Analysis*, (Macmillan, 1975).

2. Particularly the three important essays by Anne Phillips, 'The Concept of Development', *Review of African Political Economy*, no. 8, 1977; C. Leys, 'Underdevelopment and Dependency: Critical Notes', *Journal of Contemporary Asia*, vol. 7, no. 1, 1977; and H. Bernstein, 'Sociology of Underdevelopment *vs* Sociology of Development', in *Development Theory: Three Critical Essays*, (Routledge & Kegan Paul, forthcoming).

3. See J. H. Gusfield, 'Traditionality and Modernity: Misplaced Polarities in the Study of Social Change', in J. L. Finkle and R. W. Gable (eds.), *Political Development and Social Change*, (Wiley, 1966); D. Lerner, *The Passing of Traditional Society*, (Free Press of Glencoe, 1958); D. A. Rustow, *A World of Nations: Problems of Modernization*, (Brookings Institution, 1967); C. H. Dodd, *Political Development*, (Macmillan, 1972); D. E. Apter, *The Politics of Modernization*, (Chicago University Press, 1967), also, his *Some Conceptual Approaches to the Study of Modernization*, (Prentice-Hall, 1968).

4. See S. N. Eisenstadt, 'Breakdowns of Modernization', in S. N. Eisenstadt, (ed.), *Readings in Social Evolution and Development*, (Pergamon Press, 1969); S. P. Huntington, *Political Order in Changing Societies*, (Yale University Press, 1968); also, G. A. Almond, 'A Functional Approach to Comparative Politics', in, G. A. Almond and J. S. Coleman, (eds.), *The Politics of the Developing Areas*, (Princeton University Press, 1960).

5. F. W. Riggs, *Administration in Developing Societies: The Theory of Prismatic Society*, (Houghton Mifflin, 1964).

6. See for example, Almond and Coleman, *The Politics of the Developing Areas*; L. Pye, *Aspects of Political Development*, (Little, Brown & Co., 1966).

7. See for example, Apter, *The Politics of Modernization*.

8. See for example, A. G. Frank, 'The Development of Underdevelopment', in R. I. Rhodes, (ed.), *Imperialism and Underdevelopment: A Reader*, (Monthly Review Press, 1970), also, *Capitalism and Underdevelopment in Latin America*, (Monthly Review Press, 1969), and, *Lumpenbourgeoisie and Lumpendevelopment: Dependence, Class and Politics in Latin America*, (Monthly Review Press, 1972); also, Samir Amin, *Unequal Development: An Essay on the Social Formations of Peripheral Capitalism*, (The Harvester Press, 1976).

9. For example see, W. Rodney, *How Europe Underdeveloped Africa*, (Bogle L'Ouverture Publications and Tanzania Publishing House, 1972).

10. The expression 'unequal exchange' 'is used to convey the idea that on the world market the poor nations are obliged to sell the products of a relatively large number of hours of labour in order to obtain in exchange from the rich nations the products of a smaller number of hours of labour' as Charles Bettelheim puts it in his 'Theoretical Comments' on A. Emmanuel's controversial *Unequal Exchange: A Study of the Imperialism of Trade*, (New Left Books, 1972), p. 272.

11. For example, N. Girvan, *Foreign Capital and Economic Underdevelopment in Jamaica*, (Institute of Social and Economic Research, University of the West Indies, 1971); also, C. Y. Thomas, *Dependence and Transformation: The Economics of the Transition to Socialism*, (Monthly Review Press, 1974).

12. G. Beckford, *Persistent Poverty: Underdevelopment in Plantation Economies of the Third World*, (Oxford University Press, 1972), particularly ch. 8.

13. Phillips, 'The Concept of Development'.
14. *Ibid.*, p. 11.
15. First published by Francois Maspero in Paris, published in English by New Left Books, 1973.
16. Weidenfeld & Nicholson, 1969.
17. E. Laclau, 'The Specificity of the Political: Around the Poulantzas-Miliband Debate', *Economy and Society*, vol. 5, no. 1, 1975.
18. See for example, R. Miliband, *Marxism and Politics*, (Oxford University Press, 1977), J. Holloway and S. Picciotto, 'Capital, Crisis and the State', *Capital and Class*, no. 2, Summer, 1977, also, J. Holloway and S. Picciotto, (eds.), *State and Capital: A Marxist Debate*, (Edward Arnold, 1977); the latter work is a collection of essays from the debate on the state in Germany.
19. For example, see Rodney, *How Europe Underdeveloped Africa*, Preface; also, his 'Some Implications of the Question of Disengagement from Imperialism', in L. Cliffe and J. Saul, (eds.), *Socialism in Tanzania: An Interdisciplinary Reader*, (East African Publishing House, 1972).
20. D. Johnson and Ocompo, 'The Concept of Political Development', in D. Johnson, J. D. Cockcroft and A. G. Frank, (eds.), *Dependence and Underdevelopment: Latin America's Political Economy*, (Anchor Books, 1972).
21. See K. Deutsch, *The Nerves of Government: Models of Political Communication and Control*, (Free Press of Glencoe, 1963); D. Easton, *A Systems Analysis of Political Life*, (Wiley, 1965), and R. Dahl, *Modern Political Analysis*, 2nd ed., (Prentice-Hall, 1970).
22. S. S. Wolin, *Politics and Vision: Continuity and Innovation in Western Political Thought*, (Allen & Unwin, 1961); B. Crick, *The American Science of Politics: Its Origins and Conditions*, (University of California Press, 1969), also, *In Defence of Politics*, (Weidenfeld & Nicholson, 1962).
23. Almond, 'A Functional Approach to Comparative Politics', p. 3.
24. G. A. Almond and G. B. Powell, *Comparative Politics: A Developmental Approach*, (Little, Brown & Co., 1966), p. 30.
25. Almond, 'A Functional Approach to Comparative Politics', p. 7.
26. *Ibid.*
27. *Ibid.*
28. *Ibid.*
29. *Ibid.*
30. *Ibid.*, p. 8.
31. For the classic Marxist view of the origins of the state, see F. Engels, *The Origins of the Family, Private Property and the State*, (Pathfinder Press, 1972).
32. Almond, 'A Functional Approach to Comparative Politics', p. 8.
33. See for example, S. Rothman, 'Systematic Political Theory: Observation on the Group Approach', *ASPR*, vol. liv, 1960, also, C. A. Astiz, *Pressure Groups and Power Elites in Peruvian Politics*, (Cornell University Press, 1969).
34. It should be stressed that by periodisation one does not mean breaks or stops in a lineal progression but rather distinct periods of history which may be characterised according to the dominant mode of production that obtains (for example, the feudal, capitalist, etc.) and the various phases of each period.
35. Pye, *Aspects of Political Development*, p. 44.
36. Almond and Powell, *Comparative Politics. A Developmental Approach*, p. 23.
37. Poulantzas, *Political Power and Social Classes*, (London: New Left Books, 1973), pp. 41-2.
38. *Ibid.*, p. 41.
39. See V. I. Lenin, *The State and Revolution*, (Foreign Language Press, 1970).
40. See K. Marx, 'Theses on Feuerbach'; K. Marx and F. Engels, 'The Communist Manifesto', both in *Selected Works*, vol. 1.

41. See A. Wolfe, 'New Directions in the Marxist Theory of Politics' and A. Bridges, 'Nicos Poulantzas and the Marxist Theory of the State', in *Politics and Society*, vol. 4, no. 2, 1974.

42. See J. Clarke, I. Connell and R. McDonough, 'Misrecognizing Ideology: Ideology in Political Power and Social Classes', in *Working Papers in Cultural Studies, no. 10: On Ideology*, (Centre for Contemporary Cultural Studies, University of Birmingham, 1977).

43. Poulantzas, *op. cit.*, p. 51.

44. L. Althusser, 'Ideology and Ideological State Apparatuses: Notes Towards an Investigation', in *Lenin and Philosophy and Other Essays*, (Monthly Review Press, 1971).

45. Simon Clarke, 'Marxism, Sociology and Poulantzas' Theory of the State', *Capital and Class*, no. 2, Summer, 1977; see also, Stuart Hall, 'Rethinking the "Base-Superstructure" Metaphor', in J. Bloomfield, (ed.), *The Communist University of London Papers on Class, Hegemony and Party*, (Lawrence & Wishart, 1977).

46. N. Poulantzas, 'The Capitalist State: A Reply to Miliband and Laclau', *New Left Review*, no. 95, January–February, 1976.

47. See L. Althusser, 'Marxism is not a Historicism', in L. Althusser and E. Balibar, *Reading Capital*, (New Left Books, 1970); on the 'historicist' interpretation of Marx, see Karl Korsch, *Marxism and Philosophy*, (New Left Books, 1970) and G. Lukacs, *History and Class Consciousness*, (Merlin Press, 1971).

48. London: New Left Books, 1975.

49. Pye, *Aspects of Political Development*, pp. 29–30.

TWO:

Characterising the State in the Third World

Introductory note

The discussion regarding the state in third-world countries has taken place mainly under the rubric of the 'post-colonial state'. Although the expression is of little theoretical value it conjures up certain notions of a wide range of state forms found in these societies. It would appear to be descriptive of those states which emerged out of the former European colonies in Asia, Africa, the Caribbean, etc., in the 1950–60s, but not of the states in Canada, Australia and the rest of the white commonwealth although some of these countries may be considered to have dependent economies. It appears also, that the 'post-colonial state' is to be found in Latin America even although political independence was achieved early in the last century, long before the former British dominions, and some countries in the continent are not necessarily any more dependent on foreign capital. The variety of state forms that exist then, in the third world—military, authoritarian, liberal and social–democratic, etc.—continue to present considerable theoretical problems for those who wish to construct a general theory of the state in these formations.

The selections in this section reflect this situation in radical–cum–marxist political theory. This could hardly be otherwise for at the present time the available literature on the state in the third world provides, at best, only elements towards a general theory. In fact, the present literature, although instructive in many ways of these societies, tends to reveal increasingly the differences as much as the similarities between these states. What is then required is not merely a multiplicity of specific case studies, as Alavi calls for, (Essay 4), but in addition, and perhaps more importantly, theoretical constructions capable of explaining as well as describing these states. It may well be however, that in the last analysis the search for a general theory of the state in these formations may have to be abandoned and the state in these societies be seen more as an integral part of the general problem of the capitalist state. This will not entail an abandonment of the specificities of these formations because any theory of the capitalist state must take into account the specificities of different national forms. In any event, an adequate theory of the state in capitalist formations in the third world is necessarily also a theory of the state in developed capitalism.

35

In his influential article reproduced here, Alavi postulates that the post-colonial state (in Pakistan and Bangladesh and by implication elsewhere also) is characterised by (i) its 'overdeveloped' nature (vis-à-vis the socio-economic bases upon which it rests); (ii) the post-colonial state enjoys not merely the 'relative. autonomy' that the state under developed capitalism has, but rather, has a 'distinct relative autonomy' by virtue of its direct and obvious role in the economy/production; (iii) consequently, the post-colonial state is able to dispense with the usual mediatory role of politics (political parties, elections, politicians, free assemblies, etc.) in a capitalist formation. This formulation has contributed to much of the clouding and obscuring of some important similarities and dissimilarities between the capitalist state under developed and backward capitalism but it did constitute an initially stimulating discussion on the post-colonial state as is clear from the contributions by Saul and Hein and Stenzel.

Saul's piece is interesting not only because it attempts to utilise Alavi's arguments whilst correcting them in the light of African experience, but also because it represents a come-back by a Tanzaphile of long standing against attacks on his and others' defence of the loudly proclaimed 'Tanzanian socialism'. The thrust of his argument is aimed at I. G. Shivji who was largely responsible for bringing about a rejection of Saul's over-enthusiastic and optimistic radicalism which at times amounted to a denial of class struggles in Tanzania after the much misunderstood Arusha Declaration in 1967, which led to widespread nationalisation. Saul's piece is very much part of an ongoing debate regarding the post-colonial state in general and in particular the Tanzanian case and should be taken as such. His criticism of Shivji as being teleological and mechanical in the way he regards Tanzanian politics, although convincing, does not help to remove Saul credibly far from a crude reductionism – the attempts to construct socialism in Tanzania have been hampered by the bureaucracy.

Hein and Stenzel postulate a more definite dependency thesis based upon the work of the Latin American underdevelopment school, particularly that of Frank, using Venezuela as an example. There is also an attempt to utilise the growing literature on the capitalist state in Europe although the possible contrary implications that these different theories hold out for each other are not treated.

Generally then, the three pieces reflect the diversity of the state in the third world and the stage of the discussion regarding the characteristics of these state forms. In no sense therefore does this section represent a coherent, systematic view of the state in these societies. If the problems are clear then something will have been achieved.

4 HAMZA ALAVI

The State in post-colonial societies: Pakistan and Bangladesh[†]

The object of this article is to raise some fundamental questions about the classical Marxist theory of the State in the context of post-colonial societies. The argument is premised on the historical specificity of post-colonial societies, a specificity which arises from structural changes brought about by the colonial experience and alignments of classes and by the superstructures of political and administrative institutions which were established in that context, and secondly from radical re-alignments of class forces which have been brought about in the post-colonial situation. I will draw examples from recent developments in Pakistan and Bangladesh. There are, necessarily, some particular features which are specific to that context. But the essential features which invite a fresh analysis are by no means unique. In particular the special role of the military–bureaucratic oligarchy has become all too common a phenomenon in post-colonial societies. This role now needs to be interpreted in terms of a new alignment of the respective interests of the three propertied exploiting classes, namely the indigenous bourgeoisie, the Metropolitan neo-colonialist bourgeoisies, and the landed classes, under Metropolitan patronage a combination which is not unique to Pakistan. If a colony has a weak and underdeveloped indigenous bourgeoisie, it will be unable at the moment of independence to subordinate the relatively highly developed colonial State apparatus through which the Metropolitan power had exercised dominion over it. However, a new convergence of interests of the three competing propertied classes, under

† From *New Left Review*, no. 74, July/August 1972.

Metropolitan patronage, allows a bureaucratic–military oligarchy to mediate their competing but no longer contradictory interests and demands. By that token it acquires a relatively autonomous role and is not simply the instrument of any one of the three classes. Such a relatively autonomous role of the state apparatus is of special importance to the neo-colonialist bourgeoisies because it is by virtue of this fact that they are able to pursue their class interests in the post-colonial societies.

A fundamental distinction can be seen between that situation and the situation which followed the bourgeois revolution in European societies on which the classical Marxist theory of the state is based. A distinction may also be made between cases such as that of Pakistan which experienced direct colonial rule and other countries which experienced colonial exploitation under indirect rule. My analysis is confined to an example of the first type. Perhaps comparative analysis will throw light on the similarities and the differences between it and cases of the other type. Such comparative and critical studies are needed before we can hope to arrive at a general theory of the State in post-colonial societies. The purpose of this article will have been served if it focuses on fresh questions that require to be asked in relation to post-colonial societies.

Classical Marxist Theory

A focus on the central role of the bureaucracy and the military in the government and political development of post-colonial societies raises some fundamental questions, especially with reference to the classical marxist theories. What Miliband calls the primary marxist view of the State 'finds its most explicit expression in the famous aphorism of the Communist Manifesto: "The executive of the modern state is but a committee for managing the common affairs of the whole bourgeoisie," and political power is "merely the organized power of one class for oppressing another." '[1] Miliband adds: 'This is the classical marxist view on the subject of the State and it is the only one which is to be found in marxism-leninism. In regard to Marx himself, however, . . . it only constitutes what may be called a primary view of the State . . . for there is to be found another

view of the State in his work . . . This secondary view is that of
the State as independent from and superior to all social classes, as
being the dominant force in society rather than the instrument of
the dominant class.' This secondary view of the State in Marx's
work arises from his analysis of the Bonapartist State. Miliband
concludes: 'For Marx, the Bonapartist State, however independent it may have been *politically* from any given class,
remains, and cannot in a class society but remain, the protector of
an economically and socially dominant class.'

In the post-colonial society, the problem of the relationship
between the State and the underlying economic structure is more
complex than the context in which it was posed even in the
Bonapartist State or other examples which arose in the context of
the development of European society. It is structured by yet
another historical experience and it calls for fresh theoretical
insights.

The military and the bureaucracy in post-colonial societies
cannot be looked upon, in terms of the classical marxist view,
simply as instruments of a *single* ruling class. The specific nature
of structural alignments created by the colonial relationship and
re-alignments which have developed in the post-colonial situation have rendered the relationship between the state and the
social classes more complex. The two patterns of historical
development are quite different. In Western societies we witness
the creation of the nation state by indigenous bourgeoisies, in the
wake of their ascendant power, to provide a framework of law
and various institutions which are essential for the development
of capitalist relations of production. In colonial societies the
process is significantly different.

The bourgeois revolution in the colony insofar as that consists
of the establishment of a bourgeois state and the attendant legal
and institutional framework, is an event which takes place with
the imposition of colonial rule by the metropolitan bourgeoisie.
In carrying out the tasks of the bourgeois revolution in the
colony, however, the metropolitan bourgeoisie has to accomplish
an additional task which was specific to the colonial situation. Its
task in the colony is not merely to replicate the superstructure of
the state which it had established in the metropolitan country
itself. Additionally, it has to create state apparatus through
which it can exercise dominion over *all* the indigenous social

classes in the colony. It might be said that the 'superstructure' in the colony is therefore 'over-developed' in relation to the 'structure' in the colony, for its basis lies in the metropolitan structure itself, from which it is later separated at the time of independence. The colonial state is therefore equipped with a powerful bureaucratic–military apparatus and mechanisms of government which enable it through its routine operations to subordinate the native social classes. The post-colonial society inherits that overdeveloped apparatus of state and its institutionalized practices through which the operations of the indigenous social classes are regulated and controlled. At the moment of independence weak indigenous bourgeoisies find themselves enmeshed in bureaucratic controls by which those at the top of the hierarchy of the bureaucratic–military apparatus of the state are able to maintain and even extend their dominant power in society, being freed from direct metropolitan control.

The Essential Problem

The essential problem about the state in post-colonial societies stems from the fact that it is not established by an ascendant native bourgeoisie but instead by a foreign imperialist bourgeoisie. At independence, however, the direct command of the latter over the colonial state is ended. But, by the same token, its influence over it is by no means brought to an end. The metropolitan bourgeoisie, now joined by other neo-colonialist bourgeoisies, is present in the post-colonial society. Together they constitute a powerful element in its class structure. The relationship between neo-colonialist bourgeoisies and the post-colonial state is clearly of a different order from that which existed between the imperialist bourgeoisie and the colonial state. The class basis of the post-colonial state is therefore complex. It is not entirely subordinate to the indigenous bourgeoisie, in view of the power and influence of the neo-colonial bourgeoisie. Nor is it simply an instrument of any of the latter, which would have the implication that independence is a mere sham. Neither bourgeoisie excludes the influence of the other; and their interests compete. The central proposition which I wish to emphasize is that the state in the post-colonial society is not the instrument of a single class. It is relatively autonomous and it mediates between the competing interests of the three propertied classes, namely the metropolitan bourgeoisies, the indigenous bourgeoisie and the landed classes, while at the same time acting on behalf of them all to preserve the social order in which their interests are embedded, namely the institution of private property and the capitalist mode as the dominant mode of production.

The multi-class relationship of the state in post-colonial societies calls for specific explanation, and an examination of its implications. In this situation the military–bureaucratic oligarchies, the apparatus of the state, furthermore assume also a new and relatively autonomous *economic* role, which is not paralleled in the classical bourgeois state. The state in the post-colonial society directly appropriates a very large part of the economic surplus and deploys it in bureaucratically directed economic activity in the name of promoting economic development. These are conditions which differentiate the post-colonial state fundamentally from the state as analysed in classical marxist theory.

The apparatus of state does not, however, consist only of the bureaucratic–military oligarchy. Where democratic forms of government operate, politicians and political parties too form a part of it. Where political leaders occupy the highest offices in the state, formally invested with authority over the bureaucracy and military, the role of the bureaucratic–military oligarchy cannot be evaluated without a clear understanding of the precise role of politicians and political parties in the state, and the extent of their powers and their limitations. Politicians and political parties stand at the centre of a complex set of relationships. On the one hand, they are expected (ideally) to articulate the demands of those from whom they seek support; they are supposed to attempt to realize those demands by their participation in the working of government. On the other hand, they also play a key role in manipulating public relations on behalf of those who do make public policy, to make it acceptable to the community at large. For that they channel public grievances and seek to promote an 'understanding' of the situation concerning public issues which would diminish potential opposition. Their relationship with the bureaucratic–military oligarchy is, therefore, ambivalent; it is competitive as well as complementary. The ambivalence is greater where politicians who occupy high public office can influence the careers of individual members of the bureaucracy or the military.

The Mantle of Legitimacy

There are many variants of the distribution or sharing of power between political leadership and bureaucratic–military oligarchies in post-colonial societies. Political parties at the vanguard of the movement for national independence inherit the mantle of legitimacy and the trappings of political power. Nevertheless, in a large number of post-colonial countries there has been in evidence a progressive attenuation of their power and correspondingly there has been expansion in the power of bureaucratic–military oligarchies, which has often culminated in an overt 'seizure' of power by the latter. In general, however, there has been accommodation as well as tension between political leadership and bureaucratic–military oligarchies. The former do serve a useful purpose for the latter. They confer the mantle of political legitimacy on regimes and, through the charade of democratic process, they absorb public discontent and channel grievances. The role of political parties does not necessarily rule out the relative autonomy of bureaucratic–military oligarchies. The essential issue is that of the relative autonomy of the *state apparatus as a whole* and its *mediatory* role as between the competing interests of the three propertied classes, namely the domestic bourgeoisie, the metropolitan bourgeoisies and the land-owning classes. Insofar as a political leadership participates in the performance of that mediatory role and in the preservation of the relative autonomy of the state apparatus, it is valuable for the purposes of the bureaucratic–military oligarchy; it becomes their partner i.e. a third component of the oligarchy. It is only where political parties seriously challenge that relative autonomy and along with it the mediatory role of the bureaucratic–military oligarchy that conflicts arise in which, so far, the latter have prevailed. We have yet to see a clear case of unambiguous control of state power by a political party in a capitalist post-colonial society. The case of India comes nearest to that. But even in India the situation is ambiguous. The ruling

Congress Party is by no means a party of a single class; it participates with the bureaucracy in mediating the demands of competing propertied classes, while at the same time participating with it in using state power to uphold the social order which permits the continued existence of those classes, despite the socialist rhetoric of the Congress Party. Even with regard to foreign capital, the actual performance of the government of India is very different from the rhetoric of the Congress politicians.[2] What is crucial to the present analysis is that behind the apparent power of Congress politicians, the Indian bureaucracy does enjoy a very wide margin of autonomy, on which recent research has thrown some light.[3]

To understand the way in which relationships between the bureaucratic–military oligarchies and politicians have evolved in India and Pakistan one must look at the historical background of the development of their mutual relationships and especially the institutionalization of a wide measure of bureaucratic and military autonomy. Before independence members of the bureaucracy and the military were the instruments of the colonial power. One of their principal functions was to subordinate the various native classes and to repress the nationalist movement on behalf of their colonial masters. During the freedom struggle, they were on opposite sides of the political barricades from the leadership of the nationalist movement. After independence, the same political leaders whom it was their task to repress were ensconced in office, nominally in authority over them. A new relationship of mutual accommodation had to be established. The experience of partial transfer of power by stages during the twenties and the thirties had, however, already institutionalized procedures by which the bureaucracy could by-pass the political leaders who had been inducted into office, on sufferance under the umbrella of British imperial rule. These institutionalized procedures were extended and consolidated by the proliferation of bureaucratic controls and the fact that, by and large, members of the public have extensive direct, routine dealings with the bureaucracy which do not admit of mediation by political parties. An exception occurs only when individual politicians seek favours from officials for some of their supporters, in which case their relationship vis-à-vis the bureaucracy is weakened rather than strengthened. Politicians are reduced to playing the role of brokers for official favours. This mediation between the public and the bureaucracy is one of the important sources of political power in India[4] as in other parallel cases. The politician can, however, ill afford to lose the good will of the official, and this influences the overall balance of their collective relationship. The strength of the bureaucracy rests on the extensive proliferation of administrative controls and the direction of a vast array of public agencies engaged in a variety of activities.

Indonesia and Pakistan

The actual pattern of the evolution of relationships between political leaders and bureaucratic–military oligarchies varies from country to country according to differences in historical background and the evolution of political forces. In Indonesia, for example, a long period elapsed before the emergence of the overt power of the bureaucratic–military oligarchy after the overthrow of Sukarno. The underlying factors in that case are complex, but a part of the explanation must be that the bureaucracy and the military in Indonesia had to be radically restructured after independence and it took some time for the oligarchy to be consolidated. In India and Pakistan, by contrast, powerfully organized bureaucratic and military structures were inherited. In Pakistan, the military was, it is true, in bad shape at the time of independence, but the organization and bases of political parties were still weaker. The ruling Muslim League party leaned heavily on the stature and authority of its leader, Quaide Azam Mohammad Ali Jinnah, who died soon after independence. By that time the Muslim League had begun to disintegrate and its leadership had become isolated from its bases.

In Pakistan two facts stand out in sharp relief in its 25 year history. One is the dominant position of the bureaucratic–military oligarchy in the state; it has been in effective command of state power not, as is commonly believed, after the *coup d'etat* of October 1958 but, in fact, from the inception of the new state. In the first phase politicians and political parties, who provided a facade of parliamentary government, were manipulated by them and were installed and expelled from office as it suited the

bureaucratic–military oligarchy. When in 1958 the prospects of
the impending general elections appeared to pose a challenge to
the supremacy of the bureaucratic–military oligarchy, those who
already held the reins of power 'seized power' by abolishing
the institutions of parliamentary government through which
the challenge was being mounted. But, nevertheless, the
bureaucratic–military oligarchy needed politicians, who fulfil a
complementary role, and by 1962 the politicians were put to
work again in a parody of democratic politics under Ayub
Khan's system of 'Basic Democracy'. That phase ended with the
fall of Ayub Khan in 1969, after a great national political
upheaval. But still the reins of power were left securely in the
hands of the bureaucratic–military oligarchy. The latter still
needed politicians to fulfill a complementary role in government.
President Yahya Khan promised restoration of 'constitutional
government' subject to his own veto. An election was held in
December 1970 which ended in the political crisis which
culminated in the secession of Bangladesh. It is a complex history
which I have examined in some detail elsewhere.[5] In its first
phase, the period of 'parliamentary government', the true role of
the bureaucratic–military oligarchy was obscured by the political fiction under which it operated. After 1958, its dominant and
decisive role became manifest. What remains problematic is
the social character, affiliations, and commitments of the
bureaucratic–military oligarchy, or those of different sections of
it, vis-à-vis the various social classes in Pakistan and its different
regions, including the metropolitan bourgeoisies which have re-
appeared, in the plural, after British colonial rule was ended.

   The second outstanding fact about Pakistan's political history
is that the most powerful challenges to the dominant central
authority of the bureaucratic–military oligarchy came primarily
from political movements that drew their strength from people of
underprivileged regions and voiced demands for regional autonomy and for a fuller share for the regions in the distribution of
material resources as well as in state power. It was not only from
East Bengal but also from Sind, and Baluchistan and the North
West Frontier Province or NWFP—the land of the Pathans—that
such challenges were mounted. Support for regional autonomy
became an article of faith with the radical and left wing political
groups—indeed most of them were embedded in regionalist

movements. It appeared, on the surface, that the radical politics of Pakistan were conditioned primarily by ethnic or linguistic solidarities, rather than class solidarities stretching across regional boundaries. True, radical challenges were directed against class privileges. But such privileges were identified primarily in regional terms. Politically the demands of radical and left-wing political movements were for a federal parliamentary system of government and for a representation in the upper echelons of bureaucratic (and military) appointments of people from underprivileged regions. These two outstanding facts about Pakistan politics, namely the dominance of a bureaucratic–military oligarchy and the regional basis of challenges directed against it, are essentially two aspects of a single reality of the political situation in Pakistan which centres around the role of the bureaucratic–military oligarchy.

Until 1958, the bureaucratic–military oligarchy in Pakistan made and unmade 'Governments' with a succession of Prime Ministers. In 1956 it even instigated the creation of the Republic Party. A new type of constitution was introduced by Ayub Khan in 1962, after his 'seizure of power' through a coup d'etat, in 1958. Politicians were put to work again; under Ayub Khan their manipulation was perfected to a fine art. But what is significant here is the anxiety of the military leaders to retain a facade of political government. Thus, after the re-imposition of Martial Law in 1969, President General Yahya Khan was very keen that a political leadership should be installed in office as soon as possible although under the hegemony of the bureaucratic–military oligarchy. He promised elections for that purpose and immediately installed a chosen group of civilians as interim ministers. Some of his most influential military advisers were particularly insistent that without politicians in office, the military would become directly the object of public disaffection, that it would lose its mantle of political legitimacy, and that as a consequence its assumed right to intervene at every moment of crisis would be jeopardized. Thus it would be simplistic to take for granted that the bureaucratic–military oligarchy necessarily prefers to rule directly in its own name. It often prefers to rule through politicians so long as the latter do not impinge upon its own relative autonomy and power. For the bureaucratic–military oligarchy in Pakistan the elections of December 1970, however, had disconcerting results, and the crisis of 1971 ensued, resulting in the secession of Bangladesh.

Bhutto and the Army

The assumption of power by President Bhutto after the defeat of the Pakistan army in Bangladesh can be seen in a similar light. Here was a traumatic moment of crisis. It was a moment when the oligarchy more than ever needed a political leadership which would be able to manipulate an explosive political situation. Bhutto's political position in the country and the fact that his services were indispensable for the oligarchy gave him a degree of freedom. Nevertheless the dismissal by him of a clutch of generals after the assumption of power should not be taken simply as evidence of a final defeat of the bureaucratic–military oligarchy, for Bhutto is closely allied to powerful factions in the oligarchy and his actions reflect the demands of those factions. Bhutto 'dismissed' General Yahya Khan and his associates and appointed his friend General Gul Hassan as the new Commander-in-Chief of the Army, having himself assumed the office of President. But it would be a mistake to assume that General Gul Hassan was a political nonentity whom President Bhutto installed in office simply as his own nominee. General Gul Hassan in fact belonged to a powerful faction in the military establishment. As early as October 1968, before the massive political agitation against President Ayub Khan which followed a month later, was even anticipated, it was already being whispered in the corridors of power in Rawalpindi and Islamabad that Ayub would be removed and that his most likely successor would be General Gul Hassan who was then Corps Commander at Multan, one of the two seniormost field appointments in the Pakistan army. In the event, President Ayub outmanoeuvred the faction which was being aligned against him, by resigning and handing over the office of President to the man of his own choosing whom he had appointed as his Commander-in-Chief, namely General Yahya Khan. In turn Yahya Khan successfully protected Ayub Khan from retribution, which was being demanded not only by an angry public but also by powerful elements in the army itself. With Yahya Khan's fall, events had turned a full circle. In the crisis after the military debacle in Bangladesh, the intervention of the political leadership was indispensable for the military–bureaucratic oligarchy. At this moment the political leadership did assume some weight. The fact that the critical struggle for power still lay within the military–bureaucratic oligarchy was, however, soon made manifest when Bhutto had to dismiss General Gul Hassan from the post of Commander-in-Chief and instal in his place the powerful General Tikka Khan, a leader of the 'hawks' in the army who had master-minded the military action in Bangladesh. It could not but have been an unpalatable decision for Bhutto for the appointment was most inept in the context of the political necessity for Bhutto to negotiate with India and Bangladesh for the repatriation of Pakistani prisoners of war, but the supremacy of the army Junta was evidently decisive.

Big Business and the Generals

Factions in the military are based on personal groupings and allegiances, but there are underlying structural factors which influence the gravitations of groups into broader alliances. One can therefore distinguish, on the one hand, 'Conservative Right Wing' Generals. They either come from the wealthier landed families or else they (or their very close relatives) have made substantial fortunes in business. Others have made money in collusion with foreign businesses and foreign powers. Big businessmen in Pakistan have adopted the practice of awarding profitable directorships to retiring Generals, and thus they have tried to establish relationships with factions in the army. As regards dealings with foreign powers, a remarkable fact about the political situation in Pakistan has been the ability of the army to have direct dealings with foreign powers (notably the USA) over the heads of the Government in office. These varieties of affiliations and interests have resulted in powerfully entrenched positions within the army on behalf of the various vested interests. The case of the bureaucracy is parallel, for many bureaucrats come from landed families and have acquired extensive business interests; some have become millionaires.

There is, however, another influence in the army which tends to promote radicalism; but this is potentially radicalism of the right as well as of the left. The evidence so far, in fact, suggests that ultra right-wing radicalism is the preponderant element in this group. This radicalism derives from the fact that the army is recruited from one of the most impoverished and congested ؛ agricultural regions of the country, namely the unirrigated area consisting of Rawalpindi Division of the Punjab and parts of the NWFP. Whereas big farmers in some parts of the country, such as the Canal Colony Districts of the Punjab, have prospered enormously through the so-called 'Green Revolution', the smallholders in the unirrigated region have not benefited from it. Their tiny unproductive holdings do not yield even a bare minimum for their livelihood. Their sons must therefore find outside employment and it is from these districts that the army draws its soldiers and junior officers. These men have strong social grievances, especially because of inflation and the deterioration of their economic situation in recent years, but they have little political education. In general they subscribe to a conspiracy theory of society and imagine, for example, that inflation is due simply to the greed of a few businessmen (the so-called twenty families); they do not see roots of the problem in the economic system itself. The solution therefore, in their eyes, is not to be found in radical economic policies and a transformation of the social system but rather merely in the brutal punishment of 'miscreants'. The same idea of dealing with 'miscreants' was applied by them in Bangladesh. Politically these men have been reared on chauvinism and religious ideology of the extreme right wing. The influence of the Jamaat-e-Islami has been quite considerable amongst them. In recent years, however, the radical rhetoric of Bhutto's Pakistan People's Party has caught their imagination. Through them, Bhutto's political position is strongly rooted in the rank and file of the army.

'Hawks' have Objective Basis

There is also a group of Generals who have close affinities and links with the above mentioned second category of army officers and rank and file soldiers. These are the 'army generals' for whom the interests of the army as such take precedence over other considerations. It is among them that the 'hawks' in the army are to be found. The concept of army 'hawks' is not a psychological one as suggested by Tariq Ali.[6] Rather that term describes commitments which are rooted in the objective conditions and interests of the army. The 'Hawks' have been able to exploit the grievances of the army rank and file and therefore have a powerful position in the army. They thrive on chauvinism, for only on the basis of an aggressively chauvinistic ideology can they enforce increasing demands on national resources for a larger and better equipped (and more privileged) army. The massive re-armament and re-organisation of the Indian army in the last decade, following its confrontation with China, has altered the military balance in South Asia, a fact which was brought home to the Pakistani oligarchy in no uncertain terms after the debacle in Bangladesh. This will make the old policy of confrontation with India no longer credible. This confrontation has been a source of embarrassment to the two super-powers, the USA and the USSR, who have attempted for more than a decade to bring about a rapprochement between India and Pakistan. They will no doubt use their influence to restrain the 'hawks' in the army and to strengthen the hands of the 'conservative right-wing' Generals to this end. Nevertheless, the fact that the oligarchy has so far resisted the efforts of the two super-powers in this respect despite pressure for over a decade, reflects its relative autonomy; such a rapprochement would encroach on the interests of the army.

Both the bureaucracy and the military in Pakistan are highly developed and powerful in comparison with their indigenous class bases. Capitalist development in Pakistan has taken place under their corrupt patronage and close control by the bureaucracy. Because of bureaucratic controls, business opportunities have been restricted to a privileged few who have established the necessary relationship with the bureaucracy, essentially based on the cash nexus. In the late sixties the Chief economist to the Government of Pakistan revealed that 20 privileged families owned 66 per cent of Pakistan's industry, 79 per cent of its insurance and 80 per cent of its banking and that most of the rest was owned by foreign companies. That revelation, in a pre-election year, is itself an indication of the ambivalent relationship between the bureaucracy and the indigenous bourgeoisie. Even so, the local monopolists do not control any political party which can be said to represent them as a class. Indeed, the bases of political parties are primarily rural. The influence of the business community on the conduct of public affairs is primarily through its direct contact with and influence on the bureaucracy itself.

Landowning and Party Politics

Under parliamentary democracy landowners, who hold sway over the countryside, monopolize the field of party politics. They are elected to places in the national and provincial legislatures. (Even in East Bengal, where there are no big landowners comparable to those in West Pakistan, 'Sardari lineages' of rich landholders control the local votes.) The bureaucracy and the army recruit their senior officers largely from rich rural families and therefore the landowning classes have a built-in position within the oligarchy. The bureaucrats have a direct stake in the privileges of the landed classes. This link has been greatly reinforced by the grant of land to civilian and military officers, who have thereby become substantial landowners in their own right when they were not so already. Because of that fact landowners have been able to pursue their class interests effectively, despite occasional attempts by the indigenous bourgeoisie and the Metropolitan bourgeoisies to alter that state of affairs. Agricultural incomes for example, are exempt from income tax. For two decades the bourgeoisie and their foreign allies have pressed the demand that these huge incomes be subjected to tax in order to raise resources for a larger development plan, in which their own interests lie. The landed classes have not only resisted that attempt successfully; they have also obtained large subsidies of which the lion's share goes to the rich farmers and the big landlords. Nevertheless, landlords as a class, despite their close and effective links with the bureaucracy and their dominant role in party politics, cannot be said to have command over the bureaucracy. Many instances can be shown in which the interests of landowners as a class have been subordinated to those of the bourgeoisie, for example in the price policy for raw cotton, which has worked to the disadvantage of the landowners and to the benefit of the business magnates who own textile mills.

Foreign Business and the Oligarchy

Foreign businessmen like others, have sought bureaucratic favours, and have not failed to obtain them. In their case, private corruption is reinforced by governmental pressure; the greatest pressure is exercised by the Government of the United States. I have examined elsewhere ways in which US Aid has been used to enforce policies on Pakistan in support of US business to the detriment of domestic interests.[7] Competition exists not only between US and indigenous business interests but also between competing Metropolitan bourgeoisies, viz British, German, French, Japanese, Italian and others. None of them has complete command over the bureaucracy nor do they command it collectively. Neo-colonialism is, however, probably the greatest beneficiary of the relative autonomy of the bureaucratic–military oligarchy. It is precisely such a relatively autonomous role that renders the government of the post-colonial society sufficiently open to admit the successful intrusion of neo-colonialist interests in the formulation of public policy. Great emphasis is therefore placed by western ideologues on the importance of the bureaucracy as an 'agent of modernization'. Every effort is made to influence the bureaucracy ideologically in favour of policies which are in conformity with metropolitan interests. This ideology is expressed in the form of 'techniques of planning' and it is presented as an objective science of economic development. The western educated bureaucrat is regarded as the bearer of western rationality and technology and his role is contrasted with that of 'demagogic' politicians who voice 'parochial' demands. Considerable resources are devoted in the metropolitan countries to imparting training to bureaucrats of the post-colonial countries. But there are also more direct methods of influencing their outlook and policy orientations. International agencies and aid administrating agencies who vet viability of projects, advise on development planning and channelize policies of post-colonial governments along lines which suit the metropolitan countries. Influence on state policy through foreign aid as well as private corruption of bureaucrats makes this possible, even when some of the policies are blatantly against the interests of the country. Those who tend to assume the existence of mutuality in the processes of international negotiations and who suppose that if a government of a post-colonial country has agreed to a certain course of policy, it must therefore be in the interest of their country, should recognize this disjuncture between the interests of the country (however defined) and those of the corrupt bureaucracy and individual bureaucrats.

Pakistan's experience suggests that none of the three propertied classes in that post-colonial society namely, the indigenous bourgeoisie, the neo-colonialist metropolitan bourgeoisies nor the landowning classes, exclusively command the state apparatus; the influence and power of each is offset by that of the other two. Their respective interests are not mutually congruent or wholly compatible. They do have certain basic interests in common; above all, that of the preservation of the existing social order, based upon the institution of private property. But they make competing demands on the post-colonial state and on the bureaucratic–military oligarchy which represents the state. The latter mediates and arbitrates between the competing demands of the three propertied classes. This is a historically specific role of the military and the bureaucracy, the apparatus of the state in post-colonial societies. The reason for its distinctive role stems from the fact that in contrast to the ascendant bourgeoisie in an independent Capitalist state or the metropolitan bourgeoisie in a colony, both of which establish their dominance over other social classes, in post-colonial societies none of the three propertied classes exclusively dominates the state apparatus or subordinates the other two. This specific historical situation confers on the bureaucratic–military oligarchy in a post-colonial society a *relatively autonomous* role.

A Distinct Relative Autonomy

There are two senses in which the idea of '*relative autonomy*' of elements of the superstructure (such as the state), in relation to the underlying 'structure' i.e. the economic foundations of society (the relations of production) has been discussed in marxist literature, which might be clarified at this point. One is a basic philosophical sense, namely that historical materialism does not mean that elements of the 'superstructure' are determined mechanistically by the underlying structure; but that the formative influence of the latter although mediated in a complex way, is the ultimate determinant of the superstructure. This was emphasized by Engels in his well-known letter to Joseph Bloch in which he criticized mechanistic and deterministic interpretations of 'vulgar Marxism'. This fundamental, philosophical, issue should be distinguished from another, theoretical, issue. The idea of 'relative autonomy' of the superstructure is put forward in this second context as a theory, i.e. as an explanation of the relationship between the state and the underlying 'structure' in certain (exceptional) historical situations. Marx's analysis of the bonapartist State deals with the most extreme case of the relative autonomy of the State from amongst such historical examples analysed by Marx and Engels. However, in classical marxism, in the fundamental philosophical sense as well as in the specific theoretical sense, the idea of the 'relative autonomy' of the superstructure (or the state) was conceived of explicitly within the framework of a society subject to the hegemony of *a single ruling class*. The issue in relation to the post-colonial societies is fundamentally different and should be distinguished clearly from the issues which underlay earlier discussions. The classical position is summed up by Poulantzas who wrote: 'When Marx designated Bonapartism as the "religion of the bourgeoisie", in other words as characteristic of all forms of the capitalistic State, he showed that this State can only truly serve the ruling class in so far as it is relatively autonomous from the *diverse fractions of this class*, precisely in order to organize *the hegemony of the whole of this class*.' (emphasis added)[8] Such a proposition cannot apply to a discussion of post-colonial societies in which the problem arises not with reference to 'diverse fractions' of a single class, the bourgeoisie, but rather with reference to three different propertied classes, which do not constitute 'a whole', for they have different structural bases and competing class interests.

In post-colonial societies the phenomenon of the relative autonomy of the state apparatus is therefore of a different order to that which is found in the historical cases on which the classical Marxist theory of state is based. The role of the bureaucratic–military oligarchy in post-colonial societies is only *relatively* autonomous, because it is determined within the matrix of a class society and not outside it, for the preservation of the social order based on the institution of private property unites all the three competing propertied social classes. That common commitment situates the bureaucratic–military oligarchy within the social matrix. Nevertheless, the role of the bureaucratic–military oligarchy is relatively *autonomous* because, once the controlling hand of the metropolitan bourgeoisie is lifted at the moment of independence no single class has exclusive command over it. This relative autonomy is not predicated on that negative condition alone. It derives also from the positive conditions which stem from the far reaching interventions by the state in the economies of post-colonial countries, both by way of a network of controls, in which the vested interests of the bureaucracy are embedded, and a direct appropriation and disposition of a substantial proportion of the economic surplus. These constitute independent material bases of the autonomy of the bureaucratic–military oligarchy. There are perhaps parallels here in the changing role of the state in metropolitan societies also; a question which we cannot pursue here. It could be argued, however, that given the role of the State in 'promoting economic development' in post-colonial societies, the difference between the two situations is of a qualitative order. This role, it should be added, is closely interlinked with imperialist interventions in post-colonial societies, especially through the administration of economic and military aid.

Mediating Three Interests

The mediating role of the bureaucratic–military oligarchy between the competing demands of the three propertied classes is possible in the post-colonial situation because the mutual interests of the latter and their inter-relations are aligned in a qualitatively different way from that which is experienced in other historical circumstances, on which the classical marxist theory of the state is premised. In the post-colonial situation their mutual relations are no longer antagonistic and contradictory; rather they are mutually competing but reconcilable. In the colonies, the classical theory envisages a coalition between the metropolitan bourgeoisie, the native 'comprador' bourgeoisie (composed of merchants whose activities complement those of the metropolitan bourgeoisie) and the 'feudal' landowning class. The theory also envisages the interests of the rising native 'national' bourgeoisie to be fundamentally opposed to those of the metropolitan bourgeoisie. The colonial liberation is therefore characterized as the inauguration of a bourgeois-democratic revolution, 'anti-imperialist and anti-feudal' in character, which is premised as a necessary historical stage in the development of the liberated colonial society. The post-colonial state is taken to be the instrument of the ascendant native national bourgeoisie through which its historical purpose is finally accomplished. But this is not what we have actually witnessed in the post-colonial societies. This was noted, for example, by Paul Baran who wrote: 'Its capitalist bourgeois component, confronted at an early stage with the spectre of social revolution, turns swiftly and resolutely against its fellow traveller of yesterday, its mortal enemy of tomorrow (i.e. the industrial proletariat and the peasantry). *In fact it does not hesitate to make common cause with the feudal elements representing the main obstacle to its own development, with the imperialist rulers just dislodged by the national liberation, and with comprador groups threatened by the political retreat of their former principals.'*[9]

It is true that unprecedented challenges from revolutionary movements·constitute a most important element in the post-colonial situation in which the three propertied classes stand united in the defence of the established social order. But their political unity would not be possible if they were still divided by irreconcilable contradictions. That is possible because of fundamental differences in the underlying structural alignments, which differentiate the post-colonial situation from other historical parallels. The suggestion by Baran that the new unity of the propertied classes for the defence of the established social order represents a retreat from and an *abandonment* by the native national bourgeoisie of its historic anti-feudal and anti-colonial role because of its fears of the revolutionary challenge which it cannot confront alone, overlooks the fundamental differences in the underlying *structural* alignments in the post-colonial societies from those in the colonial situation on which the classical theory of the role of the native 'national bourgeoisie' was premised.

An accommodation between the native bourgeoisie and the 'feudal' landowning classes is now possible because the task of winning national independence is completed and the structure of the nation state and the institutional and legal framework necessary for capitalist development, products of the bourgeois revolution, already exist, for they were established by the metropolitan bourgeoisie. The native bourgeoisie is not confronted with the historical task of the European bourgeoisie of subordinating feudal power for the purpose of establishing the nation state. On the contrary, now the 'feudal' landowning class complements the political purposes of the native bourgeoisie in the 'democratic' running of the post-colonial state, because it plays a key role in establishing links between the state at the national level and the local-level power structures in the rural areas which it dominates. At that level it also 'contains' potentially revolutionary forces and helps to maintain the 'political equilibrium' of the post-colonial system.

The 'Green Revolution'

As regards economic aspects too, the specific nature of the relationship between the native bourgeoisie and the 'feudal' landowning classes in post-colonial societies, especially in the context of the growth of capitalist farming under the auspices of the big landowners rather than in conflict with them, has made it unnecessary for the native bourgeoisie to seek the elimination of the 'feudal' landowning class for the purposes of capitalist development. The position and the interests of the 'feudal' landowning classes were, however, challenged both from within the rural society as well as from 'radical' urban forces. In response to such pressures, perfunctory efforts were made in some countries, soon after independence, to introduce land reforms. By and large, these measures were ineffective, but their ineffectiveness has by no means impeded the development of the native bourgeoisie. In recent years in South Asia, the so-called 'Green Revolution' based on an elite farmer strategy has further helped to resolve the basic problem (for the native bourgeoisie) of increasing the agricultural surplus needed to sustain industrialization and urbanization as well as expanding the domestic market for manufactured goods. Pressures for radical action have diminished and those for mutual accommodation have increased. Contradictions remain, nevertheless, for the elite farmer strategy is having a disruptive effect on the fabric of rural society which may have consequences which reach beyond its confines. This growth of socially 'disruptive' forces in the rural areas, which may contribute powerfully to revolutionary movement, occasions concern on the part of the bourgeoisie, which seeks to consolidate the conservative alliance with the 'feudal' landowning classes to preserve the existing social order rather than contributing to the forces which seek to overthrow the power of the landowning classes in the rural areas.

As regards the relationship between the metropolitan bourgeoisies and the indigenous or 'national' bourgeoisies of the post-colonial societies, their mutual relationship is also quite different from that which is premised in the classical marxist theory. The classical marxist theory postulates a fundamental contradiction between the two. It therefore concludes that the 'bourgeois-democratic' revolution in the colonies, of which independence is only the first phase and which continues in the post-colonial situation, necessarily has an 'anti-imperialistic' character. It is true, of course, that the native bourgeoisie plays an anti-imperialist role and contributes to the national independence movement against the colonial power, but only up to the point of independence. In the post-colonial situation there is a double reorientation of alignments, both of the indigenous bourgeoisie and of the erstwhile 'comprador' class of merchants, building contractors and the like. The latter, unable to compete on equal terms with giant overseas concerns, demand restrictions on the activities of foreign businesses, particularly in the fields in which they aspire to operate. They acquire a new 'anti-imperialist' posture. On the other hand, as the erstwhile 'national' bourgeoisie grows in size and aspires to extend its interests and move from industries which involve relatively unsophisticated technology, such as textiles, to those which involve the use of highly sophisticated technology such as petro-chemicals and fertilisers, etc., they find that they do not have access to the requisite advanced industrial technologies. Their small resources and scale of operation keep the possibility of developing their own technology, independently, out of their reach. For access to the requisite advanced industrial technology they have to turn for collaboration therefore, to the bourgeoisies of the developed metropolitan countries, or to socialist states. This they do despite the fact that the terms on which the collaboration is offered are such that it hamstrings their own independent future development.

As it grows in size and extends its interests the so-called 'national' bourgeoisie becomes increasingly dependent on the neo-colonialist metropolitan bourgeoisies.

Unequal Collaboration

The concept of a 'national' bourgeoisie which is presumed to become increasingly anti-imperialist as it grows bigger, so that its contradictions with imperialism sharpen further, is one which is derived from an analysis of colonial and not post-colonial experience. The mutual relationship of the native bourgeoisie and the metropolitan bourgeoisies is no longer antagonistic; it is collaborative. The collaboration is, however, unequal and hierarchical, because the native bourgeoisie of a post-colonial society assumes a subordinate, client, status in the structure of its relationship with the metropolitan bourgeoisie. The erstwhile 'anti-imperialist' character of the native 'national' bourgeoisie changes in the post-colonial situation to a collaborationist one. The metropolitan bourgeoisies value their collaboration with the native bourgeoisies of post-colonial societies because that provides a channel through which they pursue their economic interests without political risks attendant on direct investments by themselves. Their agreements with the native bourgeoisie establish captive markets for their products as well as for their technologies.[10] The conditions which underlie the collaboration between the native bourgeoisies and the neo-colonial metropolitan bourgeoisies are therefore embedded not only in superstructural conditions namely, the threat of revolutionary movements to which Baran refers, but also in structural conditions namely, access to technology for their economic operations. It must be emphasized that even though the indigenous 'national' bourgeoisie and the metropolitan bourgeoisies are brought together into a close collaborative and hierarchical relationship they are by no means, by that token, merged into a single class. The concept of collaboration implies and describes the fact of their separateness, and hierarchy implies a degree of conflict between their interests and a tension which underlies their relationship. Convergence of their interests does not dissolve into an identity of interests. It is this element of mutual competition which makes it possible, and necessary, for the bureaucratic–military oligarchies to play a mediatory role.

Because of the powerful role of the bureaucratic–military oligarchy in post-colonial societies, positions in the oligarchy are of crucial importance, especially for aspiring educated middle class groups; and their political demands are focused on shares of positions in the oligarchy. Where the oligarchy is recruited from a narrow social or regional base, as for example is the case in Pakistan, the unprivileged educated middle class groups who are denied access to positions of influence and power in the oligarchy organize political opposition. 'Moral' principles and ideologies are invoked both by the ruling oligarchy as well as by the opposition to justify their respective interests and to rally public support on their own behalf. Differences of caste, ethnic origin, religion or language dominate the politics of post-colonial societies particularly for that reason. Opposition groups raise slogans of cultural or linguistic identity. On the other hand, the particular ethnic or linguistic (or other sectional) group which has a dominant position in the ruling bureaucratic–military oligarchy invokes in defence of its own particularistic privileges the ideology of 'national solidarity' and denounces the opposition as narrow-minded and divisive particularism. The campaign on behalf of their group is mounted by the bureaucratic–military oligarchy itself. Political issues arising out of the sectional or regional character of the bureaucratic–military oligarchy are therefore merged with broader issues of public policy as they concern different classes of people and in the political debate which ensues, political questions which concern the underlying social and economic issues are often expressed in the idiom of cultural, linguistic or regionalist demands.

In Pakistan, the ruling, predominantly Punjabi, bureaucratic–military oligarchy has taken over and put to its own particular use the slogans of Muslim nationalism, that is the slogans of the movement on the strength of which Pakistan was brought into being. It extols the virtues of 'Islamic solidarity' and denounces linguistic or regionalist opposition movements as divisive provincialism. In this way, after the creation of Pakistan, the nature and political role of Muslim nationalism and the significance of its slogans have altered. Muslim nationalism in India propagated the cause of the under-privileged Muslim educated middle classes of India, who were numerically small and educationally less advanced than those of the Hindus. The creation of Pakistan, the separate homeland of the Muslims, was the fulfilment of that cause. Therefore after the state of Pakistan had been created, the *raison d'etre* of that movement ceased to exist. At that point the Muslim League, the principal organ of the movement, disintegrated. The surviving faction, which appropriated the mantle of the Muslim League, now began to propagate its ideology on behalf of the privileged groups, especially the Punjabi oligarchs, in opposition to regionalist challenges. The ideology of Islamic unity was now employed to deny the validity of the claims and demands of the less privileged groups, namely Bengalis, Sindhis, Pathans and Baluchis, for the recognition of their distinct identity and needs.

Bengali Aspirations

The aspirations of Bengalis who (amongst others) challenged the domination of the 'Punjabi bureaucracy', were expressed in the secular idiom of the Bengali Language Movement which began with the birth of Pakistan itself. It had its first martyrs in 1952. Although the focus of the Movement was on the issue of national language, an issue which by its nature was closest to the hearts of students and the educated lower middle class, it was nevertheless instrumental in creating a radical consciousness which extended beyond the immediate interests of those who voiced the slogans of the language movement and gave it leadership. With an urban population of only 5 per cent of the total population, the educated middle class of Bengal is drawn overwhelmingly from villages and maintains close contact with the rural society. Under conditions of widespread public discontent, the problems and demands of the impoverished rural population influenced the cadres and leaders of the Language Movement and their slogans. But the aspirations of the leadership were concerned primarily with the issue of the regional share in government jobs and, especially, places for themselves in the bureaucratic establishment.

There were, therefore, two traditions in the Bengali movement. One was a petty bourgeois elitist tradition, of those who hoped to rise to senior positions in the bureaucracy or to become members of the newly created business community in Bengal on the strength of governmental financial support and subsidy. The other was a rural populist tradition which articulated the frustrations and aspirations of the long suffering sections of the extremely poor Bengal peasantry. The two traditions were intertwined, but they remained distinct. The educated sons of rich peasants had other aspirations than those of the peasantry in general. In the early fifties, the Bengali Language Movement embraced them both; at the vanguard of that movement was the old Awami League, in the form in which it was then constituted. At the head of the elitist faction of the Awami league was Suhrawardy, who aspired to public office at the cost of popular objectives. As Prime Minister of Pakistan he was an ardent supporter of imperialist powers and went to the extent of openly and vigorously supporting the Anglo–French–Israeli intervention against Egypt at Suez as well as the US alliance. Sheikh Mujib was a protege of Suhrawardy and was schooled by him in politics; his political commitments were firmly with the elitist group. On the other hand, there was a populist tradition in the Awami League, which flourished under the umbrella of Maulana Bhashani. The elitist leadership was largely concentrated in the towns and cities. The populists had large numbers of cadres on the ground in villages. As the communist party was illegal, there was also a solid core of marxists in the Awami League. Under their influence many of the populist cadres had moved towards explicitly marxist ideas. In February 1957, at the Conference of the Awami League at Kagmari, the conflict between the elitist leadership and the populist cadres was brought to a head on the issue of Prime Minister Suhrawardy's foreign policy. That led to a break, and the ousting of populist cadres of the Awami League along with their leader Maulana Bhashani. They later formed the National Awami Party. The character of the Awami League, which was left in the hands of Suhrawardy and the elitist group, and was deprived of its populist and marxist cadres, was thus transformed. It is crucial to the understanding of the Awami

League in its new form that although its populist cadres were eliminated, its mass populist base amongst the rural people remained with it. By a mistimed and badly managed precipitation of the party crisis, it was the populist cadres who were isolated. In the retention of the Party's hold over the masses, the role of Sheikh Mujib was crucial. This was because, notwithstanding his firm commitments to the elitist group, his rhetoric and even his personal style of life were populist in character. He was a man with whom the people could identify. He bridged the gap between the elitist leadership of the Awami League and its populist mass base.

As the Bengali movement progressed, reluctantly, but inevitably, the dominant Punjabi bureaucratic elite yielded some of the demands of the movement for a fair share of jobs and promotion. As a consequence, by the late sixties, the provincial administration in East Bengal was almost wholly staffed by Bengali civil servants at all levels. Bengali progress was less remarkable in the Central Government. It was not until 1969 that for the first time a few Bengali officers were installed as Secretaries to the Central Government, at the head of some minor Ministries. The bastions of power, namely, the Ministries of Defence, Finance and the Planning Commission and the Establishment Division were still retained securely in trusted West Pakistani hands.

The Bengali movement for equitable treatment reached a new level when, in the late fifties, demands began to be made for a fair and adequate share in the allocation of economic resources for development for East Bengal. East Bengali economists prepared excellent detailed studies which demonstrated the steady exploitation of East Bengal from West Pakistan. Their argument that there should be a radical reallocation of development resources and a re-alignment of economic policies, as well as demands for bureaucratic appointments, replaced the issue of the language as the principal issue in the Bengali movement. There was also a progressive radicalization of the movement and socialist ideas began to gain ground.

Creating a Bengali Bourgeoisie

In the sixties, President Ayub decided to foster in East Bengal a Bengali bourgeoisie, which, he believed, would provide him with a political base in the province and counter the influence of socialist ideas. This endeavour was blessed and backed by the Pakistani bourgeoisie. But to create a bourgeoisie the regime had to put money into the hands of men who had too little of it. Two categories of people from East Bengal were drawn into the process of 'capital formation' which was devised by the Ayub regime, to whom we can refer respectively as the 'contactors' and the 'contractors'. The 'contactors' were educated Bengalis with influential bureaucratic contacts (especially those who were relatives of bureaucrats or influential politicians) who were granted all kinds of permits and licences, which had a ready cash value because they could be sold to West Pakistani businessmen who needed them to be able to engage in profitable business transactions. This process transferred money into the pockets of a parasitic group of people, at the expense of the ordinary consumer who ultimately paid for this corruption in the forms of inflated prices. The 'contactors' lived expensively, and few of them contributed to capital accumulation or built up industries. The 'contractors' were different. They were small businessmen who were awarded construction contracts, etc., by the Government at deliberately inflated rates. The excess profits made by them were ploughed back into their businesses. They were later encouraged by generous loans and official support to become industrialists. For some industrial projects, for example, the Industrial Development Bank of Pakistan, which was set up for the purpose, would advance about two-thirds of the investment funds required and the East Pakistan Industrial Development Corporation would provide half of the remaining third of the total amount. The remaining sixth of the amount had to be raised by the prospective industrialist from his own pocket (already filled with public money) or from the stock exchange. In fact a substantial part of this equity was also subscribed by the State sponsored National Investment Trust and the Investment Corporation of Pakistan. To set up an industry, therefore, the budding Bengali industrialists needed barely 10 per cent (or less) of the capital needed. But profits were so high that it did not take

long before they became sole owners of their industries and began
to multiply their new found fortunes.

The attitude of the newly created nucleus of the Bengali
bourgeoisie towards the politics of Bengali nationalism was one of
qualified support. They profited greatly from the pressures
created by that politics. But, at the same time, they were
apprehensive because of its leftward gravitation. Moreover, their
extraordinary privileges were brought into existence because
there was a Central Government which could be pressured. The
continuance of their privileges in an independent East Bengal
was perhaps a little problematic. Not all of them supported the
movement wholeheartedly; they also provided support for right
wing movements in East Bengal, and collaborated with the
ruling oligarchy. They were particularly demoralized after the
Winter of 1968–9, when nationwide protest against the Ayub
regime, which brought about its downfall, threatened to develop
into a revolutionary movement, especially in East Bengal. Many
of them transferred substantial amounts to safer investments in
politically more 'stable' West Pakistan or, illegally, abroad.
While they supported a movement for regional autonomy and
diversion of a larger share of economic resources to East Bengal,
they also looked upon the bureaucratic–military oligarchy,
which is based in West Pakistan, as a bulwark for the defence and
protection of their own class interests; they therefore valued the
link with West Pakistan. The movement for the independence of
East Bengal cannot, therefore, be explained by reference principally to the aspirations of the Bengali bourgeoisie. Moreover, in
assessing the class basis of that movement, one must take into
account the fact that the movement existed and flourished before
the Bengali bourgeoisie was brought into being. The class base of
that movement was essentially petty bourgeois.

The massive electoral success of the Awami League in the
election of December 1970 was guaranteed by a third category of
people who had jumped on the bandwagon of the Awami
League. That was the rural elite in Bengal, which was previously
divided into many factions. The countryside in Bengal is
dominated by lineages of big farmers, the 'Sardari lineages'.
Their wealth, status and power, much of which is derived from
moneylending, enabled them to have access to the bureaucracy,
on the strength of which they mediated on behalf of their

factional supporters and thus further consolidate their local political power. These locally powerful rich farmers aligned with the elitists of the Awami League; the latter were after all their sons who had been given a university education and who aspired to big jobs in the bureaucracy.

Despite the radical rhetoric of the elitists in the Awami League, their intentions vis-à-vis the West Pakistan based oligarchy were quite ambivalent. This was because the elitist leaders were apprehensive about the radical aspirations of their own populist political base. While, on the one hand, they exploited the latter's radical sentiments in order to generate some force with which to confront those who were in power in West Pakistan and to gain some concessions, they had little wish to allow the radicalism of their followers to overwhelm them and to threaten the social order to which their own elitist aspirations committed them. It is this ambivalence which explains the anxiety of Sheikh Mujib to continue negotiations with General Yahya Khan in the first few weeks of March 1971 for autonomy within Pakistan, notwithstanding the fact that, as a consequence of an effective general strike in East Bengal he was already in *de facto* control of state power in the province; and that at a time when the Pakistan army was numerically weak and was unprepared for the action which it later launched against the people in East Bengal. This was testified to by Tajuddin Ahmed, the Prime Minister of the Bangladesh Provisional Government who, on the eve of his return to liberated Dacca, told newsmen that '*The original demand for autonomy within the framework of Pakistan had been raised by the Awami League as a whole* but the demand for independence grew when Pakistan not only refused to grant autonomy but also unleashed a reign of terror on the people of East Bengal.'[11]

The Making of Bangladesh

Since the creation of Bangladesh, the confrontation between the elitist element in the Awami League and its populist bases has re-emerged on a new level. Whereas the elitist leadership found a safe haven in Calcutta, the populist and marxist political cadres, who were once isolated, now established a new relationship with the people in the course of their armed liberation struggle. The organization and strength of the armed resistance was not yet strong enough to overthrow the Pakistani army; but it was growing. Moreover the position of the Pakistani army was reaching a point of crisis because the weak economy of West Pakistan could not sustain the long military campaign. There was an economic crisis in West Pakistan and outbursts of discontent. That opened up new prospects for the advance of the liberation forces in Bengal. It was precisely at that moment that the Indians chose to intervene, to forestall the liberation of Bangladesh by popular forces and to install the Awami League elitist leadership in power.

The picture in Bangladesh today is fundamentally different from that which existed in Pakistan at the time of its independence in 1947. The Bengali bureaucracy exists and the Awami League regime has identified itself with it and with the privileged groups in the country, but these are not backed by substantial military forces. On the other hand, the populist forces have experienced armed struggle and in the course of it they have developed organizationally. Large quantities of arms are in their possession. True, 'anti-insurgency groups' were also given training in India and were armed to prepare for the day after the liberation of Bangladesh. For the present all the political skill of Sheikh Mujib is directed to persuading the popular forces to hand over their arms or to become integrated in the organized military forces of Bangladesh—but with little success. It may yet be that a new bureaucratic–military oligarchy with outside aid will consolidate its position and power in course of time in Bangladesh. But it is equally possible that Bangladesh will be plunged into an armed revolutionary struggle, for the instruments of coercive state power at the disposal of the Awami League and the Bengali bureaucracy are weak and the economic crisis runs deep.

NOTES

1. R. Miliband, 'Marx and the State', in R. Miliband and J. Saville (eds.), *The Socialist Register, 1965*, (Merlin Press).
2. Hamza Alavi, 'Indian Capitalism and Foreign Imperialism', *New Left Review*, no. 37, June 1966.

3. C. P. Bhambhri, *Bureaucracy and Politics in India*, (Delhi: Vikas Publishers Private Ltd., 1971).
4. This 'middleman' role of politicians has been analysed in numerous studies, cf. F. G. Bailey, *Politics and Social Change–Orissa 1959*, (Oxford University Press, 1964).
5. Hamza Alavi, 'The Army and the Bureaucracy in Pakistan Politics', in A. Abdel Malek (ed.), *Armée et Nations dans les Trois Continents*, (forthcoming). Written in 1966, this article was privately circulated.
6. Tariq Ali, 'The Struggle in Bangladesh', *New Left Review*, no. 68, July–August 1971, footnote 21, p. 43.
7. Hamza Alavi and Amir Khusro, 'Pakistan: the Burden of U.S. Aid', *New University Thought*, vol. 2, no. 4, (Autumn 1962), reprinted in R. I. Rhodes (ed.), *Imperialism and Underdevelopment* (Monthly Review, 1970).
8. Nicos Poulantzas, 'Capitalism and the State', *New Left Review*, no. 58, November–December 1969, p. 74.
9. Paul Baran, *The Political Economy of Growth*, (Monthly Review, 1957), pp. 220–1.
10. This development was analysed in Hamza Alavi, 'Imperialism, Old and New', in R. Miliband and J. Saville (eds.), *The Socialist Register*, 1964 (Merlin Press).
11. *The Times*, London, 23 December 1971.

5 JOHN S. SAUL

The State in post-colonial societies: Tanzania*†

I Models for Africa

Implicitly, some crude notion of the 'autonomy' of the state lies at the root of modernization theory . . . Much the least interesting of the three broad formulations we shall mention in this section, it is a model which conceives of those who inherit the post-colonial state as 'benign elites'—the 'new middle class' or 'the modernizers'. Their role, within the trickle-down process of enlightenment from advanced countries to backward countries, is naturally, to facilitate the 'development', the modernization of their 'new nation'. In addition, there is a left variant of this essentially benign interpretation—an interpretation which, quite uncritically, sees this new stratum as a force for socialism! Of course, this has been the stuff of much political rhetoric in many centres of 'African Socialism', but Green has recently given this argument an academic formulation (albeit with primary reference to Tanzania). Quite aware that 'the elite' in many parts of Africa may, in the service of its own self-interest, abuse both its opportunity for service and the trust of the mass of the

---

* This paper was originally presented in the 'Views from the Left' Lecture Series, Toronto, Canada, February 1974. For an overview of the Tanzanian situation which spells out both the country's achievements and its continuing contradictions in much more detail than has been possible here, the interested reader may wish to refer to the author's 'African Socialism in One Country: Tanzania', in Giovanni Arrighi and John S. Saul, *Essays on the Political Economy of Africa* (New York and London, 1973), Ch. 6. The present paper is, in effect, a theoretical extension of that earlier essay. There are also the various materials collected in Lionel Cliffe and John S. Saul (eds.), *Socialism in Tanzania: Politics and Policies*, two volumes (Nairobi, Kenya, 1972 and 1973).

† Extract from paper of the same title, in, R. Miliband and J. Savage (eds.) *The Socialist Register 1974*, (Merlin Press, 1974).

people, Green nonetheless concludes that, for some unexplained reason, this does not occur in a country like Tanzania. Thus,

> in the case of Tanzania, it would be fair to say that virtually every general and specific issue raised by university critics had been posed (sometimes in even harsher terms) at least six months (and in certain cases up to two years) earlier by members of the 'neo-bourgeois bureaucratic elite' and that almost all were under active study aimed at evaluating alternative operational solutions both at official and political level. There is no reason to suppose this is a totally unique record even if it may well be atypical in degree. Further, the public sector elite has accepted material rewards substantially lower than those in neighbouring states, and than those prevailing in Tanzania five years ago, with no evident general loss of morale or loyalty. To say that shortcomings can be cited and that the elite is still far above average material standards is fair comment; to argue that it has on any broad scale deliberately obstructed or been unable because unwilling to move ahead on the implementation of the Arusha Declaration is much more dubious. There is no logical reason to assume that because technical competence need not be positively related to political commitment it must always be negatively related.[1]

It is interesting that so close an observer of the Tanzanian scene as Green could come to such a conclusion, but it must also be asserted categorically that his remarks—so sweepingly stated—cannot be squared with the findings of most other students of Tanzanian realities.[2]

At the opposite end of the spectrum from the 'benign' school are those who perceive in parts of Africa the *crystallization of a fully-formed class* around the apparatus of the state—a class with an interest quite distinct from and antagonistic to the interests of the mass of the population. Fanon hints at some such formulation, but it has been given its most vigorous scientific statement by Claude Meillassoux in his important 'class analysis of the bureaucratic process in Mali'.[3] He focuses on 'the bureaucrats', defining them as 'a body generated by the colonizers to carry out the tasks which could not (or would not) be undertaken by the Europeans themselves'. In this capacity they were entrusted with some of the instruments of power, notably with expertise. In other words, education and government (and business) *employment* are the crucial features.[4] He then argues that in Mali:

> . . . having been the instrument of the colonial power, and having turned against it to become the mouthpiece of the exploited Malian peasantry, the bureaucracy was gaining (with its access to power) some of the characteristics of a social class: control of the economic infrastructure and use of it as a means of exploitation, control of the means of repression involving a resort to various devices to maintain dominance. Some of its features are original: its opposite class is not yet socially well defined; it does not own the means of production on a private judicial basis, but controls them on a constitutional basis. There is no room here for a parliamentary system, regulating conflicts between a great number of private owners or corporations. The situation is better controlled through the single-party machine, within which open conflicts can be reduced to inner struggles between hidden factions. Appropriation of the economic bases of power cannot come from individual endeavour or entrepreneurship, nor from inheritance. It can come through co-operation by the people in position, or as the bargain lot of a *coup d'état*.

Meillassoux's findings parallel those of Alavi [Essay 4] in several respects. There is, for example, the subordination to imperialism of this 'class': 'Given the economic dependence of the country, the bureaucracy is itself a dependent group, and its origin as an instrument of western interests continues to influence its development. Instead of striving towards a real independence after winning the right to assert itself as political intermediaries with the outside world, the bureaucrats are content to return (with a higher international rank) under the rule of the old master.' Furthermore, their position is consolidated in contestation with (weak) indigenous classes: in the Mali case, an aristocracy (formerly slave-holders—a class for which there is no equivalent in East Africa) and a fairly well-developed trading-class.[5] However, having gone so far, Meillassoux remains reluctant in the end to call this group a class outright: 'it is also crucial that a distinction be made between the class proper and the dependent social elements which are the out-growth of classes, but which may, in specific historical circumstances, assume important historical functions'. Others, as we shall see, are prepared to go further in this direction, but for the moment another of Meillassoux's points may be cited. In noting the bureaucracy's attempt 'to gain certain positions of control in the modern economy and to eliminate opposition spreading from the Malian historical classes', he comments on their moves 'to infiltrate the national economy through the creation of a nationalized economic sector' as follows:

> This was done under the label of 'socialism' which provided them with a convenient ideology to bring the economy under their control, supposedly of course on behalf of the entire population. 'Socialism' permitted them to put the bureaucracy into the position of a managerial board of a kind of State corporation.

This is striking; it is almost identically the analysis that Shivji seeks to document with respect to 'Tanzanian socialism'.[6]

It also bears a remarkable resemblance to the analysis by Fitch and Oppenheimer of Ghanaian developments under Nkrumah.[7] It is therefore interesting to note that a third model of the role of the oligarchy—he does not, of course, use that term—was articulated by Roger Murray precisely in the context of a brilliant critique of Fitch and Oppenheimer's position.[8] Murray's is a model which falls somewhere between the polar opposites of the 'benign' and the 'class' models sketched above, and, like Meillassoux's argument, is of particular interest because it too foreshadows an approach to Tanzanian developments, in this case an approach very different from Shivji's. Murray is well aware of 'the sedimenting of new and gross class and power dispositions centring upon the state' in Ghana. Yet he is uneasy with Fitch and Oppenheimer's reduction of the socialist impulse there to the status of '*mere* manipulation', suggesting that in so arguing the authors lapse into 'pseudo-Marxist determinism'. A richer, more complex picture of those who inherit the over-developed state in the post-colonial period is needed.

What he sees instead is 'the accession to *state power* of unformed classes'. Concentrating on the CPP leadership and cadres,[9] he notes that

> they were drawn from the *petty bourgeois salariat* (clerks, primary schoolteachers, PWD storekeepers, messengers, etc.)—a mixed stratum which concentrated many of the political and cultural tensions of colonial society. It is precisely the socially ambiguous and unstable character of this stratum which helps us to understand its *relative autonomy and volatility* in the political arena. The CPP 'political' class did not express or reflect a determinate economic class.

Murray is trapped, almost inevitably, by the concreteness, the static and undialectical nature, of terminology here for even categories like 'unformed class' or 'class-in-formation' remain essentially teleological.[10] Thus the 'political class' to which he refers might really be best considered a 'political "x"' since any other formulation (including the term 'oligarchy') will mean that the relative social autonomy and plasticity of the political class-in-formation is lost to view. Yet this is a result Murray obviously wishes to avoid, as his further conclusion demonstrates:

> The essence of the matter is that the post-colonial state (the 'political kingdom') has simultaneously to be perceived as the actual instrument of mediation and negotiation with external capitalism, and as the possible instrument of a continuing anti-imperialist and socialist revolution. In this setting, the 'relative autonomy' of the ruling 'petty bourgeois' (we can see how unilluminating the category is at this point) stratum becomes a critical issue, whose import has to be examined in its *modus operandi* of state power.[11]

In other words, the autonomy of this 'x' is real, very real; in this 'uncertain historical moment', its members can attempt to opt for different historical alternatives, alternatives which would actually affect in *different* ways their own positions in the production process.

This is not to abandon class analysis. It is merely to highlight the 'social *uncertainty* and susceptibility to multiple determinations and influences which make the dimension of *consciousness* so crucial to the analysis—a dimension consistently underestimated by Fitch and Oppenheimer. The contradictory situation and experience of these typically transitional and partial post-colonial ruling groups is mediated through the transformations, incoherences, oscillations, 'false' and illusory representations and reconciliation at *the level of ideology.*' Thus, in discussing the CPP's left-turn in the early 1960s—a 'new articulation of ideology and organization . . . which made socialist Ghana something of a model type in possible post-colonial African development'—Murray mentions as crucial factors not only the economic crisis of the late 1950s but also 'the whole *trajectory* of ideological evolution since the 1940s'.[12] Nor is this to underestimate the determinations which encourage such elements—harassed by a 'frustrated national bourgeoisie', seduced by the easy lure of 'bureaucratic consolidation' and alternately tempted and tormented by imperialism—to entrench themselves as an 'oligarchy' of dominant 'class'. Murray states clearly that there are real limits upon what is 'historically possible' under such conditions. But he does at least affirm the possibility, in the realm of *praxis*, of a real struggle over the direction which development should take.

It follows that, if such a struggle is possible, it may take place precisely *within* this unformed 'x', between those of its members who seek to consolidate the neo-colonial set-up and those who are moved, increasingly, to challenge it.[13] Furthermore, such a model can then be interpreted as providing a scientific basis for one of Amilcar Cabral's most suggestive metaphors. For Cabral, in identifying the 'revolutionary' wing of a crucial class in formation which he dubs the 'petty-bourgeoisie' (and which is strikingly similar in many of its characteristics to that 'political class' discussed by Murray), states that 'this revolutionary petty bourgeoisie is honest; i.e. in spite of all the hostile conditions it remains identified with the fundamental interests of the popular masses. To do this it may have to commit suicide, but it will not lose; by sacrificing itself it can reincarnate itself, but in the condition of workers and peasants.'[14] As Murray demonstrates, there were no significant sections of the Ghanaian leadership who could bring themselves, ultimately, to 'commit suicide' in this sense. Nor did the CPP, the political expression of that leader-

ship, realize any such possibility, failing as it did even to attempt
the effective mobilization of that active popular base which could
alone have guaranteed forward momentum in the longer run.[15]
What of Tanzania? Clearly, Walter Rodney's application of
Cabral to the Tanzanian situation is of interest in this respect:

> (Cabral) considers the petty-bourgeoisie not as a decadent
> stereotype but as a stratum with various possibilities, and he
> includes himself. Cabral was concerned with evaluating the
> 'nationalist capacity' of the petty bourgeoisie as well as their
> 'revolutionary capacity' in the post-independence phase. He
> speaks about a 'revolutionary petty-bourgeoisie', meaning
> that section which has joined the Liberation Struggle and is
> already carrying it forward in the direction of socialist
> reconstruction in the liberated zones. In other words, the
> African petty-bourgeoisie stratum includes Shivji, the other
> TANU Youth League comrades at the University (of Dar es
> Salaam) and most of the national leadership in Tanzania—
> irrespective of political convictions. Sections of the petty-
> bourgeoisie have broken with their mentors, and individuals
> within the group have at various times wholly or partially
> opposed the external or local capitalists.[16]

II Socialism and the State in Tanzania

Turning to Tanzania, we may note at the outset that each of the
models sketched in Section 1 has found its echo in the wide-
ranging debate about the nature of Tanzania's 'socialism'. Thus,
the 'right-benign' interpretation is seen at its most sophisticated
in the writings of Cranford Pratt who eventually gives most
bureaucrats and politicians in Tanzania high marks as 'de-
velopers', despite what to him appear as the unnerving hi-jinks of
some few 'political ministers' and the occasional dangers of a
'doctrinaire determination of policies'.[17] We have already taken
note of Green's 'left-benign' variant. Both wings of this approach
present much too oversimplified an account to warrant their
further discussion here. Rather, the really significant differences
of scientific opinion lie between what are, in effect and broadly
speaking, the protagonists of the Meillassoux and of the Murray/
Cabral models.

On the one-hand and closer to Meillassoux are 'the Majimaji socialists', most notably Issa Shivji, author of two of the most important papers to have emerged from the Tanzanian debate.[18] It is in point to recapitulate his argument concerning the nature of class struggle in post-colonial Tanzania, for it is also a significant statement concerning the nature of the state there. As noted earlier, Shivji's scepticism about the socialist vocation of wielders of state power in Tanzania first found theoretical expression in his attempt to view these elements as quite straightforward agents of the international bourgeoisie. His second paper continues to stress the extent to which such elements service the interests of international capitalism, but he has gone on to develop a much more sophisticated analysis of their own stake in the system.

The class which takes power is, once again, the 'petty-bourgeoisie', particularly its 'upper level' ('the intelligentsia') identified, rather eclectically, as comprised of 'intellectuals, teachers, higher civil servants, prosperous traders, farmers, professionals, higher military and police officers'. The inclusion of the (African) 'traders' and 'farmers' in this class and in the nationalist coalition is not crucial, however:[19] 'one of the outstanding features of the petty-bourgeoisie was that they overwhelmingly came from the urban-based occupations, with some education and some knowledge of the outside world'.[20] This class spearheads the struggle against the colonial state. In doing so, their interests merely 'coincide with those of the broad masses'. The same is true, Shivji states, for the next stage of development—the struggle with the Indian 'commercial bour-geoisie'. The role of the latter class-cum-ethnic group—which has controlled the intermediate sectors of the economy—is analysed by Shivji with great subtlety; in fact, he has provided the first really convincing class analysis of the Asian community in East Africa to date. On the African side he extends his analysis in a manner which is much more controversial.

For the confrontation which Shivji sees to be taking place between petty-bourgeoisie and commercial bourgeoisie for economic power is complicated by a further development, one which emerges precisely with the accession to state power (at independence) of this petty bourgeoisie:

In an underdeveloped African country with a *weak petty-bourgeoisie*, its ruling section which comes to possess the instrument of the state on the morrow of independence, relatively commands enormous power and is therefore very strong. This was precisely the case in Tanzania. . . . The Tanzanian scene . . . comes closer to the 'Bonapartist' type of situation where the contending classes have weakened themselves thus allowing the 'ruling clique' to cut itself off from its class base and *appear* to raise the state above the class struggle. Of course, it is not that the contending classes had weakened themselves in the independence struggle. But a somewhat similar situation resulted from the fact that the petty bourgeoisie was weak and had not developed deep economic roots. This allowed the 'ruling group' a much freer hand. In other words the control of the state became the single decisive factor. For these and other reasons . . . it is proposed to identify the 'ruling group' as the 'bureaucratic bourgeoisie'. Before the Arusha Declaration, this would comprise mainly those at the top levels of the state apparatus—ministers, high civil servants, high military and police officers and such like. One may also include the high level bureaucrats of the Party and the cooperative movement, because of the important role the latter played in the pre-Arusha class struggles.[21]

Shivji does note that the weakness of the petty-bourgeoisie referred to here 'is due to the fact that it is still "embryonic"; the whole class structure is in *the process of* formation'. The same *caveat* is introduced with reference to the bureaucratic bourgeoisie. Is it 'a class *as distinct* from the petty bourgeoisie'? Not quite. 'Suffice to say that the post-independence class struggles (including the Arusha Declaration) were themselves a process leading to the emergence of the "bureaucratic bourgeoisie". The process may not be complete.' But having noted this, Shivji, unlike Murray, does not draw back from his terms. He is unconcerned with the weight of teleology which they bear. As he proceeds with his analysis, classes-in-formation behave, unambiguously, like fully formed classes. And this is the chief weakness of his argument.

For Shivji, in sum, the 'historical moment' is by no means 'uncertain'. On the contrary, he now uses this conception of

Tanzania's class structure—straightforwardly and however much the 'structure' may be 'in the process of formation'—to explain the history of post-colonial Tanzania: it is the case of 'a *non-proletarian class* after coming to political power . . . now trying to wrest an economic base' from the commercial bourgeoisie. Half-measures, like the encouragement of the cooperatives, having failed, 'the only alternative, both for further struggle against the commercial bourgeoisie and for further penetration of the economy, was state intervention': 'it was thus that the Arusha Declaration was born in 1967'. With it, and with the attendant nationalizations, a new stage in the class struggle, à la Shivji, is reached:

> Up until the Arusha Declaration, the 'bureaucratic bour-geoisie' was essentially of the politico-administrative type. Although the state played an important role in the economy it was mostly a regulatory one. With the Arusha Declaration, the state and state institutions (including parastatals) became the dominant actors in the economy. Thus a new and more important wing of the bureaucratic bourgeoisie was created. Political power and control over property had now come to rest in the same class.

Socialism as '*mere* manipulation'—Shivji comes very close to such a position. Nevertheless, he does recognize that there is some difficulty in reconciling this with the Arusha Declaration Leadership Code—a code designed to prevent leaders from involving themselves, profitably, in the private sector. Here Shivji's explanation, in order to save his hypothesis, is that 'the ideology had gained the upper hand, for even a rhetoric has its own momentum and can have important effects on concrete measures'. This would also appear to be his 'explanation' for the very real constraints (certainly as compared with other parts of Africa) on elite income and consumption which have been a part of Tanzania's 'socialism'. In addition, Shivji states, as if to reinforce his general argument, that the Code has often been flouted since its inception. This, in turn, suggests (quite ac-curately) that there was a 'spontaneous' tendency for 'leaders' to overlap into the private sector—as in neighbouring Kenya. Yet such a reality seems to contradict Shivji's emphasis. Why didn't the petty-bourgeoisie use the state to facilitate their own movement in upon the Asians on a private basis—again, as in Kenya—rather than publicly and collectively?

Shivji is aware of this problem, of course, and his explanation is of considerable interest:

> In Kenya, there were important sections of the petty bourgeoisie—yeoman farmers and traders, for example—besides the urban-based intelligentsia, who had already developed significant 'independent' roots in the colonial economy. Thus the petty bourgeoisie itself as a class was strong and different sections within it were more or less at par. This considerably reduced the power of the 'ruling clique' irrespective of its immediate possession of the state apparatus and kept it 'tied' to its class base—the petty bourgeoisie.

But this does not convince. Even if the entrepreneurial elements were stronger in transitional Kenya, the difference from Tanzania was not so striking as Shivji suggests and in any case these Kenyan Africans' commercial opponents (European and Asian) were themselves much stronger than any counterparts in Tanzania; thus the *relative* economic weight of the African entrepreneurs cannot have been that much different. Moreover, it is quite unnecessary to make such subtle distinctions. As noted, it seems obvious that large sections of Shivji's bureaucratic bourgeoisie continue to cast envious glances at their civil servant and political counterparts in Kenya and at the gross (and rewarding) 'conflicts of interest' which serve to characterize Kenyan economic and political life. And, being disproportionately drawn from commercialized, cash-cropping rural areas like Kilimanjaro and Bukoba, they do in fact have intimate (familial) connections with a 'yeomanry'. Unless contested, such a group would have had Tanzania gravitate in the Kenyan direction, a point made by Nyerere himself on more than one occasion.[22] It is difficult, in fact, to avoid the conclusion that the Arusha Declaration package of policies—the opting for collective solutions to the Tanzanian development problem—represented, first and foremost, an *initial victory* for a *progressive wing* of the petty bourgeoisie (and the announcement of its continuing commitment to the interests of the workers and peasants), rather than some cold-blooded fulfilment of the class interests of that stratum's bureaucratic core.[23]

This difference of opinion requires detailed exploration of a kind that is beyond the scope of the present paper. Suffice to say that for Shivji this kind of 'manipulation' also tends to characterize each of the specific arenas of post-Arusha policy-making, while for each such arena it can be shown that this is an oversimplification. Take, for example, the 'ujamaa village' programme (designed to promote a Tanzanian brand of agricultural collective), in Shivji's eyes merely a calculated and perfunctory gesture—an expression of 'intermittent ideological hostility' to 'kulaks'—designed to maintain for the petty bourgeoisie its 'popular peasant base'. But this was not an immediately popular policy even among much of the peasantry; support for it would have to be *created*, sometimes in a manner (as in Ismani) which challenged the local dignitaries of the party itself. Nor is it entirely true that this policy was 'not basically against the interests of the petty bourgeoisie'. The fact that in practice bureaucrats often worked hard to defuse the policy by directing it away from the 'advanced' area (Kilimanjaro and Bukoba mentioned above) and towards more defenceless, backward regions (with many fewer kulaks) testifies to their uneasiness. Nor were the extensive nationalizations of 1967 merely a charade. International capitalism was stung and the conventional wisdom of most civil servants visibly affronted. In other words, these and other initiatives represented real achievements in a transition towards socialism.[24] That the full potential of these policies' possible contribution to such a transition has not been realized is, of course, also true, a point to which we shall return.

However, there is one crucial area of inquiry which cannot be passed over here and which also sheds considerable light on the issue under discussion. Thus, Shivji argues that the main contradictions in Tanzania is now between the working-class and the bureaucratic bourgeoisie, and cites the dramatic assertions of Tanzania's working-class in recent years. Indeed, the further investigation of this subject by Shivji's colleague, Henry Mapolu, reveals a level of proletarian action in Tanzania which is virtually unparalleled elsewhere in Africa.[25] As Mapolu writes:

By any standards the progress made by the working population in Tanzania in the last few years as far as political
consciousness is concerned is astounding. To begin with, at no
other time in the whole history of this country have strikes and
industrial disputes generally been so much a day-to-day affair
as has become since 1970. But more important, at no other
time have such strikes and disputes been of such a political
nature! . . . It has indeed been a veritable revolution for the
Tanzanian workers; within a period of three years they have
moved from a state of docility, timidness, and above all
disunity to one of tremendous bravery, initiative and class
solidarity.

Beginning with the downing of tools and with lock-outs, some
Tanzanian workers had moved, by 1973, to the stage of actually
occupying factories (both state-owned and private) and continuing production on their own. And the issues were not, by and
large, of a conventionally consumptionist nature. Disputes
concerned, firstly 'the question of humiliation and oppression on
their person by managements' and, ultimately, 'issues of general
mismanagement and sabotage of the country's economy'. Pre-
dictably, such initiatives began to earn reprisals from the
bureaucracy (including police intervention and arrests), thus
polarizing the Tanzanian situation to an unprecedented degree.

But where did such a high level of consciousness come from?
This too must be explained, especially when one compares this
development with experience elsewhere in Africa. Moreover, the
Tanzanian working-class is small, even by continental standards,
and, in the past, not marked by notably radical leanings.[26] Once
again, the conclusion suggests itself that initiatives taken by a
certain sector of the leadership—notably by Nyerere and his
supporters—played an important role in bringing about this
development and in facilitating the emergence of what Shivji
calls 'the proletarian line'. Unlike their Ghanaian counterparts,
such a leadership did sense, albeit haltingly, that 'the oppressed'
could 'alone have provided the conscious support for a socialist
path of development'[27] and they therefore sought to create such a
base. Initiatives designed to facilitate 'workers' participation'
(workers' councils) and peasant participation (*ujamaa* and
decentralization) reflected this concern, despite the distortion in

practice of these programmes by the dead-hand of the bureaucracy.[28] However, most significant in this respect has been *Mwongozo*, the TANU Guidelines of 1971—a crucial document in crystallizing worker consciousness and in legitimizing, *even demanding*, the unleashing of popular pressures against oligarchical tendencies on the part of wielders of state power ('leaders'). Yet the drive for these measures did not come from below. Even Shivji must come part way to meet that reality.

In the international situation where capitalism has become a global system and socialism has been established in a large area of the world: where both internally and externally physical and intellectual wars are raging between the capitalist and socialist lines, the world-wide circulation of progressive ideas has become common-place. It is not surprising therefore that even capitalism and neo-colonialism have to be wrapped up in socialist rhetoric and vocabulary. But more important is the fact that though material *class* forces may not immediately warrant it, a few progressive and revolutionary leaders manage to push through (officially) radical ideas and policies. The adoption of the Mwongozo by TANU, with its progressive features, was such an event.

But who are these 'few progressive and revolutionary leaders'? As Shivji suggests, they do shape and crystallize, rather than merely reflect, popular consciousness; moreover, they seem to be cutting sharply against the interests of the bureaucratic bourgeoisie. It is precisely because Shivji's approach cannot fully illuminate such matters that other analysts have felt some other formulation than his to be necessary in order to explain, in class terms, the 'socialist' dimensions of Tanzania's experiment.

Indeed, it is only because it is much too evocative and dismissive a phrase that one avoids applying to Shivji's analysis Murray's epithet: 'pseudo-Marxist determinism'. Nonetheless, Murray's critique of Fitch and Oppenheimer is in many respects the best approach to Shivji. And Murray's positive formulations can also serve to promise much the most effective alternative approach to Tanzanian reality. In this respect it is worth noting that even the definitional problem (which Murray himself approached somewhat too obliquely) has been faced, quite straightforwardly, by Micheala von Freyhold—working from what is in effect, a closely related viewpoint to that of Murray. Her solution, in a recent paper, is to use the term 'nizers' for the 'x' in our socio–political equation. As she explains it:

> 'Nizers' or 'nizations' (from Africanization) is a term applied by Tanzanians to refer to that stratum or class which social scientists have called 'educated elite', 'labour aristocracy', or 'petty bourgeoisie'—those who took over important administrative and economic positions when colonialism was defeated.
>
> 'Educated elite' is an ideological term bound up with the elitist theories of dubious origin. 'Labour aristocracy' suggests a link between workers and 'nizers' which . . . does not exist. 'Petty bourgeoisie' has a double meaning: it refers to small capitalists on the one hand and all those who look to the bourgeoisie as their model on the other. As long as the educated stratum to which we refer is directly employed by colonialists or a national bourgeoisie it is necessarily a petty bourgeoisie in the second sense. In the absence of such direct employers the educated stratum can choose whether it wants to remain subservient to those by whom it has been created. Since the stratum in question may decide to become a petite bourgeoisie in both senses we would prefer to reserve the term for that particular situation.
>
> 'Nizers' is a precise and dialectical term. It refers firstly to the progressive aspect of Africanization, to the promise that those who take over the power would return this power to the people on whose behalf they took it away from the colonialists.
>
> It refers secondly to the fact that the 'nizers' have not created the existing economic and social structure but have taken it over, either adapting to it or changing the built in dependency on imperialism.
>
> It refers thirdly to the negative possibility that the original promises are not held, that the structure is not changed, that those who have taken the power will usurp it for themselves.
>
> Which of the connotations of the term 'nizers' will emerge as the decisive one is subject to the still on-going struggle among the nizers and the kind of support the different factions can mobilize among other classes—the workers and the peasants.[29]

It is precisely to this 'still on-going struggle among the nizers' that Freyhold traces the socialist impulse in Tanzania: 'In 1967 an enlightened political leadership had decided that Tanzania should not turn into a neo-colonial society. The Leadership Code was to cut the links between public office-holders and petty capitalism and nationalisations were to bring foreign capital under control. . . . Both measures were . . . a vital first step.' And the direction of further steps also remains, in her eyes, a contested matter. 'While the transformation of the nizers is an obvious prerequisite for the promised creation of a socialist society it is obvious that it will not proceed without a protracted struggle within that educated stratum itself. What the progressive parts of Tanzania's nizers envisage as their future is not yet reality. As long as the future is undecided there are still two ways in which one can look at the present educated stratum: as a nascent petty bourgeoisie which will not only be a faithful agent of international capital but which will eventually solidify into a class with petty capitalist connections and orientations or as the precursors of a socialist avantguarde.' Of course, the general definitional problem has probably not been laid to rest by Freyhold's coinage, suggestive though it is; nor does she directly address herself to Shivji's prognosis of bureaucratic consolidation *without* 'petty capitalist connections'. But the emphasis seems to me to be basically correct.[30]

To argue so is not to ignore the contradictions which mitigate, and even undermine, the achievements of Tanzania's progressive 'nizers'. Quite the reverse. In the essay cited above (note 30), I have stressed the extent to which various pressures—international and domestic—do play upon the system in such a way as to strengthen the least progressive elements in the 'present educated stratum' and to 'solidify' that stratum into a privileged class. It is quite true, as Shivji has demonstrated in another of his papers, that international capitalism can make adjustments and begin to shape to its own purposes the fact of nationalization. Corporations join with aid agencies and international economic institutions in reactivating 'conventional wisdom' and coopting those 'oligarchs' who are inclined to be so tempted. In addition, the expansion of the state sector has had the *result* (but, to repeat, not the primary purpose) of expanding the number who are prepared merely to feed off it, in the absence of countervailing tendencies.[31] If, unlike Ghana, some more real effort has been made to create a new base for the state among the workers and peasants, the pace of bureaucratic consolidation seems to be outstripping that attempt. In consequence, demobilization of the peasantry becomes the more likely result, while workers find themselves set not merely against the most conservative of managers but against the state itself and the increasingly homogeneous class which defends it.

The negative weight of 'objective conditions' has been reinforced by subjective conditions. As Murray's analysis would suggest, ideological contestation in Tanzania has been a creative factor of great importance, with Nyerere's formulations in particular being crucial to facilitating a move to the left. But this ideology of the progressive 'nizers' has also been marked by inadequacies which some might like to term 'petty bourgeois' in nature: a hostility to Marxism, for example, and the consequent lack of a fully scientific analysis of imperialism and class struggle.[32] And this problem has been compounded by a much too sanguine reliance on existing institutions of the inherited state (Ministries and Cabinets, an untransformed party) which cannot easily be turned to purposes of Socialist construction.[33] As demonstrated in my earlier essay, these factors too have made it difficult for Nyerere and others to consolidate their original initiatives. The results are paradoxical (and not pre-ordained, à la Shivji). The conservative wing of the nizers now threatens to inherit a socialist initiative and an even more 'overdeveloped' state than existed at the moment of independence) in the creation of which it had little hand but which it has sought to warp to its own purposes from the moment of the policy's first being announced. All of which is to approach Shivji's conclusion, though not by Shivji's route:

> This marks the beginning of the political struggle and the rise of the proletarian line. There is bound to be increasing opposition to bureaucratic methods of work and 'management's' dominance, themselves a reflection of the neo-colonial structure of the economy and the corresponding class structure. The struggles of the workers and peasants against internal and external vested class interests will characterize the subsequent class struggles in Tanzania.[34]

For it is necessary to reaffirm that much about this continuing class struggle has been shaped by the reality of struggle within the stratum of the 'nizers'—within the 'oligarchy-in-the-making', if you like—during the first post-colonial decade.

*　　*　　*

The critique of Shivji is also a qualification of Alavi's approach. Apart from points made earlier concerning the important differences in context which East Africa presents, and some of the implications of these differences, it can now be argued that Alavi's approach is too rigid to fully comprehend the uncertainties which define the historical process in the immediate post-colonial period. In Tanzania, his 'oligarchies' become such only more slowly and with much more ambiguous results than his model would lead one to expect. At the same time it can be firmly stated that the pressures which move the situation towards such an unsavoury result as he seeks to theorize are indeed powerful. And, as noted, there is no doubt that these pressures have been, and are continually, making themselves felt upon Tanzania. As a result, 'oligarchical' tendencies—the consolidation of Shivji's 'bureaucratic bourgeoisie' (self-interested and ever more subservient to imperialism)—seem to have been the increasingly obvious result.

Has the further development of this trend altered perspectives on practice in Tanzania? Writing two years ago I felt confident to conclude a survey of Tanzania's efforts at socialist construction in the following terms: 'Indigenous radicals will decide their own fates. Yet the fact that almost all have chosen to work within the established structures and upon the régime is no accident.'[35] And there is still some significant contestation within the 'petty bourgeoisie' and within the established institutions.[36] But where, for example, one could then argue, with some confidence, that the control of working-class organization by party and state had played, despite the costs, a positive role in curbing consumptionism and raising worker consciousness, there is now reason to be more sceptical about the logic of continuing control. Faced with 'nizers' more bent than ever upon consolidating their power, independent organization of the working-class may seem an increasingly important goal.[37] Similarly, the time may be approaching when the independent political organization of progressive elements, already a (difficult) priority in most other one-party and military/administrative régimes in Africa, becomes a priority for Tanzania as well. Smash the post-colonial state or use it? But this is really a question which can only be asked, and answered, by those engaged in significant *praxis* within Tanzania itself.

NOTES

1. R. H. Green, 'Economic Independence and Economic Cooperation' in D. P. Ghai (ed.), *Economic Independence in Africa* (Nairobi, 1973), p. 85. In fact Green's error lies in vastly *over-estimating* the progressive attributes of the Tanzanian situation—even as Shivji, in his turn, underestimates them (see below).
2. For summaries of such findings see John S. Saul, 'African Socialism in One Country: Tanzania' in G. Arrighi and J. S. Saul, *Essays on the Political Economy of Africa* (Monthly Review, 1973), Ch. 6, and Uchumi Editorial Board, *Towards Socialist Planning*, Tanzanian Studies No. 1 (Dar es Salaam, 1972).
3. C. Meillassoux, 'A Class Analysis of the Bureaucratic Process in Mali', *The Journal of Development Studies* (January 1970).
4. Interestingly, Meillassoux makes no distinction between party and administration in his analysis: 'In this situation the only people able to take responsibility and power upon themselves were those with literate, administrative and managerial capabilities, equally necessary to handle a political party or to govern a State.'
5. Thus 'if the conflict with local business was a consequence of the necessity of the bureaucracy to provide itself with an economic base, the fight against the aristocratic class was a more direct competition for political power' (Meillassoux, p. 106).
6. It is worth nothing that these extensions of the argument differ from Fanon's conclusion to what is otherwise a somewhat similar analysis, for Fanon seems to imply that such elements will infiltrate the national economy by moving in on the trading sector as entrepreneurs—viz., the very definition of this class as 'an intellectual élite engaged in trade'. Here is a very significant difference of opinion as we shall see in examining Shivji's work more closely in Section II.
7. R. Fitch and M. Oppenheimer, *Ghana: End of an Illusion* (Monthly Review, 1966).
8. Roger Murray, 'Second Thoughts on Ghana', *New Left Review*, no. 42 (March–April, 1967).
9. It should be noted that Murray tends to talk only of the members of the ruling political party when he discusses those who inherit the state; he does not really deal with the bureaucracy's role in all of this, despite his recognizing the need for 'an appraisal of the politico-administrative role and weight of the *civil service* within the state apparatus'. However, his characterization of the 'autonomy and plasticity' of 'the political class' would seem also to apply to the bureaucracy; under such circumstances they seem equally to be elements whose 'partial and "transitional" character . . . expresses itself in its absence of a determinate class standpoint grounded upon its site in the process of production'. Interestingly, Meillassoux, from his different perspective, makes little distinction between bureaucrat and politician in identifying the state-based dominants in Mali (cf. note 4 above). This is also Shivji's approach; in Tanzania the civil service and political hierarchies in-

terpenetrate and he is prepared to view members of both as candidates for his categories of 'petty bourgeoisie' and 'bureaucratic bourgeoisie'.

10. On the problem of developing terms adequate to the task of dialectical analysis of real historical processes, see Bertell Ollman, *Alienation: Marx's Conception of Man in Capitalist Society* (Cambridge University Press, 1971), especially Part I.

11. As Murray continues: 'Socially, then, the picture we have is of a petty bourgeois group projected into the power vacuum caused by the lack of objective maturation of a nationalist capitalist class and the subjective errors of aspirant bourgeois politicians.'

12. Thus, 'the whole Nkrumahist ideological complex · was undergoing profound mutation in the 1960s. This process has two particularly striking features: the attempt to transcend the "African Socialism" current of thought in favour of a more universal and scientific theory; and the related effort to institutionalize and accelerate the formation of an *ideological vanguard* of cadres who might then strive to make ideology a mass force (Winneba). This development, marked as it was by bizarre juxtapositions and unresolved contradictions, nevertheless acquires considerable significance . . .' All of which is not to deny that it was a 'misconceived, contradictory "socialism" ' which emerged, characterized by (among other things) 'the loss of any *integral commanding strategy*' (Murray, ibid).

13. Actually this struggle can even be seen to take place *within* the individual members of this unformed 'x' as they struggle with the 'bizarre juxtapositions and unresolved contradictions' in their own lives, a reality which was dramatized for me during seven years of work with young recruits to the 'petty bourgeoisie' at the University of Dar es Salaam.

14. Amilcar Cabral, 'Brief Analysis of the Social Structure in Guinea' in his *Revolution in Guinea* (Stage 1, 1969), p. 59; the point is elaborated upon in his excellent essay 'The Weapon of Theory' in the same volume.

15. Thus Murray, in 'Second Thoughts on Ghana' states that the 'implicit positive model' offered by Fitch and Oppenheimer is 'that of a political party which made the situation and demands of the most oppressed classes (urban and rural proletariat, sharecroppers, indebted tenant farmers) the absolute "moral imperative" of its organization and action. This class-based party, acting for and through the oppressed but potentially revolutionary strata of society, could alone have provided the conscious support for a socialist path of development—with all its costs and risks.' But he concludes of Ghana that 'instead, the CPP demobilized these "potential" forces'.

16. Walter Rodney, 'Some Implications of the Question of Disengagement from Imperialism' in *Majimaji* (Dar es Salaam, 1971), and reprinted in Cliffe and Saul, *Socialism in Tanzania*, (Nairobi, 1973), vol. II. The explicit reference to Shivji arises from the fact that Rodney is here reviewing Shivji. 'Tanzania: The Silent Class Struggle', (*Ibid.*).

17. See, among other of his articles, Pratt's 'The Cabinet and Presidential Leadership in Tanzania: 1960–66' in M. Lofchie (ed.), *The State of the Nations* (Berkeley and Los Angeles, 1971) and reprinted in Cliffe and Saul.

18. See note 16, above; succeeding quotations are from the second to Shivji's two papers, unless otherwise indicated. ['The Class Struggle Continues', (Dar es Salaam: 1973).]

19. Not crucial, but there is an ambiguity in the term 'petty bourgeoisie' which is revealed here, one to which we will return in discussing Freyhold's attempt to conceptualize Tanzania's class structure.

20. Shivji gives no numerical basis to his argument, but I have elsewhere cited Resnick's argument that 'out of 350,000 persons employed in wage and salaried jobs in 1968, only 44,000 fall into the "privileged" class, . . . that is, are in occupations classified as "high- and middle-level" by manpower definitions'. See I. N. Resnick, 'Class,

Foreign Trade and Socialist Transformation in Tanzania', paper presented to the Economics Research Bureau Seminar, University of Dar es Salaam (mimeo, 1972).

21. As noted above (note 9), Shivji makes little distinction between party and civil service; nor do his critics who adhere, in effect, to the Murray line of analysis—although the latter might argue that rather more representatives of this progressive petty-bourgeoisie are to be found in the party (which has, however, a tendency to become itself bureaucratized).

22. Thus Nyerere has argued that 'some Tanzanian leaders criticized the Arusha Declaration' because 'they wished to use positions of power for private gain' and 'almost the only way in which Africans could get capital to become landlords or capitalists was by virtue of their office or their seniority in the public service'; see his 'Introduction' to J. K. Nyerere, *Freedom and Socialism* (Nairobi, London, New York, 1968).

23. Such a conclusion with reference to the Tanzanian case, paralleling Murray's critique of Fitch and Oppenheimer's handling of Ghanaian developments, also raises some retrospective doubts about Meillassoux's discussion of Mali. Was the socialist assertion there as straightforwardly manipulative as Meillassoux suggests?

24. Shivji's model has been applied, with interesting results, to the educational sphere by Karim Hirji in his essay 'School Education and Underdevelopment in Tanzania', *Majimaji*, 12 (September 1973). More alert to the ideological dimensions of Tanzanian development and very insightful, Hirji's analysis suffers, nonetheless, from some of the same rigidities as Shivji's. I intend to discuss his argument in more detail in a monograph on the University of Dar es Salaam, now in preparation.

25. Henry Mapolu, 'The Workers' Movement in Tanzania', *Majimaji*, 12 (September 1973). See also Mapolu's 'Labour unrest: irresponsibility or worker revolution', *Jenga* (Dar es Salaam), 12 (1972) and Nick Asili, 'Strikes in Tanzania', *Majimaji*, 4 (September 1971).

26. For a subtle account which highlights the dialectic established in Tanzania between a committed section of the leadership and a working-class with steadily rising consciousness, see M. A. Bienefeld, 'Workers, Unions and Development in Tanzania', paper delivered to a conference on 'Trade Unions and the Working-Class in Africa', Toronto, 1973. Even NUTA, the official trade union ('that moribund organization', in Bienefeld's words) is seen to have played a role in this respect: 'For its creation did forestall the creation of the self-centred, competitive unions, whose function and mentality is so well suited to the kind of interest group politics which the most powerful interests in an open economy find congenial, and who are so easily moulded into the business unions whose existence is defined by the capitalist economy. . . . (T)he worker was freed from the mesmerising spectacle of the perpetual competition for leadership by men who fight with promises for the spoils of office, while . . . the very bureaucratic nature of NUTA made it possible for the workers' allegiance to be transferred to the government more permanently.'

27. Cf. note 15. Nyerere very early sounded the themes which were later to find expression in Mwongozo; thus, in 1967, he 'called on the people of Tanzania to have great confidence in themselves and safeguard the nation's hard-won freedom. He warned the people against pinning all their hopes on the leadership who are apt to sell the people's freedom to meet their lusts. Mwalimu (i.e., Nyerere) warned that the people should not allow their freedom to be pawned as most of the leaders were purchasable' (*The Nationalist*, 5 September 1967).

28. On the very real and disturbing distortions in practice, however, see the striking analyses of Henry Mapolu, 'The Organization and Participation of Workers in Tanzania', Economics Research Bureau Paper 72.1 (Dar es Salaam, 1972) and Phil Raikes, 'Ujamaa Vijijini and Rural Socialist Development', paper delivered to the East African Universities Social Science Conference, Dar es Salaam, December 1973.

29. M. von Freyhold, 'The Workers and the Nizers' (mimeo, University of Dar es Salaam, 1973). At the same time, it is also worth noting (as I am reminded by John Loxley) that in its popular usage the term 'nizers' is generally applied by workers and peasants in a pejorative sense!

30. Indeed, it is quite close in certain respects, to my account of the emergence of Tanzanian socialism in 'African Socialism in One Country; Tanzania'. There, however, the prognosis of bureaucratic consolidation without petty capitalist connections *is* explored and one all too possible post- 'socialist' system characterized as 'the creation of a vicious circle within which a petty bourgeoisie, on balance still relatively untransformed, demobilizes and instrumentalizes the mass of the population and guarantees, at best, a stagnant quasi-state capitalism, thereby checking further progress' (p. 298).

31. This is all the more likely to be the case precisely because this expansion of state activities into the economic sphere does expand the contact of the nizers with international corporations through management contracts, etc. and international economic agencies which are among the most co-operative of imperialism's many mechanisms.

32. Unfortunately, this tends (as again argued in my earlier paper) towards the same results as Murray noted in Ghana: 'the loss of any *integral commanding strategy*'.

33. This is the strongest point made in Haroub Othman. 'The State in Tanzania: Who Controls It and Whose Interests does it Serve' (mimeo, Institute of Development Studies, University of Dar es Salaam, Tanzania, n.d.). (also in, *Monthly Review*, vol. 26, no. 7, December, 1974—ed.)

34. Shivji, 'The Class Struggle Continues', p. 107. Furthermore, if such a polarization of classes is indeed taking place in Tanzania, it can be predicted that an increased emphasis upon the *repressive* functions of the state will also serve to enhance that state's prominence in post-colonial Tanzania!

35. Saul, 'African Socialism in One Country: Tanzania', p. 312.

36. An example is the passage of a quite progressive income tax bill in late 1973. Originally rejected by Parliament, it was passed without dissent by the same Parliament when it was reconvened for the purpose by an irate President Nyerere. The latter stated that 'I am not prepared to accept that a Bill beneficial to the majority, should be rejected simply because it is not liked by a minority. If we agree to this, we will be setting a dangerous precedent whereby an entrenched minority can prevent measures aimed at promoting ujamaa from being taken. I reject this vehemently in the name of Tanu' (*The Daily News*, Tanzania, 29 November 1973). Paradoxically, this incident reveals both some of the strength and some of the weakness of the President's role in trying to lead a socialist transition. Moreover, the President's response to worker unrest has been rather more equivocal.

37. The place of popular forces in the Tanzanian socialist equation, although it has been somewhat slighted in this essay, has been discussed further in 'African Socialism in One Country: Tanzania'. Moreover, the possible role of the 'peasants' in defining Tanzania's future raises even more complex questions than does the case of the workers. The range of variation of 'peasantries' across so large and diverse a country is vast in any case, and expressions of peasant consciousness have not been so dramatic as those of the workers. But it seems likely that the experience of 'nizer-socialism' has had some positive impact upon consiousness—and upon the future (despite the fact that bureaucratization, and World Bank 'assistance', has undermined many officially-sponsored programmes). For a suggestive case-study see Adhu Awiti, *Class Struggle in Rural Society in Tanzania* (*Majimaji*, 7, October 1972) and, for a broader overview, my 'African Peasantries and Revolutionary Change' in *Review of African Political Economy*, I, 1 (1974), especially Section V, 'Tanzania'.

6 WOLFGANG HEIN AND KONRAD STENZEL

The capitalist State and underdevelopment in Latin America: The case of Venezuela*†

Theoretical Approach
The Socio-Economic and Political Context of the State in Latin America

Theory of 'Underdeveloped Capitalism'

Our basic assumptions about the nature of 'underdeveloped capitalism'[1] are those of the Latin American dependencia literature: There exists a typical social formation of underdeveloped capitalism which is different from a pre-developmental stage of today's metropolitan capitalist countries. This social formation is the outcome of a process of continuous adaptation of peripheral societies to their exploitation by the developing capitalist centre which has been going on for more than four centuries and was one of the conditions for the industrial revolution in the metropolitan countries. In general, this 'adaptation' consisted in the growth of an export-oriented economy, concentrating on the production and exportation of very few goods (monoculture) according to an international division of labour which evolved and changed corresponding to the given historical stage of socio-economic development of the advanced capitalist nations. Furthermore, this process of adaptation led to a growing economic, political and ideological penetration of the satellites by metropolitan capital, organizations and culture, thus

* This article is part of the work in a project on Autonomy and Penetration in Venezuela, together with Jurgen Simonis and H. R. Sonntag, described in *Kapitalistate* 1/1973, p. 37.
† Extract from paper of the same title in, *Kapitalistate* 2/1973, pp. 31–48.

creating an increasing dependence on external events and decisions and inability to act politically according to their own developmental needs.

This dependence is—as A. G. Frank stresses (1971, p. 11) not only a consequence of purely external relationships, but also an 'internal' condition, 'an integral part of Latin American society, which determines the dominant bourgeoisie in Latin America'. Thus, in our analysis of the socio-economic and political context of the state, we have to consider two levels of dependence:

1) dependence as it has consolidated itself in the *social structure of underdeveloped countries*, particularly in the position of a ruling class whose interests coincide in nearly all important aspects with the interest of metropolitan capitalists to appropriate a part of the surplus produced in peripheral societies[2], and who, through the pursuit of their own political and economic interests, guarantee the integration of their society into the existing global division of labor, and

2) dependence as manifested *in the current external relations* of underdeveloped countries, which we define in the broadest possible way, including changes in the price of a country's export goods on the international market as well as foreign investment in domestic industrial projects. Besides being itself the most visible level of dependence, external relations are constantly reproducing a social structure in under-developed countries that fits into the dynamics of the international division of labour.

The class basis of the state in Latin America

An analysis of the process of political decision-making in Latin American countries as determined by the internal class basis of the state—abstracting from all effects of direct external dependence—makes it obvious that the interests of the metropolitan bourgeoisie constitute themselves already on the level of the internal political process.

This is most manifest in the period of domination of the commercial bourgeoisie. The profits of the coalition ruling from independence to the 1930s—commercial bourgeoisie and export-oriented agricultural oligarchy—were directly dependent upon exports of goods to the capitalist centre, i.e. upon the market conditions in the centre. Assuming that market conditions express at least partly the developmental needs of an economy, there is, in the periphery, a one-sided orientation toward the economic development of the centre and not toward that of their own countries because the internal market was hardly of any importance to the ruling class. The corresponding policies—often carried out by caudillo-governments—were those of trade liberalism and internal liberal reforms (expropriation of church land and of Indian community lands and their sale to private purchasers (cf. Frank, 1971, ch. 5) on the one hand, and of unconditional expansion of the export sector on the other hand. Concerning these policies, there was of course a common interest between the ruling coalition in the peripheric countries and the metropolitan bourgeoisie, consequently the policies internally decided upon seldom transcended the limits set by external conditions. Thus, throughout the liberal period, the state in Latin American countries was conserving the power structure which had already emerged in colonial times, transmitting the economic interest of the ruling coalition into political action and, on the other hand, transmitting occasional external political pressure on the internal political scene, thereby limiting the opportunity of a rising industrial bourgeoisie (in coalition with latifundistas producing for the internal market) to come into power and to implement a protective policy. . . .

The Great Depression reduced the integration of Latin American countries into the world market and created the necessity for a re-orientation of economic activities in direction of the internal market; the result was a period of relatively autonomous development of import substitution, which strengthened the internal industrial bourgeoisie. The process of import substitution continued after World War II, but changed its character with the re-expansion of world trade and foreign investments. The industrial development of the 1930s and the 1940s was not reversed, but gradually integrated into a new stage of international division of labour. Traditionally, the dividing line was between processed industrial products on the one hand and unprocessed primary products on the other; after World War II the developed capitalist countries have been more and more specializing in the export of capital goods, leaving to a group of underdeveloped countries the production of their own consumer goods—though not without the participation of metropolitan capital.

After 1945 the industrial growth in the substitution of imports slowed down (cf. Frank, p. 92), and the sector of import substitution was more and more penetrated by foreign capital. As a consequence the economic orientation toward the internal market was replaced by an orientation toward the investment interests of metropolitan capitalists (production of luxury consumer goods, automobile industry etc. instead of goods for mass consumption), especially their interest in exporting capital goods[3]; import substitution was no longer an autonomous process, but became just another industrial sector dependent on foreign interests.

In spite of this change after World War II, which of course again narrowed the limits of political action set by external conditions, import substitution, resulting in a first industrial sector that produced for the internal market of Latin American countries led to a new relationship between social and political structure, which is typical for most Latin American societies of today.[4]

The industrial bourgeoisie and the agricultural oligarchy producing for the internal market who substituted the former coalition led by the commercial bourgeoisie are interested

a) in the expansion of the internal market[5] and

b) the protection of their products from imports.

Both objectives necessitate an increasing state regulation of the national economy, broader industrial development policies in order to overcome the extreme dependence on trade, and internal social reforms in order to expand the internal market. This and the necessity to deal with a gradually growing working class and a strengthened class of agricultural workers and small farmers led to the formation of populist governments in various Latin American countries (Getulio Vargas in Brazil, Perón in Argentina, Bétancourt in Venezuela), which carried through social reform and industrial development programmes on a broad popular basis.

The potential for economic growth through import substitution of luxury consumer goods is very limited because of the relatively small internal markets for such goods. Countries like

Argentina, Brazil and Mexico reached these limits in the 1960s; economic growth was stagnating. The only solution of this crisis in harmony with the interest of the dominating industrial bourgeoisie required further change in the international division of labour: exporting consumer goods and entering the production of capital goods. Corresponding to these requirements, a change in the global strategy of some imperialist countries was and is still going on: As Junne and Nour (1972, ch. 6) point out, the export chances for industrial goods from the capitalist centre into the Third World are relatively declining while the costs for maintaining the existing state of dependence are increasing; this demands new strategies for securing the necessary supply with raw materials and chances for highly profitable investments. Besides extending economic relations with 'socialist' countries, the so-called 'key country approach' is one solution to this problem: A small number of underdeveloped countries is 'supported' more intensively while the other regions are consciously neglected. These 'key countries' are preferably some city states (Hong Kong, Singapore) and some large countries with ample mineral resources, a population large enough to constitute an internal market, and reactionary governments (in Latin America particularly Argentina, Brazil and Mexico). They are supported by the imperialist countries in their attempts at acquiring a sub-imperialist position with respect to the more underdeveloped regions, including the supply of these regions with industrial consumer goods; in addition to that the low wage level of these key countries makes the production of simple industrial products and their exportation to the capitalist centre profitable.[6]

Thus, though not without conflicts, a new fraction of the 'national bourgeoisie' (consisting of the economically most powerful parts of the old agrarian, commercial, industrial or financial bourgeoisies) gains social dominance. Their interest again corresponds to that of the ruling class in the imperialist countries. Indirect beneficiaries of this process are all those employed by the 'internationalized' sector and those belonging to the political 'management' of this form of economic development, i.e. part of the 'middle class' (intellectuals, state bureaucracies, army) and even part of the working class (Cardoso 1972, p. 93).

The corresponding function of the state apparatus is a

predominantly technocratic and repressive one: It is no longer necessary to expand the internal market of consumer goods, but to attract foreign capital and technology and to gain export markets; this requires first of all a high degree of economic manipulation—incentives for investment, for export etc.[7] On the other hand it also requires a high degree of repression as it is difficult to legitimize this kind of development policy while the situation of large population groups is deteriorating— particularly after a period of populist agitation and policies.

Up to this point, we have only discussed the relationship between the state and the dominant fraction of the national bourgeoisie (necessarily implying the relationship between bourgeoisie and the international division of labour). A full analysis of the internal class basis of the state would require detailed class analyses of Latin American societies; this cannot be done here. Two additions concerning the particular role of the so-called 'Patriziat' and the mass basis of politics in Latin America must be sufficient in this context:

1) Sonntag (1972, p. 50) characterizes the 'Patriziat' 'as a group within the ruling class whose political power is not primarily based on the ownership of means of production, but rests on their position in political and social institutions'; he distinguishes three sub-groups, the political-administrative, the clerical and the military 'Patriziat'. Although in the last instance, all groups of the ruling class are determined by their coincidence of interest with foreign capital, in the short run the Patriziat in particular may support independent developments. Sonntag attributes this fact to the structural heterogeneity of peripheric societies (1972, p. 51). Similar arguments in favour of a 'distinct relative autonomy' (Alavi) of the bureaucratic–military oligarchy can be found in other studies on underdeveloped countries (cf. Amin, 1972, pp. 366–372; Varas, 1971; de las Casas, 1971); for Hamza Alavi this particular feature constitutes the central characteristic of the post-colonial state. Whereas, according to Alavi, the state in the capitalist centre is the instrument of one class, the national bourgeoisie, and possesses only relative autonomy with respect to the different fractions of this class, the state in post-colonial societies is the instrument of three partly competing dominant

classes; the indigenous bourgeoisie, the metropolitan bourgeoisie (which is—as a consequence of their investments—
present in post-colonial society) and the land-owning classes:

> . . . none of the three propertied classes in that post-colonial
> society, . . . exclusively command the state apparatus; the
> influence and power of each is offset by that of the other two.
> Their respective interests are not mutually congruent or
> wholly compatible. They do have certain basic interests in
> common; above all, that of the preservation of the existing
> social order, based upon the institution of private property.
> But they make competing demands on the post-colonial
> state and on the bureaucratic–military oligarchy which
> represents the state. The latter mediates and arbitrates
> between the competing demands of the three propertied
> classes. (Alavi 1972, p. 71; see p. 54 this volume—ed.)

Though the cases of Pakistan and of Latin America are not
directly comparable, and Alavi's analysis seems a bit too
schematic, it can be maintained that there is an unstable
balance between the different dominating classes or factions,
i.e. no effective and lasting integration of the 'bloc au pouvoir'
in underdeveloped societies, which gives a particular autonomy to the bureaucratic–military oligarchy and represents
one explanation for the frequent change of political regimes
and of policies in dependent countries. One root of this
unstable balance in the 'bloc au pouvoir' is the structural
heterogeneity of these societies, another (in the last instance
the common root of both) the position of the metropolitan
bourgeoisie: On the one hand, it is structurally impossible to
integrate them into a Brazilian, Peruvian or Venezuelan 'bloc
au pouvoir', on the other hand this 'external ruling class' more
or less determines which fraction of the internal bourgeoisie
dominates in domestic affairs, consequently breaks up any
internal 'bloc au pouvoir' and thus effects a continuous
adaptation of peripheral societies to the dynamics of the
international division of labour.
2) The mass basis of politics in Latin America is characterized
by two elements.
a) It is very heterogeneous, being composed of a relatively

small industrial working class, a group of agricultural workers (varying substantially in size from country to country), small peasants, and a growing number of 'marginales'. As a consequence of their particular situation all these groups differ in their short-term interests, their political ideology, degree and ability of political organization.

b) Compared to the working class in the capitalist centre, the dominated classes in the underdeveloped countries have never been able to exert any relevant pressure on political institutions in their countries. This is of course due to the different socio-economic structures of both types of capitalist societies: In most underdeveloped countries exists only a small working class, which has a very limited capability of exerting pressure on the state apparatus; in addition to that the bourgeoisie in these countries has no interest in providing for the reproduction of a working force which by far exceeds the needs of today's industrial facilities. Furthermore, there was, until recently, not even a necessity for social policy as an instrument of social pacification, because neither the context of agricultural work, nor that of marginality offer favourable conditions for revolutionary political mobilization and organization.

The Brazilian situation with respect to unemployment benefits plainly illustrates the weakness of the working class in Latin America: The first Brazilian law dealing with unemployment appeared in 1965 (!); unemployment benefits amounting to 50 per cent of the minimum wages are paid if a dismissed worker has been on his last job for at least 120 days and if his company has dismissed more than 50 workers in the last two months. These benefits are paid for a maximum of three months. There exists no protection against dismissal. (Füchtner, 1972, p. 77)

Forms of dependence

The form in which dependence is mediated varies from total colonial, i.e. *overt political dependence* to different forms of *structural dependence* where there is no direct determination of any policies in dependent countries by metropolitan states or companies, but nevertheless an indirect determination through a particular trade structure, through capital movements or communication flows.

In Latin American history two types of dependence and—consequently—of integration into the international division of labour have developed (cf. Cardoso 1971, ch. II: 'Les types de dépendance et les idéologies du développement', pp. 77–117).

As long as British domination over Latin America lasted, some Latin American countries could build up an *agrarian export economy* which fulfilled a necessary complementary role with respect to the English industrial economy. This situation changed when the United States took the place of Britain, because the US-American economy was nearly self-sufficient and therefore not dependent on Latin American agricultural exports. While those countries which had developed an active export economy under English domination (Argentina, Uruguay, Brazil) could at least maintain their participation on the world market, the other countries (Caribbean, Central America, Venezuela, Colombia) which had been apart from the main flow of agricultural exports to England, never got a chance to organize their economies in a similar way. The U.S.A. had no interest in traditional agricultural imports from Latin America: their objective was to invest capital in dependent countries in order to make extra profits ('dollar imperialism'). This led to the development of *enclave economies* consisting of a modern, highly productive sector, owned and organized by foreign capitalists mostly in the field of extractive industries, and a backward native agricultural sector. Chile and Peru which had been able to organize extractive industry under local control in the course of the 19th century, fell back into the status of enclave economies when they lost control over their mining sector to external groups because of their inability to compete with modern capitalist forms of production.

These different economic bases had an important influence on the 20th century politics of the respective Latin American countries: In those belonging to the first type (agrarian export economies) the existence of a national export sector previous to the period of US-domination had permitted the formation of a ruling class which had (and in part still has) some control over the production process.

In the case of the enclave economies the economic base of local power was a poorly differentiated agrarian structure; the ruling groups acquired political power more by their capacity to exert violence and to impose an internal order which ensured the conditions necessary for the negotiations of concessions (to foreign capital) than by their capacity for economic action. In these countries all modern economic production constituted itself as direct prolongation of the economy of the centre. The goods produced in the peripheral enclaves under control of the metropolitan bourgeoisie are sold and consumed in the developed capitalist countries. . . .

Summary

As a summary of the theoretical analysis of state functions in Latin American countries we propose the following theses:

1) In the context of internal class structure and external dependence, the state in underdeveloped capitalist societies is primarily an agent of transmitting the global dynamics of the international division of labour to the national level and of reproducing the internal class and political power structure according to these dynamics.

2) State action in the context of underdeveloped capitalism does not tend to dissolve pre-capitalist formations, but to transform them into other non-capitalist elements—at this stage of Latin American development into 'marginales'. This is due to the global capitalist system which limits the range of effective policies which a capitalist state in a dependent country can enact and enforce.

The Case of Venezuela[8]

In the following we are going to exemplify the weakness of the Venezuelan state whose policies during the last fifty years have amply demonstrated its inability to carry through or even to conceptualize its own national interest against the interest of U.S. capital. The most important mechanisms in connection with this failure of dependent capitalism have been outlined above, it is now necessary to substantiate them with some relevant tendencies within Venezuelan society (for a detailed analysis we have set forth a pattern for future research in Hein Simonis/Sonntag/Stenzel, 1972). The results are especially evident in the fields of industrialization and land reform, whose combined insufficiency accounts for the staggering increase of the number of marginales, i.e. people outside the market economy and the production process.

First, we'll have to analyze the historical conditions for the penetration of Venezuelan society which today is the dominating factor in the country's economic, political and cultural reality.

The Emergence of Venezuela's Petroleum-Dominated Economy

In the 19th and early 20th century Venezuela quite clearly belonged to that second group of Latin American countries which had no export sector worth mentioning, and consequently but a negligible share in world trade. In the case of Venezuela, this was due to an almost complete lack of natural resources and a considerable shortage of manpower. The entire population did not reach 2 million before 1900. Compared with countries like Argentina or Brazil, Venezuela was just too small to have a sizeable internal market. Thus neither the export-oriented commercial bourgeoisie nor the representatives of the protection-minded industrial bourgeoisie had the same relative strength and importance they had in the countries with a large agrarian export sector. Being left out of the main flow of the beginning and rapidly intensifying system of world trade had the consequence that sufficient amounts of capital for the development and exploitation of internal resources were not accumulated. Secondly, what could be called a bourgeoisie had only a feeble and precarious economic foundation in the few and discontinuous exports.

This small group and that part of the agrarian oligarchy who produced export goods, insignificant as they were on a Latin American continental scale, nevertheless had a decisive influence on Venezuelan politics after their victory in the Federal War (1858–63) together with the prevailing fraction of the military remnants from the War of Independence under the caudillo António Guzmán Blanco. This influence resulted in a laissez-faire economic policy that neglected those economic sectors not directly connected with agrarian export activities. Therefore, when in the late 19th century copper and gold mines were discovered and had to be made accessible by railroads to be exploited, these development activities were completely left to foreign (German, English) capitalists.

The traditional export products were coffee and cacao and to a limited extent for the decade between 1880 and 1890, gold. The 12 500 tons of cacao that were exported in 1903, still comprised 10 per cent of the world production. 1923 export reached 23 700 tons, then only 5 per cent of the world production. Frequent ups and downs in output from one year to the next as well as tremendous fluctuation in world market prices prevented cacao from becoming a reliable export staple. Coffee exports, on the other hand, never reached more than 1.5 to 3 per cent of world production (fluctuation between 30 000 and 70 000 tons per year). Gold production in its heyday reached 6 tons p. a. (1884), then still 3 per cent of the total world production. But in the years after the new big finds in South Africa and Russia tripled and quadrupled world output, whereas the Venezuelan figures went down.

It is not surprising that in the whole period between 1885 and 1923 the value of exports never exceeded 10 to 25 million dollars, that of imports 15. Venezuela's share in the volume of world trade oscillated between a flimsy 0.1 per cent and 0.0 per cent. This figure is even smaller than it appears to be, because then the share of countries outside the U.S. and Western Europe in world trade was much bigger than it is nowadays when the distinctive feature of world trade is the ever more increasing concentration of trade within the industrial centre.

The big break for this almost non-existing economy was the discovery of oil in the Maracaibo Lake and on the Llanos. Production soared from a tiny 70 000 tons in 1920 to 15.8 million tons in 1928, during that time overtaking producers like Persia, Mexico, Russia, Rumania. In 1928, Venezuela had become the second largest producing country (behind the U.S.) and the leading petroleum exporting nation. During the Thirties about 1/10 of the world output was produced here. Venezuela, under the dictatorship of yet another of the caudillos Tachirenses, Juan Vicente Gómez, who administered the country according to the principles of a family hacienda with a strict spoils system for his followers, with no capital at hand, left the business to foreign, mainly U.S. capital just as long as they would pay (ridiculously low) taxes and royalties to the state and indemnities to the latifundistas whose land they took over. Whatever new bourgeois elements appeared on top of this tidal wave of foreign exchange (partly traditional export bourgeoisie switching to the new sector, partly latifundistas turned financial capitalists via the oil money they got for their lands) would again be strictly export-oriented and furthermore absolutely dependent for their profits on the investment decisions of foreign corporations who operated the by now dominating external sector of the Venezuelan economy. The value of exports, now originating almost exclusively (95 per cent and more) in this sector, went up to 150 million dollars in 1929, that of imports bought from the foreign exchange to 85 million dollars. Venezuela's share in world trade was ten times the amount realized in the traditional small scale export era before 1923 and reached 1 per cent by the end of the Thirties.

This distorted development, almost entirely founded on the expansion of one sector, was not only causing a growing dependence of Venezuela on the U.S. in all aspects of society, but also led to the stagnation and eventually regression of the traditional sector (mainly agriculture). We have already noted that agricultural exports dropped from 1920 on. Beyond that, the growth of a modern, highly productive export industry creates foreign exchange for the import of consumer goods, including agricultural products; the internal small-scale manufacturers and agricultural producers, working at a low productivity, cannot compete against the imported goods and will gradually be forced to close down and to lay off their working force. Now, as oil production is 100 times as productive as agricultural production in Venezuela, every additional worker in the oil industry will produce enough foreign exchange to import the equivalent of what 100 agricultural workers would have produced in the same time. Though this is an extreme example, it illustrates the fact that a growing export industry obliterates much more jobs in the traditional sectors than it can create.

This tendency is still intensified by the enormous population growth that set in after World War II. It is this tendency, resulting in an ever larger group of people out of work or underemployed, that has forced the state in Venezuela to attempt reforms to alleviate these consequences. Not surprisingly, then, it is only recently that the state in Venezuela has taken up any social-economic development policies. During the years of caudillismo which did not end until 1958 and were only interrupted by three years of Acción Democrática populism 1945–48, the few attempts to curb the power of the central factor in the country's economic life, the foreign corporations, were generally not supported by the dictatorial governments. Popular uprising in the Twenties and the trade union movement in the Thirties were crushed with repressive measures.

A New Stage in the International Division of Labour

It is useful to put these populist reform measures of the Venezuelan state in a historical perspective and in the context of the continuous process of capital accumulation on global scale, which through the mechanism of dependence and penetration sets the structural limits for state action in underdeveloped countries, as we have explained above.

In the stage of export-oriented economy the complementary function of Venezuela consists in furnishing to the advanced industrializing nations of the West European–North American capitalist centre raw materials from its primary sector, exclusively agricultural products first, and minerals from the new extractive industry in a second phase. The dividing line between developed and underdeveloped countries ran between processed goods and raw materials, the first being restricted to the industrialized centre. Imports from the imperialist countries consisted chiefly of luxury and other consumer goods.

For Venezuela, the starting point for industrialization was World War II and to some extent also the Thirties, when first the Great Depression and afterwards the necessities of war economy led to a breakdown of the world trade structures, since the industrialized capitalist countries were unable to provide the Third World with most of the basic finished goods, which Venezuela before could purchase abroad from the oil royalties and taxes. When they were no longer obtainable on the world market, autonomous industrialization followed slowly in a process of import substitution. Although Venezuela's exports consistently exceeded the dwindling imports throughout the 1930s, finally, in 1939, by the enormous sum of 120 million dollars in one year, the country apparently did not use its favourable balance of trade to invest into productive sectors for the internal market, but rather spent it on spectacular construction programmes to Gómez' liking or transferred it on number accounts in Switzerland or the U.S. in the case of the commercial bourgeoisie. One example is the attempt at establishing a petrochemical industry which was not subsidized by the government and obviously seemed no object for investment to the bourgeoisie either, because its production came to a halt when the oil companies who had run it on a small scale for their own purposes could not maintain it in the crisis after 1935. In the war, however, there were some attempts to build up national industries based on a labour intensive technology, since by then, capital had become scarce and expensive, plus the fact that increasing numbers of migrants to the urban areas required new jobs in the industrial sector.

After the war, when the capitalist metropoles recovered their former positions and soon expended them, the conflict between the developmental needs of the Venezuelan economy and the interests of metropolitan capital became manifest. No doubt supported by foreign capital the export-oriented commercial and financial bourgeoisie (automatically depending on maximal profits of foreign capital) overthrew the populist government in 1948 that had put national priorities (industrialization, jobs) first, thereby threatening to close one profitable export area for the consumer goods producing industries in the centre. This setback was not going to last long. Not only became the necessity of creating new jobs more urgent every year, but also did the process of concentration of large diversified capital conglomerates diminish the vulnerability of certain branches of the industrial sector in the central countries. Therefore a gradual adaptation and transition set in which redefined the complementary functions of the international division of labour in such a way that the central economies specialized on the export of capital goods, i.e. machinery, plant equipment and the like, to the underdeveloped countries to help establish their own consumer goods industries. In Venezuela, the capital engaged so far in the extractive industries was looking for new profitable outlets for its profits and now could gradually enter another modern sector.

On the internal political level this worldwide rearrangement led to the final success of Venezuelan populism in 1958 whose policies were endorsed for all of Latin America in the programme of Punta del Este ('Alliance for Progress') with active consent of the U.S. Similar developments can be traced all over the continent, some considerably earlier (Perón, Vargas), some later.

Industrialization, the State and Foreign Capital

Now that we have established a fairly abstract perspective for the analysis of populist policies in the framework of the international division of labour we can look at the structural implications of this externally dominated modernization and at the single policies enacted by the Venezuelan governments in the last decade.

We have already seen that the post-war period and the recovery of the capitalist countries changed the nature of industrialization in Venezuela. It no longer was a means toward the purpose of an autonomous internal growth connected with the establishment of a modern industrial sector *within* the country's economy (the oil sector definitely is not), taking care of internal demands, on the labour market as well as in production. In an economy dominated by a foreign-owned extractive sector like Venezuela's these objectives obviously could not be achieved. One reason is that foreign capital long ago has entered this sector. Although it is by far not as foreign-dominated as the oil sector (total existing fixed capital in the manufacturing industry: 6 716 billion bolivares, net foreign investment 2 363 billion, both 1969), it is so imbedded in a structure of dependence on metropolitan capital that it cannot afford to disregard the profit interests of the centre. Thus, a transition to a stage where capital goods industries could be part of the Venezuelan economy is effectively blocked by internal capital interests. As far as the capital is directly American or American-controlled, it will as a matter of course buy machinery and equipment from the U.S. parent companies. The trade agreement between the U.S. and Venezuela, which owes its existence and continuation to pressure from the American government, gives these goods a partly tax-exempt status and thus makes it even profitable to buy at higher prices in the U.S. As far as the Venezuelan capital is concerned, it is certainly out to maximize its profit and will therefore buy from the most profitable source, in this case, by way of some tariff manipulations, still the U.S., as we have seen.

A second reason is the problem of technological dependence. Because of the huge and continuously increasing reserves of foreign exchange, capital is relatively cheaper than qualified labour in Venezuela. This results in the import of capital intensive production technology that has been developed in the centre. At this point of the American-dictated international division of labour, Venezuela is not only excluded from the whole sector of heavy industries (mediated in the internal economic structure by the very mechanisms we are considering) but also generally from development and production of new products, new production processes, machinery and accessories involved in this, advertisement and creation of new markets. As a matter of fact, large-scale industrial production in the Venezuelan manufacturing sector is restricted to the technologically negligible stage of final assembly. There are two implications to this import of technology from the metropolitan countries.

One is concerned with the type of production. Since capital intensive metropolitan technology entails more or less automatically metropolitan machinery, metropolitan equipment, metropolitan accessories, these on their part entail orientation toward demand in the metropolitan countries. What really results is a faithful imitation of the U.S. consumption pattern, which of course is more sophisticated and based on a much wider distribution of purchasing power: thus the inadequate product structure of the Venezuelan consumer goods industry, concentration on automobiles and TV sets that are within reach of the uppermost 10 per cent of the income structure, but out of the question for anybody else. Thus the majority of industrial capacities are utilized under 60 per cent.

The second is concerned with the structure of the labour market. Stagnation in the agrarian sector and the population growth which is more than 4 per cent p. a. by now push roughly 150 000 people out of the rural sector into the urban-industrial every year. Capital intensive production technology which is the obvious choice from the point of view of the capital realization interest is squarely opposed to the national development priority of creating jobs for the unemployed urban migrants. In the decade 1960–70 the number of those occupied in the manufacturning industry has almost doubled (from 260 000 to 496 000); that, however, does not take care of more than 20 000 out of the 150 000 mentioned above. We will discuss the consequences further in the part on the land reform.

So the consumer goods industrial sector is characterized by two main shortcomings from the point of view of effective state action to further industrialization and modernization of the country:

1) internally its growth is inadequate and crippled, distorted in both the field of production, demand satisfaction and capital utilization and also in the field of the labour market, the absorption of newly emerging labour force.

2) with respect to the necessary second step of industrialization, the establishment of a capital goods industry, its direct and indirect dependence on foreign capital prevents exactly this objective.

Concerning the second point, some more details on state action seem appropriate: It cannot be denied that the state did take some cautious steps in the direction during the decade of populist reforms in the 1960s. The most important ones were the foundation of the C.V.P. (Corporación Venezolana de Petróleo) which was to get part of the oil and petrochemical production under national control and the Siderúrgica S.A. as a sub-corporation of the C.V.G. (Corporación Venezolana de Guyana).

We have shown how the domination of foreign capital prevents and sidetracks these state policies. Now it could be said that the state itself did not consequently use its political instruments to achieve success of its own modernization policies, e.g., how about the loopholes in the trade agreement, how about nationalizing petroleum or at least preventing repatriation of profits to the U.S. or restricting foreign investments to top priority sectors (heavy industries)? There have been, now and then nationalist tendencies that tried to realize all or some of these policies, but every time there has been quick and effective retaliation in form of diplomatic pressure, direct insurgency instigated by the U.S., withdrawal of production facilities and decrease of production on the oil fields (thereby lowering state revenues), increased transfer of profits, trouble with the public debt, forced devaluation of the bolivar (1964) and the like.

One essential aspect, concerning the state directly, is the fact that almost two thirds of the entire state income, e. g. in 1968 over 6 billion bolivares out of a total budget of just over 9 billion, is derived from the external capitalist sector—the oil companies and their Venezuelan holdings in other sectors (taxes, royalties). Therefore the outcome of populist industrialization policies in Venezuela has been a reduction of imports in some parts of the consumer goods area, but a triplication of the imports of capital goods instead, a feature of industrialization in dependent capitalism which makes it both profitable for the metropolitan countries and acceptable as a pseudo-progressive reform of the international division of labour that existed before. It represents, basically, another expansion of American exports and counteracts all the aims of national development.

It is very much the question whether any government within the structural limits of dependent capitalism could enforce the measures necessary to reverse this tendency, since its very existence is founded on the class alliance between the dependent national bourgeoisie and the international bourgeoisie of the central nations. At least it becomes obvious from our example that there is a fundamental contradiction between the interests of multinational capital and the requirements for an integrated national growth and development.

Agrarian Reform and the Marginales

Industrialization policy and land reform in the context of populism in underdeveloped countries are part of the same stabilization and social integration programme that tries to fence off the consequences of the disequilibrated integration of the peripheral countries into the global capitalist system without changing the principal contradiction between autonomous development of these societies and profitability of capital realization on a global scale. In the case of Venezuela and many more underdeveloped countries these consequences are accumulated in the phenomenon of marginalization.

In the field of industrial policy state action proves to be deficient, i.e. weak and uneffective—compared to that in central capitalist states—chiefly vis-à-vis the links and mechanisms of external dependence. In Venezuela the 'weak' state is a functional corollary of external dependence and economic penetration. This accounts for the fact that it has not overcome the barrier on the transition to developed capitalism which is constituted by the international division of labour. In the field of land reform state action proves deficient on account of the fact that the state does not successfully integrate the still relatively powerful pre-capitalist fractions into a capitalist development policy thereby giving unproportionate emphasis to the interests of the fraction of landowning oligarchy.

In both aspects state action proves equally deficient because of the lacking political organization of the class of marginales whose economic and social interests are at stake.

The central fact in the agrarian sector of Venezuela is its more or less stagnating productivity since colonial times that now even turns regressive. Its latifundia-property structure occupies relatively less and less of the economically active population (presently still 27 per cent); in the last decade even the absolute numbers have been going down to a mere 706 000. Its share of the national income is around 7 per cent and has been going down recently, too.

The estimated number of those who are thus forced to move off the land into the urban agglomerations has risen to 150 000 p. a. In this situation the Acción Democrática started a land reform in 1960. 10 million acres were redistributed, 165 000 families settled. But a more differentiated look at the facts reveals interesting details: In reality, only 95 300 families were finally settling on their own land, the rest gave up their allotments on the way, partly they went bankrupt because state aid was missing; even of those now settled, 80 per cent do not have a final title of possession, a fact that increases the instability and uncertainty for the whole settlement. Of the 3 billion bolivares spent on the programme almost 900 million went to the landowning class in indemnities, the rest was to be technical and financial aid. But the credit conditions for small owners soon became intolerable, and most of the financial assistance went into the hands of the agrarian oligarchy and the new agrarian capitalists who collected abandoned land reform allotments and soon enjoyed a high degree of concentration. In 1970, more money was invested in agriculture (1.4 billion bolivares) than in the entire manufacturing industry (1.16 billion), a reliable sign that if nothing else profits had gone up in this sector. The effect on creation of new jobs is negligible (slightly over 8 000 a year).

So the efforts of failed land reform and failed industrialization together still leave 120 000 people every year to underemployment, frequent change of intermittent jobs, and to plain unemployment (now 20 per cent), together to marginalization. One consequence is the inflation of the underproductive tertiary sector which already comprises half of Venezuela's economically active population in part-time or otherwise underproductive jobs. Not included in this number is frictional unemployment, i. e. of persons who are seeking employment for the first time in areas where there is still demand for labour or of those who switch from one secure job to the next. But their number is very small, and without them roughly 1/3 of Venezuela's population (dependent family members included) are marginales.

One can identify three different types (Córdova, 1971):

1) those working in the agrarian sector without being paid wages of some kind, including those living on subsistence,
2) migrants to the cities who were not able to incorporate themselves in the production process can utilize their working capacity only temporarily and/or in underproductive occupations,
3) workers who cannot maintain a status of permanent employment and fall back into the conditions of group 2.

Here now we can start illustrating our contention that the marginales, the result of failure or insufficiency of state action aiming at the capitalist transformation of the underdeveloped societies, are a non-capitalist element.

Group 3 is virtually non-existing in Venezuela. On the one hand there is a relatively continuous expansion of industry in Venezuela, on the other hand there is little fluctuation between the industrial proletariat and the marginales. The reason for that is that even simple jobs in the industrial sector require some time of on-the-job training. This investment makes it highly unlikely that a firm will exchange its skilled workers against the unqualified labour force of the marginales. Qualification is an important barrier between marginality and the industrial proletariat. Consequently there can be hardly any wage depressing function of unqualified labour vis-à-vis the proletariat. The only chance to enter wage labour status is expansion and creation of new jobs.

In connection with the agrarian capitalist concentration that is a byproduct of the land reform, group 1 is also rapidly decreasing in number. We therefore have a tendency toward a uniform group of urban marginales, distinct from the industrial proletariat.

Neither against the inherent tendency to capital intensive industries nor against the partly still latifundista-, partly agrarian capitalist-based rural power structure is state action likely. The tendency points toward an aggravation of this crisis of a frustrated transition to developed capitalism through an increasing number of economically disintegrated marginales.

NOTES

1. For a more detailed analysis of theories of underdevelopment cf. Amin (1971), Introduction pp. 9–47, and Hein, Simonis, Sonntag, Stenzel, (1972), part 2.
2. Cf. also Christiane Frelin, 1972, who interprets state structure in underdeveloped countries as an implantation of cultural as well as political and economic dependence. Regrettably she does not analyse the relationship between class structure and state structure.
3. Concerning the conformity of interest between the Latin American burgeoisie linked to the substitution of imports and the metropolitan bourgeoisie, cf. Roberto Decio de las Casas, 1971, particularly pp. 457–61.
4. Exceptions are of course Cuba, Chile, but also Argentina, Brazil and Mexico which are already expanding their industries beyond import substitution of consumer goods (cf. below, de las Casas, Cardoso).
5. In this regard, the interests of foreign investors in the consumer goods industry coincide with those of the national industrial bourgeoisie. As the former, however, are producing articles different from those most important in the autonomous stage of import substitution (automobiles, TV-sets *vs.* food, clothes etc.) they are oriented towards other consumer groups as the national industrial bourgeoisie was in the 1930s and 1940s; Today the importance of mass consumption for the sector of import substitution is decreasing while that of luxury consumption of the upper and middle class is increasing.
6. 'Supported' is used in its most general meaning, including the non-application of negotiation sanctions, capital investments, aid etc.
7. Cf. the article 'The Brazilian Miracle' in *Newsweek*, 19 March 1973.
8. Since this part of our paper is largely descriptive and an exemplification of some of the points that were made in the theoretical chapters, a general note on the material and sources may suffice here (full titles see bibliography): Amin 1971a, Araujo 1971, Banco Central 1970, Córdova 1971, now also in Córdova 1973, Córdova/Michelena 1969, Deutsche Überseeische Bank, Dominguez 1966, Hein/Simonis/Sonntag/Stenzel 1972, Mieres 1971, Orta 1970, Statistisches Jahrbuch für das Deutsche Reich 1880–1940.

BIBLIOGRAPHY

Alavi, Hamza, 1972, 'The State in Post-Colonial Societies: Pakistan and Bangladesh', in New Left Review 74, pp. 59–81.

Amin, Samir, 1971, 'L'accumulation à l'échelle mondiale', Paris.

Amin, Samir, 1971 a, 'Le cadre théorique de la problematique de transition', unpublished paper, Dakar.

Araujo, Orlando, 1971, 'Venezuela. Die Gewalt als Voraussetzung der Freiheit', Frankfurt a. M.

Banco Central de Venezuela, 1970, Informe Económico, correspondiente al año 1969, Caracas.

Cardoso, Fernando Henrique, 1971, 'Politique et développement dans les sociétés dépendantes', Paris.

Cardoso, Fernando Henrique, 1972, 'Dependency and Development in Latin America' in New Left Review 74, pp. 83–95.

Córdova, Armando, 1971, 'Empleo, Desempleo, Marginalidad y Distribución del Ingreso en America Latina', Caracas.

Córdova, Armando, 1973, 'Strukturelle Heterogenität und wirtschaftliches Wachstum', Frankfurt a. M.

Córdova, Armando, Héctor Silva Michelena, 1969, 'Die wirtschaftliche Struktur Lateinamerikas', Frankfurt a. M.

De las Casas, Roberto Decio, 1971, 'L'état autoritaire – Essai sur les formes actuelles de domination impérialiste et leurs conséquences au niveau du pouvoir local, dans un pays dominé', in Anouar Abdel-Malek (Ed.), Sociologie de l'impérialisme, Paris 1971, pp. 455–73.

Deutsche Überseeische ·Bank, Wirtschaftsberichte über die lateinamerikanischen Länder sowie Spanien und Portugal, Hamburg (monthly).

Domínguez C., Raúl, 'Las clases sociales en el campo venezolano', in: Economía y Ciencias Sociales, special issue 1966, pp. 108–23.

Frank, André Gunder, 1969, 'Kapitalismus und Unterentwicklung in Lateinamerika', Frankfurt a. M.

Frank, André Gunder, 1971, 'Lumpenbourgeoisie et lumpendéveloppement', Paris.

Frelin, Christiane, 1972, 'La diffusion de la notion d'état moderne. Quelques notes introductives', in: Revue Tiers-Monde, Tome XIII/50, April–June 1972, pp. 435–44.

Füchtner, Hans, 1972, 'Die brasilianischen Arbeiterge-werkschaften, ihre Organisation und ihre politische Funktion', Frankfurt a. M.

Hein, Wolfgang, Georg Simonis, Heinz Rudolf Sonntag, Konrad Stenzel, 1972, 'Autonomie und Penetration Venezuelas', unpublished paper, Konstanz.

Hirsch, Joachim, 1969, 'Zur politischen Ökonomie des politischen Systems' in Gisela Kress, Dieter Senghaas, Politikwissenschschaft, Frankfurt a. M.

Hirsch, Joachim, 1970, 'Wissenschaftlich-technischer Fortschritt und politisches System', Frankfurt a. M.

Junne, Gerd, Salua Nour, 1972, 'Zur Analyse internationaler Abhängigkeiten', Berlin.

Magdoff, Harry, 1969, 'The Age of Imperialism', New York and London.

Mieres, Francisco, 1971, 'Una Decada de Estancamiento Economico-Social', unpublished paper, Caracas.

Miliband, Ralph, 1969, 'The State in Capitalist Society', New York.

Müller-Plantenberg, Urs, 1972, 'Technologie und Abhängigkeit', in: Dieter Senghaas, Imperialismus und strukturelle Gewalt, Frankfurt a. M., pp. 335–55.

Murray, Robin, 1971, 'The Internationalization of Capital and the Nation State', in: New Left Review 67/1971, pp. 84–100.

Offe, Claus, 1969, 'Politische Herrschaft und Klassenstrukturen. Zur Analyse spätkapitalistischer Gesellschaftssysteme', in: Gisela Kress, Dieter Senghaas, Politikwissenschaft, Frankfurt a. M.

Offe, Claus, 1972, 'Strukturprobleme des kapitalistischen Staates', Frankfurt a. M.

Orta, Celio S., 1970, 'Ensayo acerca del desarrollo agrícola venezolana durante el período 1950–1969', in: Economía y Ciencias Sociales, No. 4, pp. 5–52.

Palloix, Christian, 1971, 'L'économie mondiale capitaliste', Paris, 2 vols.

Poulantzas, Nicos, 1971, 'Pouvoir politique et classes sociales', Paris, 2 vols.

Quijano, Anibal, 1971, 'Pôle marginal de l'économie et main-d'œuvre marginalisée', in Anouar Abdel-Malek, 'Sociologie de l'impérialisme', Paris, pp. 301–36.

Senghaas, Dieter (Ed.), 1972, 'Imperialismus und strukturelle Gewalt', Frankfurt a. M.

Sonntag, Heinz Rudolf, 1972, 'Revolution in Chile', Frankfurt a. M.

Statistisches Jahrbuch für das Deutsche Reich, 1880–1940, Berlin.

Varas, Augusto, 1971, 'Chili – Un mode de production dépendant', in: Anouar Abdel-Malek, Sociologie de l'impérialisme, Paris, pp. 243–300.

Warren, Bill, 1971, 'The Internationalization of Capital and the Nation State: a Comment', in New Left Review 69, pp. 83–8.

THREE:

Aspects of State and Society

Introductory note

The general relations between the various apparatuses of the state and between the state and society are treated in the earlier papers which attempt to depict the state in third-world societies. There is still need, however, to elaborate upon these relations. The papers in this section, therefore, treat certain definite aspects of politics and the political rather more specifically. Nearly all the papers deal with African situations where the questions involved—the relations between labour and the state, ideology, the political party, etc.—have been most urgently and interestingly posed since the 1960s.

The economically weak classes, factions of which assumed formal political power at independence in Africa were nonetheless politically strong (vis-a-vis the other social classes). But the high degree of unity they achieved around the issue of independence during the nationalist struggle could not be easily maintained in the immediate post-independence period. Generally speaking, organised labour which had joined forces with the nationalist party in the independence struggle was blamed for threatening an apparent unity by making legitimate demands for workers. This was generally interpreted as a threat by those who held state power and who wished to use this power to provide the dominant classes with secure economic bases.

Strategies towards providing such security have not been uniform: in Kenya for example, the strategy has been to encourage unabashed the primitive private accumulation of capital with the overt assistance of the state; in Tanzania, on the other hand, the Arusha Declaration of 1967 led to the promotion of state capitalism without entirely eroding private capital. In all African countries however, the response to the threat, or seeming threat, to these processes of accumulation and domination has been uniform: the eradication of all indigenous sources of power through legislation or otherwise.

Most crucially, this has meant destroying the independent trade union movement which, along with the nationalist party, presented the most organisationally developed forum for protest. Following the example of Nkrumah's Ghana where a strong trade union movement was destroyed, progressive states such as Tanzania took steps to remove the possible threats of an independent trade union movement by making the trades unions overtly part of the state apparatuses. Issa G. Shivji (Chapter 8) shows however, that in spite of this the workers in Tanzania have been able to wage proletarian class struggle through the state-controlled machinery. (It may be noted though that soon after the events Shivji relates, the Minister of Labour who is also the Secretary-General of the National Union of Tanganyikan Workers, the only union in the country, took steps to destroy the Workers' Committees which were used by the workers as a forum.)

The tight control of workers by the state has been justified by both politicians and some radical academics on the grounds that workers constitute a privileged stratum in the work force of the third world—urban workers constitute a 'labour aristocracy'. This theme dominated the literature on African labour until recently when even one of the most ardent supporters of the theory (John S. Saul) was forced to abandon it. Peace's contribution challenges this view, using the example of workers in Lagos who have a long history of struggle. It is unfortunate however, that his argument stops at an empirical answer to this grave theoretical error.

In an almost totally different context Don Harris relates the fixing of a national minimum wage to the changes taking place in the Jamaican economy. The piece is important also because it shows a different aspect of the question of labour and the state in the third world. This is taking place in a context where the struggle between labour and capital has not been significantly muted as in the African context because the state has not been required to play the same overtly dominant role. The setting of a national minimum in 1974 however, is but one aspect of the changing role of the Jamaican state as the Manley Government is obliged to take the state more and more into the social and economic life of the country in the face of growing economic nationalism. This measure taken together with the Labour Relations and Industrial Disputes Act of the same year (patterned almost entirely upon the British Industrial Relations Act passed by the Heath Government in 1971) reveals the necessity for the state to assist labour more openly as well as to institute means of better controlling it.

The second nexus of relationships treated here is that regarding the political party, ideology and how these relate to the broader and more fundamental question of class development. The classes which attempted to utilise the instruments of the state in Africa to secure or to strengthen their economic base were faced with the problem of developing new institutions or using existing ones in novel ways to assist the processes of accumulation, control and the integration of diverse socio–political elements. This problem was particularly acute in colonies where the former colonial powers did little to develop infrastructures and institutions appropriate to capitalist development. Far from being the merely parasitic and inert force Fanon and some underdevelopment theorists have portrayed, the classes assuming state power at independence have been forced by historical circumstances to be creative and take initiatives. This qualifies also the notion of 'overdeveloped' state structures inherited by these classes.

One such area of creativity has been the establishment of the single party system which functions as a force for integration and control by propounding a usually eclectic ideology. The ideology often condemns greed and ostensibly stands against accumulation whilst the structures of the party assist in this very process. The degree of stability engendered by this can be quite remarkable and has led to a wide acceptance of this type of party system. Indeed, many military regimes in Africa today are speaking in terms of moving towards a single-party state. The current popularity of this type of party no doubt springs from the fact that in the hands of the political executive (the presidency) the party becomes a very effective instrument linking politics and the state, whilst allowing the state to predominate over, and even pre-empt, the elements that make up politics.

Cournanel's thesis (Essay 10) is that a faction of the Guinean bourgeoisie has managed to use the state to develop its socio-economic base and that this has been achieved through the Parti Democratique de Guinée which purports to be socialist. My own paper is part of an intended longer work on the Tanzanian state and represents an attempt to pose some questions regarding the crucial role of the party (TANU/CCM) within the state and society. The piece presents the matter therefore in a problematic manner. Both papers treat the political party very differently from the way it has been treated by Fanon, Alavi and others following their lead.

The question of the military in the politics of third-world countries has been of considerable interest to journalists and academics as well as the public both in and outside the third world. In Africa students often pose the question of why the military so frequently enters directly into the political life of countries in both Africa and Latin America. There is of course no ready, simple, all-embracing answer. Too often and for too long, however, the problem of the military has been narrowly perceived in terms of the behaviour of individual politico–military leaders and/or posing the problem in terms of the military being the most 'modern' and therefore the 'elite' most capable of providing political leadership. Nor can the tendency towards military dictatorship and authoritarianism be adequately explained by reference to an authoritarian colonial past.

In this respect Mamood Mamdani's piece, abstracted from his important book on class formation and politics in Uganda before and after 1971, corrects this popular approach to the Amin coup in 1971 and the expulsion of the Asians soon after. He attempts to explain these events in terms of the class struggles in that society and argues that they are not acts of a madman as the British press is fond of presenting Amin, thus trivialising a deadly situation.

Roxborough et al. (Essay 13) provide us with a detailed description and analysis of some of the crucial events leading up to the bloody coup by the Chilean military against the legitimate government of Salvador Allende. As the authors show it was partly the belief in 'constitutionalism' which led to the final demise of the Popular Unity Government in September 1973. The defeat of the working-class and the progressive forces in Chile that year and the lessons drawn from this are of grave importance to progressive forces in both developed and third world countries, particularly where a 'constitutional' path to socialism appears possible.

There are some important relationships left out of this section dealing with the state and society. For example, the institutions dealing with law, the bureaucracy and the ideological value of tribalism, etc. are left out not because they do not feature prominently in the politics of the third world, particularly in

Africa, but simply because it has been necessary to be selective and in doing so care has been taken to concentrate upon some of the more significant aspects of politics and the political.

a) Labour and the state

7 ADRIAN PEACE

The Lagos proletariat: Labour aristocrats or populist militants?[†]

To enter a discussion on the nature of 'social class' in the African context is to move into treacherous territory. The somewhat elementary position adopted here can be stated briefly: the Nigerian working class are those wage-earners who stand in a consistently subordinate relationship in the industrial mode of production, whose surplus product is appropriated by those who own the means of production, whether the latter be indigenous to Nigerian society or external to it, and who on the basis of this relationship can identify a common opposition to their own economic interests and act accordingly. Quite explicitly, then, I am concerned here with social action on a class basis undertaken by factory workers in Lagos as a segment of the Nigerian working class: my experience does not extend to government and public corporation workers though I suspect that much of the analysis presented here does in fact also apply to those in the state sector.[1]

Clearly, however, while I am here concerned specifically with a sector of the Lagos proletariat, the particular as much as the generalisable characteristics of this stratum can only emerge within the context of more broadly-based theoretical statements

[†] Extract from paper of the same title, in R. Sandbrook and R. Cohen, (eds.), *The Development of an African Working Class: Studies in Class Formation and Action* (Longman, 1975), pp. 281–302.

synthesising a diversity of sociological studies of a comparative nature. Sociological theories are of value only if our understanding of particular events, social processes and institutions is thereby heightened. One such statement is the 'labour aristocracy thesis' concerning the African working class. As a general thesis, it should stand up to examination in the light of the experience of the Lagos proletariat, but, as I will try to show, it does not—indeed cannot—do so. In my view, the labour aristocracy thesis, widely accepted as it is, represents a serious barrier to an accurate understanding of the present (and probably future) responses of Lagos wage-earners to their class position. A markedly different perspective is outlined in this paper: if this has any wider application its value can only be judged by others with experience and opinions quite different from my own.

The labour aristocracy thesis

As with most sociological theories concerned with the economic development and underdevelopment of sub-Saharan Africa, the labour aristocracy thesis has somewhat diverse and eclectic roots: it thus brings strange bedfellows together. Historically, the first commentators were the colonial administrators themselves, who feared the development of exceptional rural-urban divisions where early wage-earners could force up their wage rates by collective action (a by no means unimportant consideration for this paper). Contemporaneously, perhaps the greatest influence is found in the writings of Frantz Fanon, most notably in *The Wretched of the Earth*. But the most systematic academic contribution is the work of Giovanni Arrighi and John Saul, who in an early article entitled 'Socialism and Economic Development in Tropical Africa' initially set down views they have subsequently elaborated at greater length.[2]

Arrighi and Saul's central concern is with the dominant patterns of extraction of economic surplus produced within the new African nation-states following political independence. They argue correctly that economic surplus produced by the peasantry, rather than being reinvested to the benefit of the mass of the people, is for the most part repatriated by overseas companies or consumed wastefully by indigenous elites. Such established processes in their turn militate against increased productivity generated by a discontented and hostile peasant class.[3] For present purposes, attention is to be focused on one particular area of surplus consumption, for it is here that Arrighi and Saul identify a source of class conflict crucial to their overall thesis. The roots of such conflict are to be found in the colonial period, but the outcome is of the greatest importance for the present time:

> The higher wages and salaries [established during the colonial period] foster the stabilisation of the better-paid section of the labour force whose high incomes justify the severance of ties with the traditional economy. Stabilisation, in turn, promotes specialisation, greater bargaining power, and further increases in the incomes of this small section of the labour force, which represents the proletariat proper of tropical Africa. These workers enjoy incomes three or more times higher than those of unskilled labourers and together with the elites and sub-elites in bureaucratic employment in the civil service and expatriate concerns, constitute what we call the labour aristocracy of tropical Africa. It is the discretionary consumption of this class which absorbs a significant proportion of the surplus produced in the money economy.[4]

Here, then, Arrighi and Saul identify in Africa a critical deviation from the classic theory of increasing class conflict between ruling class and proletariat as economic development proceeds apace. Far from bourgeoisie and proletariat being forced into increasingly irreconcilable camps, their economic interests and political ideologies become increasingly complementary over time to a point at which they are virtually indistinguishable. Since Arrighi and Saul concentrate almost exclusively on the peasant-produced surplus, the only inevitable major polarisation occurs with the peasantry on the one hand and the forces of elite, sub-elite, and wage-earners—'the proletariat proper'—on the other. In contrast to the Marxist model of increasing exploitation *within one mode* of production, the dominant pattern of class exploitation occurs *between two modes* of production.

Such complementarity of elite, sub-elite and wage-earners' politico-economic interests has not emerged in an entirely uniform fashion. The economic superiority of the elite and sub-elite is firmly rooted in the colonial situation when the functional indispensability of the early African middle class ensured a high economic return relative to the peasantry and the forerunners of the modern labour force. Though some measure of economic superiority over the peasantry was achieved by wage-earners during the colonial period, their inferior standing relative to elite and sub-elite was substantially corrected by the advent of international capitalist oligopolies into the manufacturing arena immediately before political decolonisation. After independence, such enterprises moved to break out of the 'vicious circle [of] "high [labour] turnover—low productivity—low wages—high turnover" [which militated against] the development of a semi-skilled, relatively highly paid labour force'[5] by paying sufficiently high wages to stabilise its composition: this strategy in its turn began a 'spiral process' involving both expatriate companies and African governments equally concerned to make permanent their respective labour forces and win over skilled workers from one sector to another.

While acknowledging some differentiation between elite, sub-elite and wage-earning class, nevertheless Arrighi and Saul feel justified in treating them as an entity. They do, however, point to one further division within the wage-earning class which is of considerable importance here:

> . . . the wage-earning class is polarised into two strata. Wage workers in the lower stratum are only marginally or partially proletarianised as, over their life cycle, they derive the bulk of the means of subsistence for their families from outside the wage economy. Wage workers in the upper stratum, generally a very small minority, receive incomes sufficiently high (say 3–5 times those received by wage workers in the lower stratum) to justify a total break of their links with the peasantry. This is a type of 'optional proletarianisation' which has little in common with processes of 'proletarianisation' resulting from the steady impoverishment of the peasantry.[6]

Only the 'upper stratum', characterised by their complete

reliance on their urban-industrial experience, are to be included in the labour aristocracy. Though one may question the notion that the 'lower stratum' constitute a 'marginally or partially proletarianised' class—in my view once a worker enters the factory floor then he is 'proletarianised', though he does not, for example, necessarily act similarly to his West European counterpart—nevertheless one may accept this distinction here.

More important in this context is the separation of distinct courses of political action for the two sub-groups within the wage-earning class as a whole. Arrighi and Saul maintain that the close identification of the permanently employed 'upper stratum' with the elite and sub-elite remains valid: but 'this lower stratum, consisting of workers and unemployed who retain strong links with the peasantry, has in fact interests which are antagonistic to the present order'.[7] Notwithstanding the fact that to date, members of the urban lumpenproletariat have proved the most politically promiscuous of all socio-economic strata in Africa, constantly at the beck and call of the highest bidder, Arrighi and Saul suggest that Fanon's view of the lumpenproletariat as the urban spearhead of a peasant-dominated revolutionary movement has considerable relevance.[8] Such antagonism is not, however, a part of the elite-proletariat relationship where only minor differences have emerged. For example, 'where wage restraint began to be demanded of those junior partners to the "aristocracy" its imposition was made difficult by the un-ambiguously privileged position of its other members, the politicians and the salariat'.[9] Yet such differences are of slight importance alongside the overriding consensus and filiation.

Before moving to a critique of the Arrighi-Saul position by setting it against the Nigerian experience, one can point to certain merits. First, the existence of economic classes with distinct socio-political interests is granted rather than regarded as problematic. Second, the major problem is identified in terms of the sources, mode of extraction, pattern of expropriation and manner of consumption of the economic surplus. Third, certain socio-political processes general to a fairly wide range of African states, such as the general absence of labour radicality and the occasional embryonic peasant rebellion, can be accommodated, though not adequately explained, in terms of the labour aristocracy thesis. But there are very considerable limitations to which I now turn.

There are three possible interpretations by which the African wage-earning class is viewed as exceptional among the urban masses—as an economic elite, a status elite, and as a political elite. Arrighi and Saul concentrate on the first and last, as outlined above, while a number of sociologists have added the second.[10] It is noteworthy that Lagos is a most convenient location for testing the labour aristocracy thesis in the West African context. Here is one of the longest established wage-earning forces and one of the first to be organised under the umbrella of colonial rule. And currently, minimum wage-rates in the Lagos area stand at £13 per month while in the Western State where the vast majority of the population are farmers (by no means the poorest occupational category in Nigeria) the average income is probably no more than £35 per annum. It is, however, precisely such concentration on objectively measurable criteria such as differential wage-rates which imposes the greatest restraint on the explanatory value of the labour aristocracy hypothesis. Economic return is most certainly of considerable significance, but one needs to go further, looking at other characteristics of the wage-earning population, such as how they respond to their class situation and why they do so.

The nature of the Lagos proletariat

An economic elite?

At first sight, urban wage-earners' minimum income rates throughout the colonial and post-colonial periods appear to have given this class of employees substantial economic benefits over other urban and rural strata. The 1971 minimum wage of £13 per month represented a return several times higher than the average for the population of Western Nigeria as a whole. Further, successive commissions of inquiry into wages and salaries have, in recognition of rises in the cost of living, adjusted the minimum wage rate over time.

But throughout, this has quite emphatically been a *minimum* wage rate calculated to cover the subsistence level of *the individual workers.* No account has been taken of the costs for the maintenance of workers' wives and children in a society where, in the past more than at present, wage-earners frequently had two domestic units. Nor did it allow of any unforeseen hazards facing the wage-earner or his family. Because Nigeria, like any other colony, had to be self-supporting, the most profitable extraction of the surplus product of the peasant population partly depended on the cheap construction of a suitable infrastructure, an integral element in which were exceptionally low wage-rates for the small labour force.[11]

Against a background of continuing labour surplus, successive wage commissions had to do no more than periodically raise wage rates in acknowledgement of (though not correspondence with) rises in the cost of living: increases in real wages were considered unnecessary. Throughout the colonial period, the emphasis was on eradicating even the potential for the emergence of rural-urban differentials which might afford the wage-earning class a higher standard of living and improved life-chances by comparison with the peasant class. Rare occasions of labour shortage which allowed concerted industrial action against prevailing wage-rates, such as the Lagos strike of 1897, achieved little more than strengthening the resolve of the administration not to allow similar conditions to recur.[12] Particularly in Nigeria, this was facilitated by the absence of other employers of wage labour whose interests conflicted with those of the administration. In contrast, in certain East African territories, the different labour market demands of the white planter population encouraged wages above subsistence level: in Kenya for example the legal minimum wage acknowledged the requirements of the worker, his family, and their 'obligatory and socially desirable expenditure' such as taxes and school fees.[13] In Nigeria, only on occasions did members of wage commissions consider such generous notions as 'need' and 'minimum living standard' worthy of note: invariably the government did not.

Not only did substantial qualitatively different standards of living for wage-earners fail to emerge during the colonial period: post-independence developments have reinforced government-stipulated wage rates as being the minimal payments necessary to keep unskilled labour in the wage-earning sector rather than returning to the land or entering into the lowest and most unstable reaches of trading. Two examples of official concern will suffice to illustrate this feature. The Morgan Commission of 1964 estimated the minimum cost of living for a young unskilled labourer entering wage employment for the first time, and sufficient to meet the requirements of himself, a wife and a child, at £202 per annum in the Lagos area. In the commission's own words, this minimum cost of living by comparison with prevailing wage levels confirmed that 'most workers are living under conditions of penury'.[14] Despite this, Morgan further acknowledged that implementation of these wage rates would bring economic ruin and so cut the zonal rate for Lagos to £144. Though under pressure from a general strike, the federal government reduced this further to £110 per annum. Seven years later, notwithstanding an equally sympathetic wage commission under Chief Adebo, and despite extreme inflation generated and compounded by the civil war, the attempt to alleviate '*intolerable suffering at or near the bottom of* the wage and salary levels' by raising the minimum daily rate from 7s. 6d. to 10s. was eradicated by inflation in the course of a few months as the prices of foodstuffs and accommodation soared uncontrollably to a new peak.[15]

The central point, then, is that wage and salary rates tell us little if anything unless complemented by data on the cost and standard of living in African urban areas. On the economic plane alone there are clearly very considerable limitations on the value of the labour aristocracy thesis of Arrighi and Saul when applied to the Nigerian case. Since economic standing and political interest-expression of the wage-earning class are intimately related in the thesis, the latter too requires critical examination. Before this, however, I wish to consider briefly the possibility of viewing the workers as a status elite in the urban arena for two reasons. First, status considerations can assuredly (if not to the same degree as economic ones) drive a wedge between wage-earners and other urban groups and the peasantry and thereby influence their political alliances in the national arena. Second, status relationships are of considerable importance for the view outlined below that the Lagos wage-earning class is best seen as a political reference group for the urban masses in general.

A status elite?

A most frequently observed development in African urban status systems involves the acquisition by Africans of Western cultural elements exhibited by the white colonial elite and the educated indigenous elite of the present. Such a search for 'civilised' or 'Westernised' status attributes appears to seep down to the lower reaches of the hierarchy, involves a rejection of rural culture and the creation of a cultural bond between the national elite and members of the employed class.[16] Where the ruling elites have the means whereby such status attributes can be dispensed to the masses, the potential for an appeal to common interests on a political basis is at least present. Of all proponents of the labour aristocracy view, Fanon is most explicit on the importance of this bond between national elite and wage-earning class. He writes of the latter: 'Their way of thinking is already marked in many points by the comparatively well-to-do class, distinguished by technological advances, that they spring from. Here "modern ideas" reign.'[17] A number of sociologists with Fanonist inclinations have laid considerable emphasis on this cultural symbiosis between the two classes.

Such an emphasis on acquiring the artifacts of 'civilised' status cannot, however, be so emphatically applied to the Lagos proletariat. The majority of workers drawn from the Yoruba of the Western State have an extended history of pre-colonial urbanisation;[18] so the dominant elements of the existing cultural system are as appropriate to the modern urban context such as Lagos·as they are to the more established ones such as Ibadan. Unlike the majority of African migrant workers drawn from scattered rural villages with little experience of urban conditions, Yoruba wage-earners enter the Lagos arena with substantial cultural resources on which they can freely draw, so that the customary division between 'modern' urban townsmen and 'traditional' rural farmers is, in Lagos, inapplicable.

Certainly there are some status-enhancing features attached to the role of permanent worker, most notably relative stability and security in both public and private employment. But precisely in these factors lies the rub since these create new obligations. Wage-earners frequently form the focal point of urban networks comprised of kinsmen in less fortunate circumstances who constitute a serious drain on whatever financial surplus permanent workers may accumulate. This development of mutual support systems is too well-known to require further expansion here. But one point is of considerable significance. Because relatively secure wage-earners are relied upon by a host of others in marginal unstable employment and yet move quite outside the 'employed' category, the political activity of the wage-earning class and its success or failure in gaining higher wages by collective action has quite direct repercussions for these same urban dwellers, including those quite outside the dependent capitalist mode of production. Not only do these share the benefit of collective action: they closely empathise with whatever interpretations permanent workers place on the activities of management and government, operating autonomously or in concert. And in such an association of interests those marginal to wage-employment are not alone, as indicated below.

On the other hand, a most significant nexus of deference-entitling properties centre on the role of the private entrepreneur, a role taking multifarious forms but one admired by wage-earners and non-wage-earners alike in Lagos society: it is to this position that the majority of workers aspire. Not only prevailing low wages but the nature of factory employment itself indicate to workers that only marginal socio-economic mobility is possible for most. Highly rewarded skilled posts are few in number in the technologially advanced private companies and these are often filled by older workers with specific technical qualifications gained before entering factory employment. Such skills as can be developed on the shop floor are limited to specific tasks and are not easily transferable. By contrast, the realm of the entrepreneur working and living in the suburban neighbourhoods and communities around Lagos has far greater potential. Through such occupations as transporting, trading and contracting, illiterate and semi-literate men have achieved considerable economic standing and in many instances political power, often from humble origins. A variety of factors, ranging from sheer entrepreneurial expertise to immense good fortune, figure in their personal histories: but the precise combination of influences rarely detracts from the deference and admiration such individuals receive from all quarters. Further, the business organisation of such men (finding new clients, responding to changes in trade, exploiting new opportunities for trade), requires them to live alongside the class of urban poor from which they have emerged. Spurning the aloofness of well-educated industrial managers, bureaucrats, white-collar salary-earners and teachers who live in the more exclusive suburbs, the successful independent man thus acts as a constant reference point for the young worker living alongside him and associating with him or his kinsmen in neighbourhood and community affairs. In these circumstances, the factory worker views wage employment as a means to the end of entrepreneurial activity; over an extended period of time he hopes to save capital and develop skills which will place him on the lower reaches of the entrepreneurial scale.

So, though wage-earners are differentiated from other urban strata on certain criteria, there are other factors which unite these strata. Furthermore, a crucial link is the fact that the economic activity of the entrepreneurial class depends substantially on the wage and salary structure. Collective action by the proletariat to force wage increments will, if successful, promote further opportunities for the individual entrepreneur. For the present, however, the emphasis is on the important sharing of prestige elements by members of the lower strata of Lagos society. Values and sentiments attached to the wide range of entrepreneurial activity promote unity, not division, between those inside and outside the industrial mode of production.

A political elite?

So one arrives, by a somewhat crude deductive process, at the possibility of the Lagos proletariat as a political elite. But the perspective suggested here is markedly different from the Arrighi-Saul formulation whereby the urban proletariat (or at least their representatives), elite and sub-elite constitute a triumvirate of political power dividing between themselves a peasant-produced surplus. In contrast, it is argued that the Lagos proletariat is best viewed as the locally-based political elite of the urban masses, a reference group in political terms for other urban strata who substantially rely on the prevailing wage structure for satisfaction of their own interests in the urban arena, and, furthermore, look to the wage-earning class for expressions of political protest against a highly inegalitarian society. In this sense the Lagos proletariat may be termed 'populist militants': 'militants' in the sense that they have the organisational capacity and resolve to oppose firmly those actions of the ruling groups which they consider to be most iniquitous, 'populist' in that they thus express through their class actions general grass-roots sentiments of strong antagonism to the existing order. The value of this perspective is best judged by reference to class action by the proletariat as such, but there are certain structural considerations which *prima facie* provide background support.

Consider first the distinctive features of the industrial mode of production. In the Lagos arena, the extreme division between those who own the means of production and those who do not has no parallel in the broader system of socio–economic relationships. This division contrasts strongly with relationships in the entrepreneurial realm. In the case of a trading or transporting business involving several dozen workers headed by a self-made entrepreneur, the distinction between 'owner' and 'employee' is viewed primarily as a division of labour and thus does not encourage the growth of class consciousness among the latter directed against the former. The distinctiveness of modern technological production is reinforced by the concentration of private expatriate companies in large industrial estates within the Lagos metropolitan area, each estate having a labour force several thousand strong.

Second, the life-styles and life-chances of the Lagos proletariat are intimately bound up with the strategies and tactics of the national ruling elites in a formally institutionalised manner. This is obviously true of most lower class Nigerians, but of wage-earners it is accurate to an exceptional degree precisely because of the 'minimum wage level'. State intervention can suddenly and substantially affect the buying and saving power of the workers as a whole. In addition, the relatively recent arrival of large-scale expatriate manufacturing oligopolies has further compounded rather than detracted from this clear dependence on the political class. Though such enterprises do frequently pay higher wages than government, nevertheless, the majority of workers begin on the minimum wage level and remain close to it: and since private enterprises invariably match all-round increments stipulated by state decree, private sector employees expect as of right that they will receive similar benefits. So the link from the shop floor to the corridors of national political power has been reinforced by the advent of the new imperialism.

Third, owing to the density of the wage-earning population in Lagos and the slightly higher wages in acknowledgement of the prevailing cost of living, wage increments have substantial repercussions throughout the breadth of Lagos society. Here the economic interests of the labouring class merge with those of others. Such interdependence was most graphically expressed by an illiterate market woman who, on hearing of nearby workers successfully gaining wage increases, commented: 'So our young men have got more money? It is good for now we shall eat.' With the greater part of low wages being spent on rent and foodstuffs, landlords and market women are the major beneficiaries: traders, craftsmen and suppliers of other urban services also share such increments, as higher prices immediately follow general wage and salary awards. Gains made by the working class are, then, shared by an inestimably wider population.

Fourth, there are important historical precedents whereby the proletariat have emerged as the stratum most ready to articulate political grievances felt by the urban masses. Of all socio-economic groups created by the colonial situation, the Lagos wage-earners were most immediately and enduringly cast in the role of concerted opposition. Whereas the colonial adminis-tration exhibited deep-felt paternalism towards the peasantry and established at least a working relationship with the African middle class, wage-labourers became Nigeria's awkward class in the eyes of administrators, eager to translate their class ex-perience into political institutions and actions, most notably trade unions and strikes.[19]

Finally, there is the fact that the wage-earning force is composed of 'our young men', i.e. men characterised by their youth, level of education and high expectations. Particularly the Action Group party's policy of free primary education in the Western Region released finances for the secondary education of favoured sons, thus raising simultaneously educational and aspirational levels among Yoruba youths. In turn this creates certain expectations of workers by the predominantly illiterate population: a higher degree of political sophistication is anti-cipated in consequence of their ability to read newspapers, understand commentaries in English on the radio, converse and organise freely across tribal divisions, and so on. This collective status ascribed by others contributes substantially to the role of the proletariat proper as a reference group on matters of political import: this role is strikingly confirmed when class action does occur on a broad basis. . . .

Conclusion

By contrast with the Arrighi–Saul labour aristocracy hypothesis in which the elite, sub-elite and wage-earning class have primary economic interests in common and develop political alliances accordingly, it is suggested here that the Lagos proletariat has the organisational capacity and class consciousness to wrest wage increments from those competing elites which collectively comprise the contemporary Nigerian ruling class. Such material benefits coincide with those of members of other urban strata, but additionally workers' class action has a populist character in that, in the words of T. S. di Tella, 'it is also supported by non-working-class sectors upholding an anti-*status quo* ideology.'[20] In the view of the present writer, a central weakness in the Arrighi–Saul formulation is the assumption that marginal increments in wages and salaries benefit workers alone when, in effect, such increments have repercussions throughout the urban arena and promote economic and political identification between the labour force and non-wage-earners. Wage-earners also express a sense of generalised social injustice not yet compounded by the development of distinct sectional interests which divide the lower strata among themselves. Therefore, should a radical movement from below emerge, social categories who have no established avenues for political protest—such as traders and the lumpenproletariat—will follow those who have. In Lagos this applies above all to the proletariat.

Furthermore, the unambiguously exceptional case of Southern Africa apart, the Arrighi–Saul model fails to give weight to the scale and tactics of exploitation *within* the industrial sector as such. Since, according to their argument, wages and salaries are high, the extent of surplus extraction within the industrial mode of production scarcely merits attention. But the root of widespread political protest is the nature of such exploitation, based as it is on minimum wage and salary levels. The upshot of such processes are crucial in promoting identification *between* workers and the peasant class. For example, during the Adebo strikes*, comparisons were frequently drawn between the urban protest movement and earlier rural ones, notably the *agbekoya* peasant uprising in Nigeria's Western State: 'What farmers were doing recently, we are doing now'; 'workers, like farmers, have to get better prices by all means'; 'the farmers' uprising and our strikes are one and the same for the *mekunnu*† are all one against the rulers'.[21] Such comments indicate that, far from being in opposition to one another, peasantry and proletariat have a similar socio-economic status, that of producing classes equally exploited by surplus expropriators. For those involved, it appears that the mode and degree of exploitation are of less importance than the fact of exploitation itself, as expressed quite simply in the recurrent expression: 'We are all suffering'.

This is not to reject the labour aristocracy thesis in its entirety: it does appear to have considerable explanatory merit when applied to certain East African states where labour demands were such as to require wage rates allowing Africans above-minimum standards of living. The experience of Tanzania in particular, from where Arrighi and Saul draw the greater part of their illustrative material, is certainly a case in point of substantial rural-urban living standard differentials being rooted in the colonial experience.[22] Further, a case could be made for terming the highly-skilled, well-paid West African industrial workers an aristocracy relative to the urban masses as a whole, but only with very substantial modifications of the thesis such as to make it unrecognisable from its present form. This category (it is no more than that and certainly not a group or class), is extremely small and widely dispersed; its members depend on paper qualifications and highly personal contact with influential managers to gain promotion or better salaries. And because of its size and distribution in a multiplicity of public and privately-owned work places, its political significance is negligible.

But when the labour aristocracy thesis is applied to the majority of unskilled and semi-skilled Lagos wage-earners, its

---

* A section on the Adebo affair which demonstrated the political will of the Lagos proletariat, is omitted in this selection—ed.

† Common people—ed.

explanatory value is slight indeed. There are obviously economic and status differences within these strata, too, but these are of limited significance; with the possible exception of more educated white-collar workers, such distinctions do not appear to influence trade union membership or propensity to industrial action. The influence of such wage differentials is frequently mitigated by non-work considerations. The more a worker receives, the more pressing become demands from kinsmen and acquaintances both in urban and rural areas. Such intricacies cannot be developed here: the central point remains that, though the great majority of workers have broken their links with the peasantry and become wholly reliant on the industrial urban experience (for Arrighi and Saul the definitive indicators of 'optional proletarianisation'), their relationships with the national elites are characterised by hostility and conflict rather than acknowledgement of congruity of essential interests.

More tellingly perhaps, *if* academic debate *is* to be made relevant to socialist goals of development, serious conceptual or empirical shortcomings in the former ill serve the political strategy by directing attention away from important areas of exploitation. To concentrate on the flow of economic surplus from the peasant economy to the urban-industrial sector rather than explore the exploitative nature of both is, as Gavin Williams puts it, 'a classic example of the "displacement" of the "primary contradiction" between the interests of the exploiting and the exploited categories on to a "derived" contradiction between exploited classes.'[23]

In sum, then, Lagos workers are acting in response to a deeply felt sense of exploitation. Throughout the colonial period and a decade of political independence, the wage-earning class has been forced into a substantial degree of accommodation to the prevailing distribution of scarce resources in their society. From time to time, however, in circumstances of exceptional duress— the general strike of 1964 or the Adebo affair of 1971—the existing framework has been unequal to the pressures imposed on it by the underlying contradictions of a neo-colonial economy.

Such protest is not the monopoly of the proletariat, as illustrated by the *agbekoya* movement of Yoruba cocoa-farmers. But by comparison with the peasantry, the wage-earning class is continually involved in developing and refining those organisations which reflect a growing class consciousness determined by their consistently subordinate relationship to the industrial mode of production. A class-based act such as the one described here is not to be seen as an isolated experience under exceptional circumstances. It is, more importantly, a particularly overt manifestation of on-going socio-political processes. In Nigeria, as elsewhere in Africa, the relative absence of prominent and widespread political activity by the proletariat can be too easily explained in terms of apathy, indifference, the absence of class consciousness, and the like. One is reminded most vividly of a costermonger's salutary comment to Henry Mayhew on mid-nineteenth-century England:

> People fancy that when all's quiet that all's stagnating. Propagandism is going on for all that. It's when all's quiet that the seed's a-growing, Republicans and Socialists are pressing their doctrines.[24]

NOTES

1. The research on which this paper is based was financed by a grant made by the Social Science Research Council (UK) to Dr P. C. Lloyd of the University of Sussex, for the study of social stratification among urban Yoruba. I would like to thank Richard Sandbrook, Robin Cohen, John Saul and other members of the Toronto conference for critical comments on an earlier draft of this paper. Responsibility for the views expressed remains, of course, mine alone.
2. Giovanni Arrighi and John S. Saul, 'Socialism and Economic Development in Tropical Africa', *Journal of Modern African Studies*, vol. 6, no. 2, 1968, pp. 141–69.
3. *Ibid.*, p. 142.
4. *Ibid.*, p. 149.
5. Giovanni Arrighi, 'International Corporations, Labor Aristocracies and Economic Development in Tropical Africa', in Robert I. Rhodes, *Imperialism and Underdevelopment: A Reader*, (Monthly Review Press, 1970), pp. 220–67.
6. Giovanni Arrighi and John S. Saul, 'Nationalism and Revolution in Sub-Saharan Africa', in Ralph Miliband and John Saville, *The Socialist Register*, (Merlin Press, 1969), pp. 137–88.
7. *Ibid.*, p. 169.
8. Frantz Fanon, *The Wretched of the Earth*, (Penguin, 1967), ch. 2.
9. Arrighi and Saul 'Socialism and Economic Development . . .', p. 162.
10. Robin Cohen and David Michael in 'The Revolutionary Potential of the African Lumpenproletariat: A Sceptical View', consider the emergence of a Fanonist tradition. *Bulletin of the Institute of Development Studies*, (University of Sussex, July 1973).
11. John F. Weeks, 'Wage Policy and the Colonial Legacy—A Comparative Study', *Journal of Modern African Studies*, vol. 9, no. 3, 1971, pp. 361–87.

12. A. G. Hopkins, 'The Lagos Strike of 1897: An Exploration in Nigerian Labour History', *Past and Present*, 35, 1966, pp. 135–55.

13. Weeks, 'Wage Policy and the Colonial Legacy . . .', pp. 363–71.

14. *Report of the Commission on the Review of Wages, Salaries and Conditions of Service of Junior Employees of the Federation and in Private Establishments* (The Morgan Report), (Federal Government of Nigeria, Lagos, 1964).

15. *First Report of the Wages and Salaries Review Commission* (The Adebo Report 1), Federal Ministry of Information, Lagos, 1971. See also, *Second and Final Report of the Wages and Salaries Review Commission* (The Adebo Report 2), (Federal Ministry of Information, Lagos, 1971).

16. J. C. Mitchell, *The Kalela Dance*, Manchester University Press, 1956; A. L. Epstein, *Politics in an Urban African Community*, (Manchester University Press, 1958); Valdo Pons, *Stanleyville: an African Community under Belgian Administration*, (Oxford University Press, 1969).

17. Fanon, *The Wretched of the Earth*, p. 86.

18. Peter C. Lloyd, *Yoruba Land Law*, (Oxford University Press, 1962), ch. 3; P. C. Lloyd, B. Awe and A. L. Mabogunje, *The City of Ibadan*, (Cambridge University Press, 1967); A. L. Mabogunje, *Urbanisation in Nigeria*, (University of London Press, 1968).

19. Arnold Hughes and Robin Cohen, 'Towards the Emergence of a Nigerian Working Class: the Social Identity of the Lagos Labour Force, 1897–1939' (Occasional Paper, Faculty of Commerce and Social Science, University of Birmingham, Series D, No. 7, 1971); Wogu Ananaba, *The Trade Union Movement in Nigeria*, C. Hurst, 1969.

20. Torcuato di Tella, 'Populism and Reform in Latin America', in Claudio Veliz, *Obstacles to Change in Latin America*, (Oxford University Press, 1965).

21. Gavin Williams, 'Political Consciousness among the Ibadan Poor', in Emanuel de Kadt and G. P. Williams (eds.), *Sociology and Development* (Tavistock Publications, 1974). See also the forthcoming volume by C. E. F. Beer, based on his 'The Farmer and the State', Ph.D. thesis, University of Ibadan, 1971.

22. G. K. Helleiner, 'Socialism and Economic Development in Tanzania', *Journal of Development Studies*, vol. 8, no. 2, 1972, pp. 183–204.

23. Gavin Williams, 'The Political Economy of Colonialism and Neo-Colonialism in Nigeria', unpublished paper.

24. Quoted by E. P. Thompson, *The Making of the English Working Class*, Penguin, 1968, p. 781, from Henry Mayhew, *London Labour and the London Poor*, 1862.

8 ISSA G. SHIVJI

The post-Mwongozo
proletarian struggles in Tanzania[†]

The struggle

The post-*Mwongozo* 'downing of the tools' or strikes by the
workers have been the most intense on the industrial scene in
Tanzania since the establishment of NUTA in 1964. Table 8.1 is
an indication of the various phases of class struggle. The strike
figures correspond to these various phases remarkably
accurately.

As noted earlier, the workers' strikes in the late 1950s played a
crucial role in the struggle for independence. In the three years
(1958–60) just before independence, there were 561 strikes
involving 239 803 workers with 2 194 212 man-days lost, the
greatest number to be recorded. But soon after independence the
struggle between the different sectors of the petty bourgeoisie –
based in the government and the trade union – broke out. The
high number of strikes between 1961–64 bears this out (362
strikes involving 99 382 workers with 613 778 man-days lost).
The demands as before revolved around wages and conditions of
work mainly. In its attempt to curb TFL opposition the
government passed the Trade Disputes Act 1962, which prohibited strikes unless the established machinery was exhausted.
This made strikes virtually impossible. Although the number of
strikes in 1963–64 went down to half that of the previous two
years, the trade-union opposition to the government continued.
The decisive step in this intra-petty bourgeois struggle was the

---

[†] Extract from the author's *The Class Struggles in Tanzania* (Tanzania Publishing
House, 1975), ch. 13.—ed.

banning of TFL and the establishment of NUTA in 1964. NUTA came virtually under the government control. The post-1964 strike figures consequently show a drastic fall. In the six-year period, 1965–70, there were 74 strikes involving only 9308

TABLE 8.1

Industrial disputes involving strikes 1958–73

		Year	Number of strikes	Number of workers involved	Number of man-days lost
Petty bourgeoisie- +workers v. metropolitan bourgeoisie		1958	153	67 430	296 746
		1959	205	82 878	402 693
		1960	203	89 495	1 494 773
	(1)	Total	561	239 803	2 194 212
Intra-petty bourgeois struggles		1961	101	20 159	113 254
		1962	152	48 434	417 474
	(2) (a)	Total	253	68 593	530 728
Government based v. trade union based		1963	85	27 207	77 195
		1964	24	3 582	5 855
	(2) (b)	Total	109	30 789	83 050
Petty bourgeoisie v. commercial bourgeoisie		1965	13	884	1 825
		1966	16	2 062	8 845
		1967	25	3 224	7 224
	(3)	Total	54	6 170	17 894
Rise of 'bureaucratic bourgeoisie' disintegration of commercial bourgeoisie		1968	13	1 906	5 757
		1969	4	876	2 141
		1970	3	356	726
	(4)	Total	20	3 138	8 624

Table 8.1—*continued*

	Year	Number of strikes	Number of workers invovled	Number of man-days lost
	1971 (From Feb.)	15	11 043	31 915
Workers v. 'bureaucratic bourgeoisie'	1972	10	8 360	17 030
	1973 (Until Sept.)	6	3 305	14 701
	Total	31	22 708	63 646

Sources: L. R. Patel, *East African labour régime*, op. cit., p. 412 and the same author's personal files.

Mapundi, 'Post-*Mwongozo* downing of the tools' (unpublished), p. 39 for 1971–73 figures.

Notes:
(1) Independence Struggle.
(2) (*a*) Trade Disputes (Settlement) Act, 1962 making strikes virtually illegal.
    (*b*) NUTA (Establishment) Act, 1964 requiring General Council's sanction before going on strike, Banning of the TFL.
(3) Permanent Labour Tribunal Act, 1967, establishing compulsory arbitration procedure for settling disputes.
(4) Adoption of the TANU Guidelines. (*Mwongozo*).

workers with 26 518 man-days lost. The few strikes were sporadic and spontaneous without NUTA leadership. The NUTA Act itself prohibited strike action unless sanctioned by the General Council which is under the leadership of government appointees. Moreover, in terms of class struggle, it was the contradiction between the petty bourgeoisie and the commercial bourgeoisie which was being ironed out during this period.

Meanwhile, although subdued some NUTA leaders continued to pose embarrassing questions to the government as at the same time the membership complained about their organization.[1] The year 1967 saw the passing of the Permanent Labour Tribunal Act making strikes virtually illegal and establishing compulsory arbitration by the Tribunal for solving trade disputes. The number of strikes between 1968–70 was only 20, involving 3138 workers with 8624 man-days lost. But by 1971, having cleared all the ground, the fundamental contradiction between the 'bureaucratic bourgeoisie' and the workers came to the fore and asserted itself in a dramatic way in the post-*Mwongozo* 'downing of the tools'. This time, unlike the strikes before, the leadership was generally not in the hands of organized trade unions or even of the petty bourgeoisie, but of the workers themselves through, in many cases, the workers' committees. Between February 1971 and September 1973 there were 31 'downing of tools' involving something like 28 708 workers with 63 646 man-days lost. In terms of workers involved and man-days lost, this is over twice the figures for the previous six-year period, from 1965–70. Incidentally, these figures do not even include the numerous disputes against bureaucratic managers (to be discussed below) not resulting in strike.

It is the latest phase that we now propose to discuss in some detail. The post-*Mwongozo* workers' struggles may be divided roughly into three phases, *à la* Mapolu.[2] The first phase was dominated by *downing tools*, i.e. stoppage of work. Later, in the second phase, the workers increasingly began to *lock-out* the officials whom they did not want, meanwhile continuing to work. The beginning of the third phase was the factory *take-overs* which elicited the harshest response from the government – *en masse* dismissal of workers as in the case of the Mount Carmel Rubber Factory.

In practice these phases overlapped. Besides, the workers also used other methods, such as resorting to protest marches to the offices of the Prime Minister, the President, or TANU.

Jack Sperling and Sri Nimpunoo[3] have recorded these disputes as reported in the daily newspapers. Of course, all the disputes do not get reports in the newspapers and therefore the figures calculated from their tables are likely to be rough estimates. But they do bring out the essential features of the struggle.

Their tables show that between the period July 1971 and March 1974 there were roughly 45 industrial disputes affecting both the private and the public sectors. About two-thirds of the disputes were in the state sector, i.e. the wholly state-owned enterprises and others where the state directly, or through state corporations, has some ownership interest. The fact that a particular enterprise was publicly owned did not deter the workers: as we noted earlier, class relations have little to do with legal relations.

In the majority of these disputes the trade union, NUTA, was not involved. In fact it came to the scene more as a conciliator than as a workers' representative. The workers have tended to look upon NUTA with suspicion. As early as 1966, one of the major complaints recorded by the Presidential Commission[4] against NUTA was:

> A number of leaders enter into suspicious associations with employers. Business is conducted in privacy, through telephones or in English, a language which most members do not understand.[5]

And in the Rubber Industries case (1973) the workers said:

> We do not want NUTA officials because the firm's director has told us time and again that the whole of the NUTA organization is in his control and that therefore we would never be listened to by that organization. We have also proved that his words are very true for we have been requesting the NUTA official to come and deal with our problems since April 9th but all in vain. They have not even answered the three letters we wrote to them.[5]

The institution which the workers used most was the workers' committees and in some cases the TANU branches. . . . In a few cases where the workers' committees had obviously become puppets of management the workers demanded the resignation of the committee members and even organized to overthrow them (Rubber Industries). Thus, the post-*Mwongozo* disputes clearly brought out the trade union as an instrument of the 'bureaucratic bourgeoisie'.

The immediate causes or reasons which were publicly put forward by the workers for either downing tools or locking-out management may be put under two broad categories: (1) those connected generally with remuneration; and (2) non-wage demands revolving around the treatment of the workers by the management. It is the second category which was predominant. The management was accused of being oppressive, indifferent to workers' grievances, disregarding them, contemptuous, and so on. The workers accused the management of breaching the *Mwongozo* and in particular clause 15, which states that 'a Tanzanian leader . . . must be forbidden to be arrogant, extravagant, contemptuous, and oppressive.' Clause 33 which states that the Party must ensure that parastatals do not use surpluses extravagantly, was also cited against the managements accused of being corrupt, misusing the funds of the enterprises, etc. In short, the workers enthusiastically quoted the *Mwongozo* as their ideological weapon in the struggle. But the bureaucracy of course would not oblige. It was one thing to issue a declaration for mobilizing the masses in the interest of their own class security, but quite another to implement it.

The response of the bureaucracy became increasingly harsher. It accused the workers of being irresponsible, misinterpreting the *Mwongozo*, and undermining the economy. But let us see whose economy was being undermined? The following recent case of the Tanganyika Motors dramatically illustrates the issue. Tanganyika Motors Ltd which mainly repairs the Peugeot cars is a privately owned company. The workers of the company locked out its four top officials on the grounds that they were indifferent to their grievances and looked down upon the African workers. The manager retaliated by closing down the enterprise. A NUTA official, trying to get the workers back to work, 'reminded the workers that Peugeot motor vehicles for which their company is agent were very much used by individuals and Government institutions'.[6] True, the Peugeot car is a status symbol for the members of the petty bourgeoisie: it was therefore the economy of the Peugeot owners and the comfort of the Peugeot users which were being undermined. No wonder, a representative of the workers said that human dignity was more important than the economy of the country.[7]

The climax of the bureaucracy's reaction was the mass expulsion of the workers in the case of Sungura Textile Mill and Dar es Salaam Motor Transport (DMT). Between June 1970 and August 1972 the workers at Sungura Textile stopped work over eight times. In August 1972, the government picked on 31 workers as ringleaders and instigators. They were taken into the police custody and dismissed from their jobs. The government statement issued at the time strongly condemned 'downing tools' as harmful to the economy. It harped on the figures of losses incurred in the privately owned Sungura Textile as a result of the work stoppages and warned that strong measures would be taken against instigators and agitators.[8]

Between 27 November 1972 and 4 January 1973, the drivers and the conductors of Dar es Salaam Motor Transport (DMT) went on strike twice. DMT is the government owned passenger transport service in the country. Because of these strikes the city public transport came to a complete standstill. When the workers went on their first strike on 27 December 1972, four of them were arrested and prosecuted. The workers were promised that their grievances would be looked into and settlement reached by 1 January. On 4 January, having heard nothing from the authorities, they again stopped work. This time the government dismissed all the 676 drivers and some 452 conductors.[9] The government statement issued at the time reads:

> This act now means that there is no negotiating but competing between the Government and the workers concerned. The Government has no need for competing with a person or persons. Therefore the decision of the Government is that as from the time those drivers and conductors decided to strike to the present, the Government no longer recognizes them as workers of DMT . . . . If there are some who went on strike because of being instigated or threatened, yet they would like to continue with their work wholeheartedly, those are given this chance. Special orders are being made in writing and any one who would like to continue with work should from 12 this afternoon to 6 this evening report to the DMT office in the Pugu-Msimbazi Street; he will be given these orders; if he accepts them he should sign them; thereafter he will be allowed back to his work. If not so, then he should quit.[10]

What alternative did the drivers and the conductors have but to rejoin the company. The large majority of them signed the forms.

The full story of the struggles in the various enterprises following the *Mwongozo* has still to be told. Research[11] on these issues by a number of people has just begun but it will be some time before results become known. The following brief accounts of two famous disputes bring out some of the important features discussed in the foregoing sections.

Manager Locked out: The BAT Case

The British American Tobacco Co. Ltd (BAT) of Tanzania is a subsidiary of the National Development Corporation (NDC) which owns 60 per cent of the shares. The company has a general management and technical consultancy contract with BAT Ltd. BAT is a British company ranking fifth among the British firms and with capital employed of B£461 106 000 (1967) on which a net profit (before interest and tax) of B£103 033 000 was made. The company has 100 factories in 50 countries including South Africa. It has a virtual monopoly of the East African market.[12]

On the 23 May 1973[13] when the Personnel Manager of the company, one Mr Kashaija, came to the factory, a fire alarm bell was sounded and all the workers stopped work. Some workers walked to his office and threatened to pull it down if he did not leave the premises. 'Peace' was not restored until police armed with guns and tear gas arrived at the scene at the request of the management.

The workers refused to work until some decision was taken on the fate of Mr Kashaija. Finally, as a result of a meeting between NUTA and the management the workers' complaints were forwarded to the Permanent Labour Tribunal.

At the hearing of the case before the Tribunal Mr Kashaija was helped by Mr P. Hayward, BAT's secretary and an advocate provided by the state-owned Tanzania Legal Corporation, they being BAT's legal advisers. One of the witnesses who consistently defended Mr Kashaija was the expatriate General Manager of the company, Mr MacDonald. The alignment of the forces could not be clearer.

The stoppage of work was a result of the accumulated grievances of the workers against Mr Kashaija, which were voiced for the first time as early as 1971. The main complaints of the workers were as follows:

(a) That Mr Kashaija used the company's resources extravagantly in breach of the TANU Guidelines paragraphs 15 and 33. The two of the more important incidences cited were that Kashaija used the company's Range Rover to attend his father's burial in Bukoba. This cost the company as much as 5820Sh. Secondly, Mr Kashaija used 6100Sh of the company to throw a grand party to which something like 194 people were invited.

The party enraged the workers very much. It was held at the Kunduchi Beach, a tourist resort area. The invitation card from Mr and Mrs Kashaija gave the duration as follows: On the 3rd March, any time after 8.00 p.m. 'The party started at 8.00 p.m. on the 3rd ran throughout the night, and ended on the 4th at around 1.00 p.m.' No workers or even their representatives were invited. In his evidence the General Manager said that the purpose of the party was to strengthen the relations existing between the company and the general public. Kalokora has given a cross-section of the invitees which constituted the 'general public' at this party:

Guest of Honour:
Minister for Economic Affairs and Development Planning.

Others:
Minister for Communications
Minister for Agriculture
The NDC General Manager
The Managing Chairman, National Bank of Commerce
The General Manager, National Housing Corporation
The General Manager, National Insurance Corporation
The Chairman, Pyrethrum Board
The Chairman, Civil Service Commission
Gynaecologist, Muhimbili Hospital
A Senior Medical Officer, Muhimbili Hospital
The Manager, Cooper Motor Corporation
The BAT Wholesale Manager
(Someone) from the Army Headquarters
The Manager, Development Bank
The Personal Assistant to the President
The Principal Secretary, Ministry of Information
The Director, Ministry of Foreign Affairs
The ex-Ugandan Foreign Minister and his 5 friends
An important Dar businessman (African)

The Commissioner for Lands
A Professor of Economics, University of Dar es Salaam
The General Manager, NATEX
The General Manager, TANESCO
An accountant from Cooper Brothers
A Police Public Prosecutor
The General Manager, State Trading Corporation
The Tanzanian Ambassador to the Peoples' Republic of China.[14]

There could not be a better cross-section of the representatives of the international bourgeoisie (managers of foreign companies); members of the Tanzanian 'bureaucratic bourgeoisie' and the upper sector of the petty bourgeoisie. Surely, it was to strengthen the relations among the dominating classes, if not the 'general public'!

(*b*) The other set of complaints accused Mr Kashaija of tribalism and favouritism. It was alleged that Mr Kashaija tended to employ people from his own area, i.e. Bukoba.

The Tribunal found that 12 per cent of the overall work force were *Wahaya*. Comparing it with *Wachagaa*, who constituted only half the *Wahaya* at the factory, the Tribunal concluded that the only way such a large proportion of *Wahaya* could be explained was that they had been employed through tribalism.

(*c*) Thirdly, the workers accused Mr Kashaija of practising segregation and discrimination. For instance at one time or another he was alleged to have encouraged separate canteens for workers and top bureaucrats.

At the hearing one worker witness said that while the Junior BAT staff were given 'prison food' the senior management members took 'delicious dishes of tourist standards'.[15]

In its decision the Permanent Labour Tribunal found that a number of allegations against Mr Kashaija were justified and recommended that he should be removed from the company.

Meanwhile the workers had voluntarily worked overtime—*unpaid*—to compensate for the losses incurred as a result of the strike.

Factory Taken over: The Mount Carmel Case

'The Rubber Industries Limited workers scratched the first match, the curtain raiser; they were followed by the five hundred nightwatchmen who refused to watch other people's property while theirs was being pillaged; then came the Mount Carmel Rubber tragedy where the Carmel having locked its master out of the tent was removed from the tent by super-powers and condemned for ever to suffer in the blizzard and the harmattan, because it refused to be mounted! The tradition at Mount Carmel is that the "Carmel" must always be mounted.' (Mihyo.)

The highest stage after downing of the tools and the lock-outs in the workers' struggles was reached with the takeover of the factories.

The first successful takeover was at Rubber Industries Ltd. This factory was owned by a group of Tanzanian Asians in partnership with Industrial Promotion Services (IPS), which is dominated by the Aga Khan and is NDC's partner in a number of Tanzanian enterprises. The story of how the takeover was organized by the militant workers has been competently told by Mihyo in great detail and I need not repeat it. This was a successful takeover supported by the government.

The second takeover was that of the Night-Watch Security Company whose owner had in fact left the country.

The third takeover, which resulted in the workers' dismissal, was that of the Mount Carmel Rubber Factory, situated just opposite Rubber Industries.

The Mount Carmel is owned and managed by one Mr Yadzani. The conditions at the factory were deplorable. 'When on the 17th of March, 1971, the factory inspector visited the Mount Carmel Rubber Factory, he found that it was in a terribly unhealthy situation. The set up of the factory was itself a violation of the letter and spirit of the . . . Factories Ordinance. This inspection report has revealed that contrary to section 13 of the said ordinance the factory was not kept clean—that indeed it was stinking. Dirt was lying about in heaps as if it was a raw material or a commodity for sale.'[16] The boiler was not adequately housed; it constituted a danger to human life. There were no adequate drinking facilities for the workers. When asked about this by Mihyo, the employer replied that there was shortage of water in Dar es Salaam and added cynically: 'I am of course not a rain maker!'

Out of the 70 or so workers employed at the factory, 20 or more were casual employees. They were in even worse conditions, because they would not be entitled to any terminal benefits nor was their employment secure. Thus the working conditions at the factory were as bad as could be.

There was no workers' committee at the factory until 1971. NUTA had hardly done anything for the workers. It was only after the formation of the committee that a collective agreement was drafted. However, it was never enforced. In January 1972, the workers, led by their committee, had threatened to go on strike. A meeting of the workers was called but nothing substantial came of it.

It was under such circumstances that the workers finally decided to take over the factory. In this they were encouraged by the neighbouring factory.

Thus, sometime in June 1973, when the factory's personnel manager tried to enter the factory gates he was met by the workers, shouting and booing. He was told by the Chairmen of the TANU branch and the workers' committee that the workers did not want him or the Managing Director, Mr Yadzani. The workers had taken over the factory. While some of them kept guard at the gates, others continued production. Some of the placards posted at the factory read:

'Long live Mwalimu* and Mwongozo.'
'We are ready to work night and day if allowed to take over the factory.'
'For 21 years now from 1952 to 1973, there has been no improvement at the factory.'
'The factory belongs to the workers. It is in Dar not Persia' [reference to the employer's origin].

The workers refused completely to see the NUTA or other labour officials despite a warning by the Labour Commissioner that refusing to meet officials 'was very serious and would lead to punishment'. The then Regional Commissioner, Mr Kisumo,

---

* Reference to President J. K. Nyerere, a former schoolteacher who is popularly referred to as Mwalimu (Teacher in Kiswahili)—ed.

who had approved the Rubber Industries takeover a few days ago, vehemently opposed this takeover. He tried to persuade the workers to allow their employer in, but they would not budge from their decision. Next day the regional commissioner again appeared at the factory, this time with a contingent of policemen, but the workers remained adamant:

'The workers told the regional commissioner who advised them yesterday to abide by the Party's ruling that they were prepared to leave the firm any time if they would be provided with transport and land to establish their own *Ujamaa* village, rather than accept their employer as the leader of the firm. (Mr Kisumo told them): "TANU advises you to allow your employer to enter the firm's premises and wants you to work together with him." Amid applause a worker assured Mr Kisumo that their decision was firm and that all workers in the firm were members of TANU, therefore their decision was still in line with Party policies.'[17]

The workers accused their employer of being a neo-colonialist and involved in importing raw materials which were obtainable locally.

Meanwhile, the workers of the Hotel Afrique were reported making preparation to take over their 'factory'. Mount Carmel was setting a bad precedent. This could not be allowed. Next day, at 11 a.m. a labour officer accompanied by police and trucks appeared at the factory gates. Let the *Daily News* report take up the story in full: 'An official from the Ministry accompanied by a number of policemen called at the factory in Chang'ombe and issued to all the workers what he called a Government order. He said that those workers who were not ready to work under Mr Yadzani should stay apart from those who accepted his leadership. All workers who refused to accept their employer's leadership were ordered to enter packed vehicles. Sixty-two were driven away to the Central Police Station leaving the industry with only 15 workers.'[18] All the members of the workers' committee and the TANU Branch Committee including their Chairmen were among those arrested.

Having had their finger-prints taken, and after staying in the police custody for a few days, the workers were repatriated to their respective 'home' (!) areas.

The government statement issued on the occasion warned the workers against 'the habit of unilaterally taking over factories' and that it would not 'tolerate such unruly behaviour on the part of the workers'. The statement triumphantly declared that 'early yesterday morning the Government re-instated the owner of the firm in his factory and opposed the workers' demands to take it over'.[19] And, as usual, the Government daily, the *Daily News* joined in the celebration. The editor in his *Comment* on the dismissal, had a 'brilliant brainwave':

'Socialism is coming,' he wrote,
'This no one can prevent. . . .
The action was not meant for
the benefit of a capitalist or a group
of capitalists. In the final analysis
it was for the benefit of the workers
of Tanzania themselves.'[20]

The state thus asserted its class character regardless of the ideology. But in so doing it laid bare the fundamental contradiction between the exploited and the exploiter. It is this contradiction which is going to be the dominant one henceforth. True, the workers' struggles we have described have been sporadic and not necessarily couched in conscious class ideology. The reaction of the workers has been more a consequence of their class instinct, rather than because of definite class consciousness. But class consciousness does not come spontaneously. It is the role of proletarian ideology to develop class *instinct* into class *consciousness*. Meanwhile, the workers have definitely declared that the stage of history when they were used as cannon fodder in the intra-petty bourgeois struggles to be fast coming to an end. This time it will be their own struggles—their own class war—and the struggle of their fellow exploited class, the poor peasants that they will fight, not to replace one exploiter with another but to begin to replace the very system of exploitation.

NOTES

1. See generally, L. R. Patel, *East African labour régime*, (mimeo, 1972), ch. 11.
2. H. Mapolu, 'The workers' movement in Tanzania', *Maji Maji*, no. 12, (TANU Youth League, September 1973).
3. Unpublished.
4. *Report of the Presidential Commission on the National Union of Tanganyika Workers*, (Government Printers, 1967), p. 1, para. 5.
5. *Uhuru*, 26 May 1973. Quoted in H. Mapolu, 'The workers' movement in Tanzania', p. 40.
6. *Daily News*, 16 January 1974.
7. *Ibid.*
8. *Tamko Rasmi la Serikali kuhusu migomo*, (mimeo), (n.d.).
9. See the *Daily News*, from 28 December 1972, to 9 January 1973.
10. Quoted in K. F. Ileti, 'Workers' disputes', Unpublished student course-work (1974), Faculty of Law, University of Dar es Salaam.
11. Some of the course-work Papers done by the Undergraduates in Labour Law (1973–74) at the Faculty of Law, University of Dar es Salaam will be published in the forthcoming issues of the *Eastern Africa Law Review*. (I am indebted to Messrs Mihyo, Kalokora, Ileti and Mapundi for letting me use some of the material from their papers.)
12. National Christian Council of Kenya, *Who controls industry in Kenya?*, (East African Publishing House, 1968), p. 106.
13. This account is based on Kalokora, I. Bwesha, 'Labour disputes in Tanzania: a case study of selected incidents', (1974), (unpublished).
14. The full list, according to Kalokora, was attached to the BAT statement of Defence.
15. Quoted in Kalokora, 'Labour disputes in Tanzania'.
16. P. Mihyo, 'Labour unrest and the Quest for workers' control: three Case Studies', (tentative title), Student Undergraduate dissertation, (1973), published in *Eastern Africa Law Review*, vol. vii, no. i, 1974. The account that follows is also based on Mihyo, Course-work Papers; Mapolu, 'The workers' movement in Tanzania', and newspaper reports.
17. *Daily News*, 20 June 1973. Quoted in Mapolu, 'The workers' movement'.
18. *Daily News*, 21 June 1973.
19. *Daily News*, 21 June 1973.
20. *Daily News*, 22 June 1973, quoted in Mapolu, 'The workers' movement'.

9 DONALD J. HARRIS

Notes on the question of a national minimum wage for Jamaica[†]

1. Wages and Employment in a Capitalist Economy

In order to arrive at an adequate understanding of the question of a National Minimum Wage for Jamaica, it is necessary to start from a correct theoretical analysis of the nature and operation of the wage system in capitalist economy and the specific historical forms of that system which have developed in Jamaica.

It is evident from such an analysis that what is at issue in the current discussion of a national minimum wage, is the inherent inability of the wage system itself, or the system of capitalist employment, to provide productive employment for our people at a wage which would enable every worker and his or her family to enjoy a standard of living that is consistent with some socially acceptable minimum.

This inability is inherent in the wage system as such. This is because it is a system which is based on the employment of labour at whatever level the wage settles on the market, and with the overriding objective that such employment return a profit which is acceptable to the capitalist employer. (We leave aside, for the moment, areas of wage employment such as domestic service and the civil service that are outside the orbit of direct profit-making activity). In the operation of the labour market under the capitalist rules of the game, the employer seeks to keep wages as low as possible so as to make profits as large as possible. The workers struggle, within the limits of their organised strength, to

[†] From C. Stone and A. Brown (eds.), *Essays on Power and Change in Jamaica* (Jamaica Publishing House, 1977), ch. 8—ed.

resist this pressure and to improve their living and working conditions. There is no guarantee that the wage which the market thus determines will be sufficient to provide for the minimal requirements of the worker and family. It may well fall below that minimum for large groups of workers in unskilled occupations in the least organised sectors of the economy.

As between capitalists and workers, the wage relation is an *antagonistic* relation. For, the capitalists can increase the rate of their profits only by lowering wages; the workers can increase their wages only through a reduction in the rate of profits. This antagonism is inherent in the nature of production. Because of this, any attempt to raise the wage above the level which it would otherwise reach may be expected to incur the active resistance of the capitalists. One way out, for the capitalists, is to introduce mechanised techniques of production which raise the productivity of labour and thereby increase profits. But not all capitalists, and especially not the smallest ones (the petty capitalists), can obtain the finance required for investment in such techniques. For the workers, on the other hand, introduction of such techniques may involve a reduction in employment.

Once the capitalist labour market has determined what amount of employment is profitable at the going wage, and with existing techniques of production, the workers that are left without jobs must try to squeeze out a living in whatever way they can, in domestic service, by self-employment, begging, or theft, or by relying on relatives. The size of this pool of labour is augmented over time by the systematic erosion of traditional forms of petty commodity production (small-peasant cultivators, self-employed shopkeepers, craftsmen and seamstresses) due to expansion and concentration of capital (as in bauxite mining, supermarket retailing, textile manufacturing, etc.) and by fluctuations and technical reorganization of production in capitalist industries.

It is the continued existence of this pool of labour—*the reserve army*—which aids the capitalists in holding down the wage of workers employed in unskilled and semi-skilled occupations. This is because the ready availability of the reserve army weakens the bargaining power of employed workers. Furthermore, because of the large size of this reserve army, there is no necessity or compulsion, from the point of view of the circulation and reproduction of capital as a whole, for the capitalists to pay to employed workers a living wage. A living wage would consist of the necessaries of food, clothing, shelter, medical care, etc., that are required to sustain the workers' ability to continue to work. These are the *necessary costs of reproduction* of the workers' capacity to labour or labour-power. But, since the capitalists can recruit from the reserve army as much labour-power as is required for production, there is no imperative to pay a wage (either directly or through taxation of profits by the state) adequate to meet these costs. The objective evidence of this is in the malnutrition, disease, illiteracy, poor housing and high rate of early mortality among the masses of working people.

The predominance of low-wage unskilled and semi-skilled jobs in the available total of capitalist employment in Jamaica is a reflection of the backward level of technology which continues to prevail throughout the economy, both in traditional large-scale agricultural activities producing for export (sugar, bananas, etc.) and in small-scale farming, as well as in the innumerable activities of petty-capitalist enterprise in the manufacturing, commercial and service sectors. In the case of traditional export agriculture, the existing conditions of production are inherited from a long past history of colonial control of the economy and reflect the continued subordination of production to the requirements of international capital. All such activities continue to survive chiefly because of the existence of a huge reserve army of cheap labour and in the degree to which they are sheltered in one way or another from competition of other capitalists.

Expansion of total employment depends on the rate of re-investment from the total pool of surplus produced in the economy. The more capital-intensive the techniques that are involved in this investment the less rapid is the expansion of employment, and *vice versa*. For the existing pool of unemployed labour to be absorbed there has to be a *sustained* and rapid expansion of total employment. A net transfer of labour out of low-wage employment requires, further, that there be a sufficiently rapid expansion of employment in high-productivity industries. However, in a dependent capitalist economy thoroughly integrated into international capitalism as is the Jamaican economy, there is little or no prospect of such a sustained expansion of employment. This is for a number of reasons. In the first place, a substantial share of the available surplus is drained away through repatriation of profits by foreign corporations and banks, payment of interest on foreign loans, and consumption of imported luxuries by the wealthy classes. This drainage from the national economy is not on average offset by new foreign investment. Secondly, the overall rate of investment tends to vary sharply in accordance with recurrent crises in the international capitalist economy. Thirdly, much of whatever new investment occurs tends to embody highly capital-intensive techniques that are adapted to the profit requirements of capitalist firms and to the pattern of consumption of the wealthy classes, therefore giving rise to a very small gain in employment. All of this means that the predominance of low-wage jobs along with the existence of widespread unemployment tends to become permanent, in-built, features of the economy.

Thus, the problems of unemployment and sub-standard wages in Jamaica are neither arbitrary nor accidental. For reasons indicated in the foregoing analysis, *they are definite and mutually related products of the same system, the particular system of capitalist employment which exists in Jamaica.* There is therefore no way of eliminating these problems so long as that system continues to be the chief source of employment for the masses of people.

In conditions of economic backwardness such as those which currently exist in Jamaica, the only system which has concretely demonstrated the ability to solve the problem of unemployment and at the same time raise the living standard of the masses of the people to a decent and reasonable level is the system of socialism. This is abundantly clear from all the evidence for the socialist economies of China and Cuba. The reason for this is also clear. With a system of social ownership and control of national production, it becomes possible to restructure the pattern of employment and production so as to make maximum use of available labour, to seize hold of the available surplus for ploughing back within the national economy in accordance with a rational plan for development, and to distribute the available output of consumption goods among worker-families so as to ensure a reasonable minimum of consumption for every family while eliminating the luxury consumption of the rich.

In capitalist economies, whether backward or advanced, various types of legislative action, expenditures by the state, and economic reform have been developed in response to the struggles of workers to improve their conditions of work and living standards. Such measures sometimes serve to alleviate, to a limited extent, the material conditions of some sectors of the working class. Taken by themselves, however, such measures do not eliminate the basic causes of those conditions.

It is in this light that the current proposal for a national minimum wage in Jamaica must be examined.

2. History of the Minimum Wage Law in Jamaica

A Minimum Wage Law came into existence for the first time in Jamaica in December 1938. This and other related developments (like the Moyne Commission Report) were a direct outcome of the worker-peasant revolt which occurred earlier that year, forcing upon the national consciousness an awareness of the desperate economic conditions facing the majority of the people.

The Law empowered the Minister of Labour to fix a minimum wage-rate for any or all sectors of employment in the economy and to appoint Advisory Boards for advising the Government on specific sectors. The first Advisory Board to be established (in 1940) was that for the sugar industry. Subsequently Advisory Boards were established for other sectors as follows (with dates of establishment in brackets): Beverages (1943), Printing (1944), Dry Goods (1945), Catering (1947), Hotels (1951), Laundry and Dry Cleaning (1954), Retail Petrol (1954), Drugs (1954), Garment Making (1961), Frozen Confectionery and Dairy Processing (1964). A minimum wage (without an Advisory Board) was introduced in the baking trades in 1965. It thus took about twenty-five years for coverage to be extended to this limited range of sectors, and coverage has remained limited to those same sectors up to the present time. (A National Minimum Wage covering all sectors of the economy was announced by the Government in early October, 1975). The actual fixing of a minimum wage is even more limited: only seven of those sectors actually have an established minimum wage. These were indicated in Table 9.1, which shows the level of the minimum wage

TABLE 9.1

Weekly minimum wages fixed under the minimum wage law, and consumer price indices

Sector	1967	1968	1969	1970	1971	1972	1973	1974
Banking								
Urban	10.05	n.c.	n.c.	15.05	n.c.	n.c.	n.c.	22.05
Rural	8.41	n.c.	n.c.	13.40	n.c.	n.c.	n.c.	20.40
Printing								
Newspaper	6.95	n.c.	13.00	n.c.	15.00	n.c.	17.50	n.c.
Job Printing	6.70	n.c.	7.83	n.c.	10.00	n.c.	12.00	n.c.
Dry Goods	3.75	n.c.	n.c.	n.c.	4.22	n.c.	n.c.	n.c.
Retail Petrol								
Urban	2.30	n.c.	n.c.	3.36	n.c.	n.c.	n.c.	n.c.
Rural	2.00	n.c.	n.c.	2.80	n.c.	n.c.	n.c.	n.c.
Laundry & Dry Cleaning								
Urban	3.00	n.c.	n.c.	3.00	n.c.	n.c.	n.c.	n.c.
Rural	2.40	n.c.	n.c.	3.20	n.c.	n.c.	n.c.	n.c.
Hotels & Guest Houses	4.80	n.c.	5.00	7.20	n.c.	n.c.	n.c.	n.c.
Catering	4.67	n.c.	n.c.	n.c.	7.01	n.c.	n.c.	n.c.
Consumer Price Indices								
Urban: Food & Drink	100.0	104.2	111.2	118.4	131.4	141.8	146.3	184.0
All Items	100.0	103.2	109.4	116.2	127.5	136.0	144.0	171.6
Rural: Food & Drink	100.0	107.9	110.8	116.8	132.0	142.4	150.5	189.2
All Items	100.0	106.4	109.4	114.8	126.9	135.9	143.4	172.6

Source: Government of Jamaica, Economic Survey, 1973, 1974.
Notes: (1) Wages rates are quoted in Jamaican dollars.
(2) Price indices are annual means with base January 1967 = 100.
(3) n.c. = no change.

established in the different sectors and the revisions that have been made at various times since 1967.

It is evident from Table 9.1 that there has been a substantial lapse of time, averaging about 3 to 4 years, between revisions in the level of the minimum for each sector. With sizeable increases in the cost of living in the interim, this has meant a sharp *decrease* in the actual purchasing power of the minimum wage between increases. The increase in the minimum when it comes, has usually been insufficient to compensate for the previous decline in purchasing power.

The legislated pattern of minimum wage involves a sizeable spread in the level of the minimum between sectors, the difference being about 8 to 1 between the highest (Urban Baking) and the lowest (Rural Retail Petrol). This pattern reflects in part the difference in reproduction costs of labour-power and organizational strength of workers in the different sectors. It reflects also, and more importantly, the imperative to preserve a profit margin in each sector so as to allow the individual capitalists to survive. For, given the difference in labour productivity and capital per man between sectors, a difference in the minimum wage is required to ensure an adequate margin of profit for each capitalist. *In general, this imperative is especially great from the point of view of petty capitalists and agrarian landlords* operating usually with a small margin of profit in low-productivity sectors and with a labour force of mostly unskilled and semi-skilled labour. *It is less great for big monopoly-capitalists* operating with a large profit margin and with a well organised labour force of mostly skilled labour paid at a rate which is significantly above the minimum. It is therefore an imperative which derives from the needs and interests of petty-capitalists and the influence which they have exercised up to now in Jamaica over the policies of the state. The failure of extension of the coverage of the Minimum Wage Law reflects the same set of factors and influences. A policy of setting a higher minimum for sectors in the low-productivity range would be consistent with this imperative if it were accompanied by a system of state-financed subsidies to preserve the profit margins of those sectors. But such a policy would require increased taxation of profits of the big monopoly-capitalists and would therefore run up against the resistance of those capitalists.

The considerations outlined in the previous paragraph suggest that a policy of differentiated levels of minimum wages that are low on average while falling off sharply in the lower range may be in the mutual interest of all sectors of capital at a particular time. However, changes in that policy may come about at other times in accordance with the changing interests of the different sectors of capital, changes in their respective degree of control over the state, and the changing conditions of the workers' struggle. Some reasons for this in the currently changing situation of the Jamaican economy will be considered below.

Enforcement of the existing law has been entrusted to authorized officers who are staff members of the Labour Department. They are empowered to enter employers' premises, inspect records, investigate complaints and undertake legal proceedings against alleged offenders.

Failure of the enforcement mechanism is one of the chief complaints that are often made. Such failure has an objective basis in the small size of the staff entrusted with enforcing the law, in complicity between employers and the state apparatus, and in the disorganised state of the workers, which, along with the pressure of the reserve army, dictates the submission of the workers to sub-standard wages.

3. Current Situation of the Jamaican Economy

The raising of the issue of a national minimum wage at this time is by no means an arbitrary or accidental occurrence. It has, rather, a certain necessity deriving from objective conditions existing in the Jamaican economy at this time. At one level, this necessity arises now, as in 1938, from the crushing economic conditions facing the masses of people, workers and peasants, which conditions have deteriorated sharply in recent years. At a deeper level, it derives from contradictions associated with those conditions and with the particular needs and requirements for continued expansion of the major sectors of capital in the contemporary period. These contradictions dictate a range of policy solutions and overall programme of economic reform of which the national minimum wage proposal constitutes but one part.

As to the facts of the contemporary situation, much can be gleaned from available statistics. Though the statistics are not entirely adequate for present purposes, some are nevertheless relevant and these are presented in the accompanying Tables.

One of the most striking conditions, observable with the naked eye, is the great disparity in incomes between different groups of the population, with a concentration of high incomes among a small few at the top and the great majority receiving incomes below what by any standard could be considered a reasonable level. This is attested to by all the available statistics.

In a study reported in 1971, it was estimated that the poorest 60 per cent of the Jamaican population received only 19 per cent of the total national income while the highest income group constituting 5 per cent of the population received 31 per cent of national income as their share.[1] Lying behind this pattern of income distribution and giving rise to it is, of course, a similar pattern of concentration of property and wealth. In this connection, the study showed that the situation in Jamaica is an extreme one by comparison with other countries. In only 6 other countries, from a listed total of 44, was the income share of the poorest 60 per cent less than that estimated for Jamaica.

Latest available data (for 1973) on income distribution are equally revealing (see Table 9.2). Take as a measure of the bare essentials of survival in 1973 an average weekly income of $20, which is approximately (allowing for inflation) what the state currently pays to unskilled labour employed in 'make-work' projects under the Impact Programme. Then it is evident that about 76 per cent of the employed labour force received an income below this level. The position of females was somewhat worse than that of males: 81 per cent of females fell below this level and 73 per cent of males; but together, as members of the same dispossessed class, they shared in the same conditions of deprivation.

Table 9.3 gives a more detailed picture of income distribution in terms of the sectoral pattern. It reveals sharp inter-sectoral variations in the pattern of distribution. The proportion of the employed labour force in each sector receiving a weekly income of less than $20 varies from a high of 94 per cent in agriculture to a low of 8 per cent in mining. The highest concentrations of

TABLE 9.2

Distribution of employed labour force by average weekly income: cumulative percentages

Income group	Total employed labour force	Males	Females
No Income	7.8	7.5	8.1
Under $10	45.8	41.8	51.9
$10–$20	76.4	73.1	81.4
$20–$30	86.9	86.1	88.3
$30–$40	93.4	92.7	94.4
$40–$50	95.7	95.0	96.7
$50–$75	97.8	97.4	98.5
$75–$100	98.7	98.5	99.0
$100 and Over	100.0	100.0	100.0

Source: Department of Statistics, *The Labour Force 1973*.

deprivation (more than 70 per cent of the sectoral labour force receiving less than $20 per week) are in agriculture, commerce (wholesale–retail trade, financial intermediaries, etc.), and other services (domestic and personal services, schools, hospitals, hotels, etc.). These are also the sectors which contain the great majority, 63 per cent altogether, of the total labour force. On the scale of concentrated deprivation, the manufacturing sector is not far behind these, with 65 per cent of the labour force in that sector getting less than $20 a week. The lowest concentrations are in mining and public utilities.

A disaggregated picture in terms of different social strata and economic groupings of the population can be had from the household savings survey of 1972 (see Table 9.4). The data show that there is much less concentration of deprivation among wage employees of the state than among private-sector employees, and much less among all wage-earners taken together than among self-employed persons (petty commodity producers of various sorts). When viewed in terms of different occupational and skill strata, it is among craftsmen, semi-skilled, unskilled, and 'other skilled' categories that the greatest concentration of deprivation occurs.

To complete the overall picture regarding the existing pattern of deprivation in the Jamaican economy, consideration must be given to the prevailing high rate of unemployment which, by

TABLE 9.3

Sectoral distribution of employed labour force by average weekly income: cumulative percentages

Income group	Agri., For. & Fishg.	Ming., Quarg., Refng.	Mfg.	Constr. & Instl.	Pub. Util.	Comm.	Trsp., Stor. & Com.	Pub. Admn.	Other Serv.	Ind. not Stated
No Income	11.9	0	9.1	6.4	0	8.1	1.3	0	3.0	9.3
Under $10	66.6	5.9	33.0	19.2	5.4	46.1	9.7	10.1	41.7	24.8
$10–$20	93.8	7.9	65.4	52.9	19.3	79.2	31.2	33.4	83.0	57.0
$20–$30	98.0	17.7	80.3	81.1	46.2	89.5	63.2	52.1	91.0	91.2
$30–$40	99.2	35.3	89.5	93.3	64.2	92.8	83.2	79.7	95.2	93.1
$40–$50	99.6	49.5	93.4	96.4	79.1	94.9	90.2	87.2	96.7	93.1
$50–$75	99.8	75.6	96.3	98.2	96.2	97.2	94.8	95.0	97.7	100.0
$75–$100	99.9	93.1	97.6	99.0	96.3	98.3	95.6	97.5	98.3	–
$100 & Over	99.9	100.0	100.0	100.0	100.0	100.0	100.0	100.0	100.0	–
	100.0									
Percentage of Total Employed Labour Force	32.0	1.9	12.4	6.2	1.0	14.3	3.3	10.9	16.8	1.1

Source: *The Labour Force Survey 1973*, unpublished data.

TABLE 9.4

Income distribution of savers classified by worker status: cumulative percentages

Annual Income	Total Savers	Government Employees	Non-Govt. Employees	Self- Employed	Not Classified
Under $500	57.9	29.2	49.3	75.2	80.6
$500–$999	78.0	53.6	75.4	88.3	90.1
$1,000–$1,999	91.3	83.8	89.6	96.4	94.1
$2,000–$3,999	97.4	96.7	96.4	98.8	98.5
$4,000–$4,999	98.4	98.3	97.8	99.3	98.5
$5,000–$9,000	99.2	99.7	99.0	99.6	98.5
$10,000 and Over	100.0	100.0	100.0	100.0	100.0

Source: National Savings Committee, *Household Savings Survey, 1972*.

official estimates, has remained at around 22 per cent of the labour force. Unemployment is relatively more severe among women than men and is concentrated among the 14–24 age group (the rate being about 41 per cent in this group) and among service occupations, clerical and sales personnel, and unskilled occupations.[2] The significance of unemployment in the present context is that it adds to the total number of non-earning dependents in each worker-family and reduces thereby consumption per capita within the family. The current situation is such that every 3 employed persons in Jamaica have one unemployed person to support in addition to 6 other dependents too young or too old to work.

Essentially, these data point to a basic structural condition of *uneven development* which has been characteristic of the national economy through all phases of its history. This condition has, however, become intensified in the past 15–20 years. This is due to the specific form of development that has occurred during this period, consisting of a large expansion of production in mining based on foreign capital and accompanied by rapid growth of national and international capital in construction, public utilities and various manufacturing activities. Employing mostly skilled labour with highly mechanized techniques of production, these sectors have generated small pockets of high-income employment which accentuate the pattern of income inequality in the system. Property income (dividends, interest, rent) in these sectors and among the bigger merchants and traders has also grown correspondingly.

The process of capitalisation of agriculture has not kept pace with these developments, due to the much higher rates of profit to be made elsewhere in the system. There seems to have been even some significant decumulation and running down of existing plant and equipment in some areas of traditional export agriculture such as sugar production. As a result, agricultural productivity has failed to rise and incomes in agriculture have remained low relative to other sectors. At the same time there has been a systematic erosion of sectors of petty commodity production based on handicrafts and peasant farming as a consequence of competition from imported consumer goods and concentration of land under the ownership of foreign mining companies, local big landlords and real-estate speculators. This process has created pools of dispossessed labour, forced to enter other forms of low-productivity, petty-commodity production, to migrate or to join the reserve army of unskilled, unemployed labour. In these various ways, the concentration of deprivation at one end of the social system and polarisation of high incomes at the other end, are a direct product of the process of expansion and concentration of capital under the control of both national and international capitalists.

Account must also be taken of the rapid *inflation* in consumer goods prices in recent years, accelerating to an annual rate of some 25 per cent or so for the food and drink category which forms the major component of working class budgets. The effect of this has been to erode further the *real* income position of working class households, peasant families and fixed-income groups, while swelling the incomes of merchants, traders and industrial capitalists. Inflationary conditions have existed in Jamaica for some time prior to the recent 'energy crisis' and general crisis of world capitalism. Though aggravated by the current crisis, inflation cannot therefore by fully explained in terms of that crisis. Inflation is rather to be understood as *an outcome of the process of uneven development itself* by which some sectors expand ahead of and at the expense of others. Once the expansionary momentum of the advancing sectors gets underway, capitalists, merchants and middlemen of various sorts attempt to take advantage of the attendant shortages by raising prices above values seeking thereby to increase profit margins. The greater the monopoly position of each of these groups, the greater is the upward pressure on profit margins. As prices rise, workers react by pressing for wage increases to offset the reduced purchasing power of their money incomes. Cost increases due to rising wages then feed the inflationary process. The whole process is sustained by the struggle between workers seeking to defend their real incomes and property owners seeking to increase their respective shares in the total pool of surplus value.

4. Thesis on the Current Phase of Capitalist Development in Jamaica

Deeper analysis of the concrete conditions of the Jamaican economy and the process of its historical evolution up to the present is required in order to reveal the central contradictions of the current phase of capitalist development in Jamaica. Only in this light can the specific role of the proposed national minimum wage and the general programme of economic reform which constitutes the main task of the state at this time be firmly grasped. There is a pressing need for such analysis which still remains to be done. Meanwhile, the following *theoretical* arguments could seem to be warranted.

There is, first of all, a basic contradiction in the polarization of incomes and in the restricted consumption of the masses of the people associated with the existing pattern of income distribution. This contradiction can be explained as follows: Capitalism tends to produce and reproduce in the course of its development the polarization of incomes. The restricted incomes of the workers engaged in wage employment are the very basis upon which the owners of property are able to continue to appropriate a share of the product. The owners gain an additional share of the national product through the inequality of exchange with non-capitalist producers (peasants and petty-commodity producers) which depresses the living standards of those producers. But, at the same time, in order to realize the surplus value which is produced in this way, capitalism requires a growing mass market for the sale of the increasing quantities of commodities that are produced in the expanding industries. *The restricted consumption of the masses of the people is an obstacle to the development of that mass market.*

There are a number of ways in which the capitalist state can act to speed the growth of a mass market. These include, as at the present time in Jamaica, (a) the expansion of state expenditures to provide increased employment of labour in the state sector, (b) efforts to raise the wages of the most depressed sectors of the working class through provision of social security and improvement of the minimum wage law, (c) various ongoing attempts to improve and expand trading relations with other states in the Caribbean region and elsewhere. While providing short-term remedies these efforts cannot, however, resolve the basic contradiction involved. For that contradiction is rooted in the existing structure of ownership of property, which directly produces the polarization of incomes, and in the continuing drive for expansion of surplus value which is the fundamental motive force of capital.

It is necessary also to take account of the role of *imperialism*. Imperialism produces, by reason of the global interests of international capital, the drain of surplus value from one sphere of the world capitalist system to be used for re-investment in other spheres. In any *one* country, as in the case of Jamaica, the inflow of capital may at one time (in the heyday of 'bauxite expansion') exceed the outflow, but subsequently this relation may be reversed. The surplus which then drains out of the national economy is not available for re-investment and hence development of the productive forces is thereby retarded. *This is the basic contradiction of imperialism.*

The basic contradiction of imperialism is the contradiction of capital itself. Specifically, it is the contradiction of capital to seek continuously to expand the production of surplus value, while holding back the full development of productive forces. But the specific form and implications of this contradiction may differ as between one country and another, or between one sector of capital and another, and at different times. Generally, one form of appearance of this contradiction is in the inability to realize the whole of the surplus value produced, as manifested in recurrent realization crises. Under imperialism, however, the realization problem need not be faced *directly* by capital *in the country in which surplus value is immediately produced.* This is especially the case where capital is invested mainly in production of raw materials, minerals, foodstuffs and tourist services that are intended chiefly for export and *not* for direct sale on the domestic market. This has been predominantly the case in Jamaica up to now. It is an essential feature of the 'bauxite–tourism phase' of capitalist development in Jamaica. However, it seems that a transition is now occurring from this phase and, while that feature continues into the newly emerging phase, it is not the dominant one or, at least, its relative significance is considerably reduced.

These theoretical considerations have a direct bearing on the problem at hand. The important feature of the new phase of capitalist development in Jamaica is the emergence of an increasingly significant base of *national* industrial capitalists with an increasing degree of control over the state. It is the relationship between *imperialism*, with its contradictions that in reality have now become obvious, and *the interests of this particular group of capitalists* which dictates some of the main tasks that have to be carried out by the state in this period. Specifically, because this relationship involves a number of (non-antagonistic) conflicts, some structural readjustments are called for in the economic system.

In this connection, what is most important for present purposes is that, unlike the foreign capitalists, the national capitalists, relying essentially on the national market for sales of their product, *do* face a realization problem. They face also the need for the development of basic infrastructure in the domestic economy for the purpose of facilitating further investment. These problems are also aggravated by the low rate of re-investment by foreign capitalists in the national economy. In this situation an increase in the minimum wage plays a significant role. To the extent that it raises wages in foreign-owned enterprises, it cuts down on the outflow of current revenues and increases thereby income and demand in the domestic economy to the advantage of the national capitalists. Of course, in the longer run, the wage increase may also have a distinctive effect on new foreign investment. This is especially likely in the case of 'run-away shops' which are most immediately attracted by low wages to begin with. For this and other reasons the outcome is neither entirely unambiguous nor completely controllable. It becomes all the more important, therefore, for the state to seek to *capture directly* some of the outflow. By gaining control in this way over a greater share of the available surplus, the state at the same time secures a greater ability both to control the direction of investment activity in the interests of the national capitalists and to make a larger pool of new capital available to the national capitalists for their own investment. All of this accounts for a policy of increasing levies and taxation on foreign corporations as well as a policy of outright nationalization in some cases. These together form a part of a total policy package or general programme of economic reform, along with the introduction of a national minimum wage. This particular set of policies cannot, however, be pushed too far without an adverse reaction on the part of international capital. This, in turn, sets a decisive limit on the ability of the state to continue to pursue those policies. Such a limit arises out of the basic needs and requirements of *national capital itself*, in terms of finance, technology and markets, which drive such capital to become increasingly dependent upon and subordinated to international capital.

There is a contradiction also in the relations between industry and agriculture, or between town and country, deriving from the conditions of unequal exchange between the two and from the conditions of uneven development. There are complex reasons for this, which can be briefly stated as follows:

The expansion of industry sets up increased demand for the products of agriculture in the form of food items and raw materials for industrial processing. But the ability of the agricultural sector to respond to these demands is severely constrained due to the backward techniques and organisation of agricultural production, including patterns of land tenure, and to the limited availability and high cost of finance which inhibits investment in fixed and working capital, thereby perpetuating the existing low level of productivity. Furthermore, the proliferation of layers of middlemen between agricultural producers and consumers eats into the share of the revenues which return to the producers, despite rising prices of agricultural products. This factor, together with the rising prices of commodities which the peasants buy from the industrial sector cuts down on peasant incomes, forcing the peasants to sell their labour into wage employment in industry, or to emigrate, thereby reducing the output of agricultural commodities. At the same time, the rising cost of reproduction of labour-power in agriculture, due to the rising price of commodities which agricultural labourers consume, pushes up agricultural wages. This eats into the profits of small capitalist farmers forcing some of them out of business, thereby reducing further the output of agricultural commodities or its rate of expansion. The effect of all this would be to retard the growth of industrial production were it not for the ability to continue to import the required commodities. This ability is in turn constrained by the outflow of surplus from the national economy.

One way of breaking these constraints is for capital itself, or rather, *big* capital, to take command of agricultural production, restructuring the organizational forms and scale of production through increasing concentration of ownership, while pumping credit into the system to provide fixed and working capital. But the low rate of expected return from this form of investment relative to other alternatives makes it less attractive to international capital. And the drainage of surplus from the national economy inhibits the ability of the state and national capitalists to move in on a substantial scale.

What are the implications of a national minimum wage in this context? The implications are twofold and contradictory. In the short run, an increase of the minimum wage may force some small farmers out of business, thus compounding the problems of agricultural output. But in the long run, this is likely to speed up the process of rationalization of agricultural production through forcing the *less efficient* farmers out of business and enabling the concentration of land ownership in the hands of the more efficient. In the meantime, while contributing to some loss of agricultural employment, the minimum wage serves to raise the incomes of those agricultural workers who are able to remain employed. In seeking to resolve these contradictory effects, the state is likely to pursue a policy of *gradual increase* of the minimum wage in the agricultural sector, allowing time for adjustments to take place. But this policy, by itself, does little to resolve the underlying contradiction in the relations between industry and agriculture. It therefore has to be supplemented by other policies, which are no more effective, such as for instance, state ownership and leasing of land (Project Land-Lease).[3]

There is a contradiction, moreover, between big and small capitalists, whether they be operating in industry or in agriculture. This contradiction derives ultimately from the expansionary momentum of capital which drives individual capitalists into competition with each other. In the particular case of big and small capitalists, it derives from the ability of big capital to command a larger pool of surplus value and greater access to finance for investing in relatively advanced techniques of production, marketing and distribution of the product. Big capital in the process of its expansion therefore eats up small capital through mergers, take-overs, or erosion of the latter's markets. *The effect of a minimum wage here is to enhance the position of big capital relative to small capital.* It does this by raising the labour costs of small capitalists operating usually with more labour-intensive methods of production, cutting down on their profits and forcing some of them out of business. Big capital is thereby able to capture additional markets as well as expand its available labour force of skilled and semi-skilled labour from the displaced workers.

All of these contradictions converge upon and receive *political* expression in a growing militance on the part of workers and poor peasants with reactions taking place among capitalists of all sorts, rich peasants and landlords. The policies of the state must be seen as arising out of, and responding to, the shifting forms of confrontation between these various groups.

5. Thesis on the Proposed National Minimum Wage

Minimum wage laws have been developed in all capitalist countries at one time or another in response to the struggles of workers to improve their living and working conditions.

The experience of all such countries shows that the adoption of a minimum wage law, while bringing about certain (relatively minor) adjustments in the economic system, has never been the cause or the basis of a major structural readjustment in capitalism.

On the contrary, effective implementation of a national minimum wage may, for various reasons that have been shown here, directly serve the interests and needs of capital and especially *big* capital in the course of its development.

It is the organizational weakness of *independent* workers' movements in Jamaica, along with the rebellious mood of the urban and rural poor facing severe economic deprivation, which accounts for the attempt on the part of the ruling party to project itself forward at this time as defender of the poorest workers calling for a national minimum wage.

It is the most backward sectors of capital, the smaller merchant capitalists and petty capitalists, along with big land-owners and middle peasants, and middle class employers of domestic servants, who would most resolutely oppose the implementation of a national minimum wage. This is for reasons deriving from their objective position in the economic system.

All sectors of capital would of course oppose a significant increase in the overall level of minimum wages since it would mean a substantial reduction in the overall rate of profits. But a less significant increase could be relatively easily absorbed by big capital and may work to its advantage. The bigger capitalists are thus likely to support such an increase.

Political considerations arising at a different level from that at which the present analysis is located enter into the actual determination of the national minimum wage in Jamaica at this time. But all indications point to the likelihood of a slight increase in the overall level of the minimum, special concessions being made to backward sectors, especially in agriculture, so as not to require too severe adjustments in those sectors in the immediate future.

To press for a substantial increase in the minimum wage along with a wide range of other 'welfare' schemes, is to support the struggle of workers against the grinding conditions which they face in their daily life. But at the same time it is necessary to oppose *economism* and *reformism* which seek to uphold the minimum wage as an end in itself, failing thereby to expose the true nature of the system which produces and reproduces the daily life of the workers.

NOTES

1. See I. Adelman and C. T. Morris, 'An Anatomy of Income Distribution Patterns in Developing Nations', *Development Digest*, October 1971, p. 27.
2. See *The Labour Force 1973*, (Department of Statistics, Jamaica).
3. See Carl Stone's article 'Tenant Farming Under State Capitalism', in *Essays on Power and Change in Jamaica*, C. Stone and A. Brown (eds.), (Jamaica Publishing House, 1977), ch. 9.

b) Class development, ideology and the political party

10 ALAIN COURNANEL

Ideology and development in Guinea *

Class struggles and the single party

(*I*) The political crises which have marked the history of Guinea ever since independence have simply been manifestations of the class struggle, which is always closely linked to fluctuations in the development strategy.

The search for a self-maintaining growth and the adoption of a 'non-capitalist way' received the active support of the unions and the left (whose approach was that of the Parti Africain de l'Indépendance, P.A.I., which had asked its Guinea section to merge[1] with the Parti Démocratique de Guinée after independence). But at the same time, a whole series of measures contradicted the reality of this orientation: the nature of the nominations to posts of responsibility, or of candidates presented at the first election of the Party organisations after the ref-

* First published as 'Idéologie et Développement en Guinée', in *Africa Development*, vol. II, No. I, February, 1977–translated from the French—ed.

erendum, the anti-democratic take-over of the unions and youth movements, significant fluctuations[2] in foreign policy. It was over the plan that the decisive battle was to be joined. At the Kankan conference, summoned to adopt the Three Year Plan, Sékou Touré intervened to declare: 'we are not a communist régime,'[3] and again 'we define ourselves according to Africa and it is Africa that we choose. People tell us we have to choose between capitalism and socialism, but I decline to do so; and between ourselves, we are practically unable to define what capitalism is and what socialism is'.[4]

At the time the plan was launched, it had been obvious for several months that there was no strict ideological line or clear programme. In such a context, the intervention of Sékou Touré, according to Benot, 'gave the lie to everything at a decisive moment in the history of independent Guinea. Far from helping the unity he boasted of, he forced each person to ask questions about what the chosen course really was; and ideological rifts, like social rifts, were to become more accentuated in the months which followed'.[5]

Although we agree entirely about certain effects of this intervention, we do not think that it 'gave the lie to everything', in the sense that the global movement could only be explained by coming back to the system of relations of production. The President's speech was at best decisive in the sense that it marked the turning-point of the plan (in the muffled struggle which had been going on for more than a year) and the direction in which the governing powers wished to settle things. The reinforcement of the state bourgeoisie and the growth of the commercial bourgeoisie quickly brought pressure to bear on the workers' standard of living. At the end of 1961, a violent clash arose between the governing powers and the unions,[6] which resulted in the breaking down of the Marxist bias which controlled the majority of the unions which made up the C.N.T.G. (Confédération Nationale des Travailleurs Guinéens). It is significant that the unionists arrested were charged[7] with being partisans 'of an egalitarianism exaggerated beyond all bounds' or of being 'pseudo–Marxists'.

As from 1962, the interpenetration of public and private capital, and the measures of liberalisation adopted in the commercial sector, accelerated the rise of the 'private' bourgeoisie (essentially commercial). It had an important part to play in the framework of a policy of growth founded on the appropriation of a surplus derived from national production activities, with the state bourgeoisie linking commercial capital (situated 'above' agricultural production) and the international market. After the turning-point of 1962, the state bourgeoisie, unable to ensure an enlarged reproduction of national capital, chose to rely on the mining income and ally itself more explicitly with international capital. From then on it could keep its distance from the commercial bourgeoisie which had made spectacular strides from 1960 to 1964 and was becoming politically dangerous.

In 1964 and 1965, economic and political measures struck at this section of the bourgeoisie and its allies in the state bourgeoisie: these were the limitation of the number of traders, which had the effect of favouring concentration; an attempt to verify the origins of acquired goods; the exclusion of traders from posts of political responsibility; and the repression of the 1965 'plot' which proved the existence of a private bourgeoisie equally keen to gain political power.

There was a new period of crisis from 1967 to 1969. The seriousness of the economic and financial situation (stagnation, inflation, generalisation of rationing) was to exacerbate class conflicts.

The governing powers decided upon a series of 'economies' in businesses (reduction in salaries, suppression of seniority bonuses and overtime) which because they particularly affected workers and employees, aroused the discontent of the unions without giving rise to an open conflict. The problem was overcome in stages: the integration of the C.N.T.G. with the Parti Démocratique de Guinée (P.D.G.) in 1967, the entry of the party into business in 1968 (by the creation of Business Committees) and, in 1969, compulsory union membership for workers. The union became more than a driving-wheel: it became a further element of political control and centralisation of claims.[8]

Parallel to this, a much more violent conflict broke out at the heart of the state bourgeoisie. As we have seen, the growth of the state bourgeoisie implied the formation of 'preserves' of private capital, and thus the extension of the field open to private investment. But the economic difficulties which Guinea was experiencing restrained the state bourgeoisie's possibilities of expansion more and more, at a time when the governing powers were controlling the private sector very closely. The struggle between factions (the commercial bourgeoisie supported some of them) became more severe, and the integration of new generations into the state bourgeoisie posed a problem which was hard to resolve in an economy which was in a state of complete stagnation. The stake in this clash was crucial: it was the conquest of the main political and economic areas of the state-controlled sector, but it was also the possibility of internal economic liberation, and thus of an opening up in all directions to foreign capital (whereas the régime in power intended to limit this opening up to certain forms of co-operation with foreign capital in defined areas). This struggle implied as clearly as could be the possibility of a change of régime in the position of power. The blossoming of the state bourgeoisie implied a less dictatorial style of government but also in the long run the dissolving of the state power as it existed in the country. The 1969 trials and the 1971 purges struck down elements of both the state bourgeoisie and the 'private' bourgeoisie. But the state bourgeoisie was not attacked as much as most. It was to be subject to an intense revival which, by putting a temporary end to the struggle between minorities, solved the problem of integrating the new generations.[9] On this point we agree entirely with Claude Rivière when he writes 'the purging of the sympathisers of the would-be "fifth column" in 1971 occasioned a radical renewal of the élite groups and brought a brutal response to a crucial question'.[10]

In 1968–1969 the threat came from within. In 1970 an invasion attempted to overthrow the régime, which took advantage of this contingency to finish off the purging begun in 1969, with the Conakry trials. In both cases, it was the most general interest of the state bourgeoisie which triumphed through the actions of the ruling powers. In the event, the materialisation of known projects will lead to new strides for the state bourgeoisie, but also to an increase in proletariat numbers.

(*II*)   New contradictions among classes and at the heart of the ruling class ensued. The sole party, the Parti Démocratique de Guinée, played a frontline role in driving back class conflicts. Its implantation in Guinean society had been intimately linked with the penetration of marketing relations and capitalist relations of production, at the recovery of initiative aroused by almost half a century of colonisation. The P.D.G. in its ascendant phase was representative of the common interests of the different classes in their struggles against the colonists. Nevertheless, major rifts opened at the heart of the party under the influence of events that are now well-known: collaboration with colonial authorities, political disalliance from the Rassemblement Democratique Africain (of which the P.D.G. represented the Guinean section) and with the French Communist Party, breaking off with the French C.G.T. and the creation of the Confédération Générale des Travailleurs Africains (C.G.T.A.). These rifts resulted from the new strategy of the R.D.A. in the fifties.

As Alpha Condé writes, 'the economic interests of the various social strata which make up the united front do not necessarily need the same solutions. Certain social strata may find the solution to their problem in an adaptation of the colonial system; for others no solution is possible within that framework. As long as the administration maintains an attitude which is hostile to any collaboration, not one of these social strata can hope to achieve its aims. Thus it is inevitable that the first divisions should necessarily appear from the moment that the administration decides to collaborate'.[11]

After independence, the parties which had opposed the P.D.G. on a reactionary basis scuttled themselves; and their members joined the P.D.G., which immediately conferred important responsibilities on a number of them. The P.A.I., which had recently been created, quoted Marxism–Leninism and upheld an argument diametrically opposed to that of the P.D.G. on the existence of social classes in Africa. But analysis of the P.A.I. led to the need to form a National Front (this conclusion was later reinforced by the arguments on national democracy of the Conference of eighty-one communist and worker Parties). It is understandable that in these conditions and despite major ideological differences, the Guinean section of the P.A.I. should have joined the P.D.G. in its turn.

The internal situation of Guinea and the international state of affairs in 1958–1960 favoured a relative balance of social classes; this balance was characterised by the fact that the maintenance and development of capitalist relations of production passed through the emergence and then the hegemony of a state bourgeoisie. This implied a relative automony of the state power, particularly strong in the early days, and thus the return to dictatorial methods and a complete subjection of the state bourgeoisie and other classes, in the name of the survival of the state and the national interest.

The P.D.G. was to constitute an essential instrument for the governing power. Interfering in absolutely all areas, even those most traditionally 'private', it allowed the Bureau Politique National* (B.P.N.), whose members coincided with the essential members of the government, to lay its hands on all issues (individual or collective) likely to have political repercussions. B. Charles[12] has clearly established the predominance of the executive in the political system of Guinea, that is to say, in the end, the predominance of the President of the Republic (who is also Secretary-General of the Party) and the B.P.N.

In 1964, the Party numbered 10,250 regular committees and thus the same number of leaders at that level, 10,250 special women's committees (with 132,500 people carrying responsibility), 10,250 youth committees (and 132,500 people carrying responsibility), 177 committees in charge of sections and 2,125 leaders etc.,[13] in other words, one elected member for every eleven inhabitants. Party affiliation was obligatory, as the party's intervention was indispensable for acts as vital as marriages, divorces and provisioning, and so this proportion of one to eleven did not represent a particularly democratic method of party functioning, but rather the extent of the political infiltration effected by its intervention. This process of political control was accompanied by a spectacular reduction in the size of the governing nucleus. In 1964, when the B.P.N. still had fifteen members, 'delegate ministers' were created, a sort of 'over-minister' who each supervised one of the four great natural regions. The 8th Party Congress in 1967 reduced the B.P.N. and regrouped various ministries rechristened 'State Secretariats'.

Today (in 1976) there are eight domains: those of the President, the Prime Minister (army, foreign affairs, planning, financial control), Interior and Security (which also includes justice and regional development), Culture and Education,

---

* National Political Bureau

Social (health, social affairs, labour and civil service), Commerce and Communications, Economy and Finance (also including industry, mines, banks) and finally the rural domain. Each domain is controlled by a member of the B.P.N., and six of its eight members have belonged to this organisation since independence.

The reduction in the number of B.P.N. members coincided with a spectacular vesting of all powers in the person of Sékou Touré (President of the Republic and Secretary General of the Party). Any trend which is expressed in the P.D.G. is suspected of being a plot. The political monopoly conferred on the P.D.G. has led to the radical contesting of all freedom of association,[14] of expression (including cultural and scientific), and of meeting, in the context of an exacerbated class struggle and increased exploitation.

Through the Party, the state power repressed tendencies which were truly favourable to an evolution towards socialism, and the threat periodically represented by the 'private' bourgeoisie, and safeguarded the most general interests of the state bourgeoisie. The relative balance of the beginning had been modified to the advantage of the bourgeoisie, notably the state bourgeoisie. The growth of this sector resulted in a new challenge to the autocratic style of government at the point when the offensive against the working-class's standard of living had reached its zenith. This conjunction of circumstances, in the interest of the state bourgeoisie as a whole, demanded a move to a higher level of repression, but a higher level also of the ideological discussion which accompanied it.

Official ideology and the development of state capitalism

(*I*)   In 1958, the orientation of Sékou Touré and thus the official Party doctrine was extremely precise on the problem of classes. Sékou Touré denied the existence of social classes, not only in Guinea but in Africa. Describing the situation in Guinea, Sékou Touré wrote: 'The struggle set 80 per cent of the population against the feudalism used by the colonial régime under the cover of chieftainship. Well, that feudalism was abolished by the team in power under the régime of the Cadre Law in 1957. The second conflict set the intellectual elite against the mass of the rural people, for in the concrete domain of this intellectual elite's position, there was a series of advantages and guarantees which were quite foreign to the lives of the immense majority of people, and which constituted privileged conditions in relation to the conditions of the people. In the end, the internal conflicts were minor. The troubles were fomented by embittered people and racists; other conflicts grew out of individual behaviour prompted by egoism, opportunism or by professional critics'.[15]

On the other hand, Sékou Touré recognised the existence of the class struggle at the international level, between nations:

> The analogy between the proletarian class of the modern world and the *proletarian peoples* is not fortuitous, it is the inescapable consequence of the plundering which has been practised, of the fraudulent buying up of goods, in fact of the usurpation of controls which colonial powers use illegally in places where they have been able by various means to install themselves and rule.[16]

As Wallerstein also quotes, Sékou Touré goes even further, because he states clearly: 'If we prove that without a class struggle a profound transformation is possible in our country, we will have made our contribution to the world and to political and social science'.[17]

This statement can mean in the extreme that outside Africa too, the class struggle could be shown to be unnecessary. This analysis stems not from a concern for theoretical knowledge on the part of Sékou Touré, but from the purest pragmatism because it was a questioning of the maintaining by bias, a unity (at the Guinean and African level) which was considered indispensable. At best, he admitted the existence of social strata: country people, salaried workers, planters, property owners, tradespeople, contractors, small industrial people. As Y. Benot pointed out, this 1961 list added planters and small industries to an analagous list which figured in a speech of 1 May 1959.

Tradespeople, industrial people and high-ranking civil servants were 'inclined to become bourgeois', as the author went on to state, 'to distinguish themselves from the mass of the people'.

The bourgeoisie was characterised by its way of life, by its reflexes, its resistance to democratic practices. It hurled anti-mobilising orders and the most sterile of criticisms at the revolutionary movement. The 'financial bourgeoisie' used economic corruption and sabotage (currency trading, illicit price increases). The bureaucratic bourgeoisie readily showed itself by 'intellectual speculations', poisoning the minds of the masses by their opportunist and reactionary doctrines.[18]

These strata were a product of the incomes policy followed during the colonial period. The colonists had unceasingly tried to transform the feudalists into land proprietors, to create 'a little national bourgeoisie made up of most of the few existing natives who had reached managerial level and the former students who had gained diplomas, psychologically won over by the theory of assimilation', while the hardworking masses were impoverished. But these privileged strata, destined to become agents of neo–colonialism, emerged late in Guinea and thus had 'no means likely to realise a primitive accumulation of capital for these means were in the hands of neo–colonialism'.[19]

In the writings of Sékou Touré, the refusal to admit the existence of classes seemed to be tied to the low degree of social differentiation which resulted from colonial action. But more fundamentally, the class Front achieved by the P.D.G. during its period of struggle against the colonial authorities, and again during the first months of independence, was essentially the reason behind the position adopted by the Secretary of the P.D.G. Still in support of his thesis, Sékou Touré invoked, pell-mell, the fact that the Guinean labourer received an income which was twice that of a peasant, and that the country population had not been exploited (forgetting the feudalism which he had so often noted, unless he thought that the abolition of chieftainism had sufficed to efface the existence of relations of exploitation).

Sometimes exploitation and the private ownership of means of production were denied, and their non-existence explained by the intensity of colonial exploitation. Sometimes the possibility of relations of exploitation was admitted, but the division of Guinean society into classes was rejected in the name of the common objectives realised at the end of the colonial period.

The analysis of pre-colonial Africa was carried out in terms which were both peremptory and vague. Sékou Touré declared that colonial intervention in Africa had happened in a feudal period, 'which was still deeply marked by a communocratic spirit', a statement which seems at the very least to demand further developments which we are not granted. On the other hand, the author proclaims without any argument: 'The organisation of the means of production was at that time neither analogous to slavery, nor assimilable to the kind of organisation known as Asiatic'.[20] The essential thing for Sékou Touré is the way in which colonisation used traditional structures (and in this respect, he emphasises a fundamental problem, even if his analysis is very superficial, not to say erroneous). From that point stems one whole aspect of the P.D.G.'s ideology, an explicit opposition to a series of institutions or values tied to tradition: chieftainism, statutory inferiority of women and younger sons, sorcery and fetishism. The P.D.G. set itself up and developed itself against tribalism and racialist or sectarian after-effects. The search for an authentically African personality (but the rejection of the negro ideology), and the idealisation of African heroes, are rather conceived as the material, or moral springs, which are indispensable to the construction of a new Africa. But we feel that it is too linear to write that 'the most obvious continuity in Guinean politics since independence (and even before, under the Cadre Law) has been that of a pitiless struggle against ideologies and structures termed traditional'.[21]

Studies[22] on ethnic groupings have shown the predominance of the Malinkés in regional administration (as governors, regional secretaries, local heads) and in national enterprises, in other words in the state bourgeoisie's key sectors. Exactly the same observation could be made for the B.P.N. According to B. Charles, this was perhaps an important factor in explaining the solidarity of the régime.[23]

Let us add that at the heart of the state bourgeoisie, very close ties were formed on the basis of family and ethnic relationships. The growing class differentiation in the 'sixties was accompanied by compensatory phenomena due to the persistence and vitality of family, ethnic and regional solidarity. But one must go further: the seriousness of the economic crisis, the stagnation in inflation and penury, reactivated social relationships and traditional values. This was evident in a rural environment when the country population turned to self-subsistence to escape from inflation. But in an urban environment, family relationships allowed the most underprivileged to lessen the most flagrant penury and partially escape from their class situation. This reactivation of pre-capitalist social relations coincided with the return in force of sorcery and marabout practices which certain resounding affairs bore witness to. Once again, ideology and real historical evolution kept up ambivalent relations, to which we will return.

(*II*)   The problem of classes was thus made void, or at least reduced to an after-effect (in the strict sense) of colonialism, and this lasted until 1967. The Eighth Congress was marked by a new ideological departure, as Sékou Touré then put forward the notion of lumpenbourgeoisie: 'The idle and shirking petite bourgeoisie, ready to hire out the nation to the imperialist power which is on hand'.[24] Joined to this category was the group of corrupt high-ranking civil servants. The whole thing was a class of counter-revolutionaries. In fact, the type of analysis remained strictly the same.

The governing powers were looking for scapegoats, when the corruption and the accentuation of dependence were merely consequences of their policies. Certainly real problems were being emphasised: such as the managerial personnel who considered as their private property the sectors with whose running they had been entrusted. Sékou Touré once more referred to the 'emerging bureaucratic bourgeoisie'.[25]

From then on, the President of Guinea would find it expedient to develop the thesis of two stages:

1. National democracy was a means of associating all classes with the construction of the state, with the aim of economic development.
2. At a second stage, the working class and the rural population (to whom were added the progressive elements supposed to include the leaders and some others) controlled all sectors which were fundamental to economic and social life.

We will come back later to the reality of this thesis. From a logical point of view, this thesis of two stages contradicted the basic reasoning of Sékou Touré. The existence of classes could only be explained in two ways:

a. either the 1959 analysis was not correct, and the diagnosis of the P.A.I. and the left in the Union Générale des Travailleurs d'Afrique Noire (UGTAN) was justified;

b. or it failed to admit that as classes did not exist at the end of the colonial era, their appearance was linked to the adoption of the non-capitalist course of development. This is nonetheless surprising.

The fundamental approach, despite certain tactical modulations, remained constant. Classes and the class struggle were not analysed in respect of relations of production. The basic criteria were still political and ideological 'conscience', and 'behaviour'. In short, the bourgeoisie was assimilated to a sum of individuals characterised by critical or subversive behaviour in relation to the governing powers.

It was not a question of studying the relationship to the means of production, the role of work in the social organisation, or the appropriation of extra work by a class of non-producers, but of limiting oneself to a social psychology reducing the bourgeoisie phenomenon to a type of deviance dangerous for the régime. Relations of exploitation were secondary and finally there was no real emergence of new classes, but rather of new negative behaviour.

The refusal to recognise the existence of classes took on its whole meaning only when associated with the theory that all states are dictatorships and with the 'four-fold identity',[26] People–Party–State–Nation. Identified with the Nation and the People, the Party was moreover implicitly reduced to its direction.

As Y. Benot has written very aptly:

Society is here and now presented as a harmonious whole, in which the individual simply has to occupy the correct place which has been assigned to him . . . If the individual has no right outside society, that means, and this is confirmed in practice, outside society as it exists now in Guinea, or in another African country; *this society is thus thought to be balanced, with the exception however, of certain negative phenomena* here and there, which are in a way the wants of a healthy social body.

Neither non-conformism nor any displays of resources and creative initiatives of strong personalities can be tolerated; with this exception, that as it is necessary for someone to set out the philosophy of the P.D.G. and as no way of speaking except through an individual has yet been found, it is the Head of State who assumes the task and by that fact ensures that he has a monopoly of it. And it is perhaps a detail in the picture as a whole that Sékou Touré takes care never to name African writers who exist here and now. . . . *In reality, the system of values extolled here aims to impose submission to the State and not to society, to avoid all discussion of the tactical turning-points in official policy, and to prevent the Guinean intelligentsia from fulfilling the whole creative function in the building up of the country, which it might do . . . .*[27]

Let us add that the identity of intellectuals and individualism was often postulated by Sékou Touré, who brutally revealed his deepest thoughts in the following lines: 'We are perfectly aware that the Guinean revolution has greater need of men who are aware, committed, devoted and hardworking, than of clever minds.'[28]

Consideration of the State takes precedence in the context of an ever more intense class struggle. As the Secretary of the P.D.G. explicitly writes in 'Revolutionary Technique', the Party is the sole source, the melting-pot which must make our concepts uniform, and harmonise our attitudes. And when he adds that the people are the sole source of legitimacy and legality, he is still talking about the Party.

The reality of the dictatorial methods used does not prevent Sékou Touré from claiming that freedom is the basic means used to achieve this uniformity. This freedom is the kind that is based on the masses accepting the explanations put forward. And they reach this point 'by getting to know the philosophy of the Guinean revolution'.[29] What one is up against here is one of the distinguishing features of the ideology as Louis Althusser defines it: 'The individual is called upon as a (free) subject to submit himself freely to the Subject's orders, thus to accept (freely) his subjection'.[30] This is what Althusser calls the double reflection structure of the ideology:

This means that all ideology is *centred*, that the Absolute

Subject occupies the single place at the Centre and summons around him the infinity of individuals his subjects, in a double reflection relationship which *subjects* the subjects to the Subject, while giving them, in the Subject in which each subject can contemplate its own image (present and future) the *guarantee* that it really is about them and about him, and that as everything is happening in the family (the Holy Family: the family is essentially Holy), God will recognise his own, that is to say, those who have recognised God and have recognised themselves in him, they will be saved.[31]

For Sékou Touré, ideology (which he assimilates to philosophy), is something quite different: Science of the sciences, a 'force', a 'technique', a 'superior way of life'. It is a 'historical truth' and a 'methodological truth', it 'uses' science and 'necessarily covers all the activities of development'.[32] The official ideology is omnipotent and omnipresent, it has priority in the social evolution, since the Cultural Revolution in Africa must advance and prepare the political, economic and social revolution in order to wipe out the after-effects of colonial capitalism.[33] (Sékou Touré tends to equate capitalism and colonialism.)

Ideology 'uses' science, in other words it is 'treated as the maid of all work for the political decisions of the day'.[34] It is a characteristic of the pragmatism which Sékou Touré displays elsewhere in a provoking fashion: 'It is not necessary to talk about the correctness of a political line, it is the result which bears witness to its correctness'.[35] Theory was reduced to the role of developing considerations of State. The priority of ideology meant, in the Guinean context, that no real solution was envisaged outside the present system, outside the course of State capitalism.

The abundant ideological output of the Guinean leader was the expression of a historical blockage, the inability to have an effect on real history without questioning the system of relations of production, and of a search for imaginary solutions. This inability to bend real history is particularly apparent in certain fundamental areas. The need to gain economic independence, to be free, has been recurring in all the official speeches for years. But the course of state capitalism periodically renews the threat represented by the continual rebirth of a private bourgeoisie, having as a corollary the return to more direct forms of subordination with respect to international capital. Besides we have shown sufficiently clearly that this course in the present context causes a real dependence with regard to imperialism. The historical blockage which we have noted was objectively linked to the persistence of the present relations of production. Certain formulae arose out of pure demagogic movement, as when a year after the conflict with the Marxist left, Sékou Touré declared that Guinea was embarking on a 'socialist development starting from the real condition of the country population'.[36]

But we prefer to emphasise here certain developments of official ideology after 1967. For in fact they seem typical of the relations which this ideology has with the real relations of production and with the class situation.

(*III*) Socialism became the official objective after the Eighth Congress of the P.D.G., whereas in fact the standard of living of the proletariat had deteriorated drastically (provoking a latent but unquestionable discontent), the country population turned even more than in the past to self-subsistence, and the State bourgeoisie was preparing to stage a come-back.

As the corrupt speculators and public officials were put to scorn, the holders of power could only bring the working-class and peasantry out of their imaginary reality to take control of social and economic life, using the theory of the two stages[37] of the Revolution. In this respect, the setting up of the Pouvoirs Révolutionnaires Locaux*, (P.R.L.) and the Collèges d'Enseignement Révolutionnaire† (C.E.R.) was extremely instructive.

The creation of the P.R.L.s once more mobilised the villages by entrusting to them assignments concerning the economy, local public works, health, defence, and communications, through setting up various brigades, 'which gather together on a voluntary basis, which is more or less respected, the people necessary to fulfil their tasks'.[38] Traditionally, village committees already had a number of powers: political, judicial, administrative. The establishment of the P.R.L.s gave them com-

---

* Local Revolutionary Powers
† Colleges of Revolutionary Education

plementary powers in matters of defence (which does not require particular explanation in the context of 1969 and the following years) and economy. X. Leunda, after setting out at length the details of these institutions, recalls the continuous problems of the P.R.L.s concerning the tradespeople 'whose interests are harmed by the direct collective selling of the harvests in the state commercial network'[39] and ends with the following conclusion: 'The institution certainly seems well adapted to the Guinean village: it is likely to guide it towards a self-sufficient development, culminating in the long run in a certain form of collectivism—which somewhat recalls the Chinese people's commune at the brigade level'.[40] The opinion of the author of this statement upheld the intentions of the official ideology. We will come back to it. But it must be remembered to begin with that the 'socialist' transformation of the Guinean countryside resulted in the first place from the C.E.R.s. These colleges of secondary education produced degree students who after a supplementary year of final training in agricultural techniques (for those who did not pursue their studies into higher education) would create socialist co-operative settlements on the spot. As these C.E.R.s assured an immediate link between general training and productive activities (variable according to the place, but usually agricultural), there would be no break between the co-operative settlements and the C.E.R.s from which they drew their members.

The C.E.R.s had about 50,000 pupils in 1970,[41] the first co-operative settlements were to be started in 1974 and 5,000 degree students were to be taken in by the settlements in 1975. Tractors and livestock had to be provided for the C.E.R.s, as well as arable land. The sums invested for national education by the Ministry of Education and other ministries were relatively high (5 per cent of the expenditure of the Seven Year Plan, according to X. Leunda).[42]

The functioning of the P.R.L.s was linked to that of the C.E.R.s and the socialist settlements by the following schema: 'The P.R.L.s contribute to the creation of the C.E.R., the mould into which will be poured a man who has been removed from the domination of the old ways, and provided with more modern technical knowledge, having had seven years experience of a community life which prefigures the new society'.[43]

In return, the co-operative settlements born out of the C.E.R.s became a model for the P.R.L.s by the superiority of their scientific and organisation level, in fact by their whole way of life. At the bottom of this schema was the idea that the reform of men's education and training could play a major part in the socialist transformation of the country, without changing the relations of production in the other sectors and even in agricultural production outside the socialist settlements.

Although the C.E.R.s could have variable productive activities (which in the end had to meet the cost of amortisement of material, the expense of feeding the pupils and other running costs—the large initial investments and the teachers' salaries were not their responsibilities), the settlements were essentially conceived as agricultural units of production. However, the problems of equipment and lodging,[44] indeed of staffing were not solved. We have already pointed out that the Five Year Plan only devoted between 3 per cent and 4 per cent of its investment to agriculture, whereas agriculture contributed to provide half the P.I.B.* in 1969.[45] And yet Sékou Touré in person, when presenting the Five Year Plan, insisted on 'absolute priority for the production of foodstuffs'.[46]

Confronted with a growing insufficiency (or even a regression, depending on the products and the years) of its agricultural production, the governing power attempted to solve the problem in various ways. After the failure of co-operation between 1960 and 1964, parallel with the experiment of the P.R.L.s and the C.E.R.s, the government relaunched modern rural co-operatives in exchange for deliveries of goods designed to nourish state commerce which had been 'systematically forsaken'.[47] After trying to round up the 'falsely unemployed' to assign them to productive tasks, as 'prisoner workers', in the hope that eventually they would voluntarily integrate themselves into the co-operatives, the ruling powers, who were not able to redirect the education boom politically,[48] attempted to solve the problem of the costs of this by using the C.E.R.s essentially in agricultural production, and to restrict the state bourgeoisie's access by establishing a growing number of degree students in the agricultural sector. Investments in agriculture showed the extent

---

* Gross industrial product.

of the effects of this enterprise. It is strange to think that generations of graduates, in the Guinean context where the transition to socialism has never passed the verbal stage, will agree to live in the country. Both the country population, through exploitation by the domestic community, and the working-class have been under constant pressure. In what respect might this context miraculously lend itself to a purely bureaucratic creation of co-operative socialist settlements? This utopian socialism still counted on human investment (with M. Sangaré stating[49] that investments for agriculture in the Five Year Plan did not include the cost of human investment). Finally, this was certainly the main result expected from an attempt which was not to get very far: to release a sufficient quantity of free labour into the agricultural sector in order to get over the most acute penuries while waiting for the beneficial effects of mining exports.

The problem we have just touched upon is full of lessons, in that it allows one to underline several aspects of P.D.G. ideology: in the first place, and this is the most obvious, a desire for independence in relation to European cultural models, and for an adequate response to national realities. But the idea of adequate here is much more complex than it seems at first sight. This setting up of socialist settlements by decree in a rural world more and more marked by social inequality since independence, strongly resembles that search 'in the imaginary domain of original short cuts'[50] of which Y. Benot speaks. These institutional innovations seen by certain observers as indications of a socialist transformation, were merely concretisations of official ideology, which prolonged it in its attempt to act (but in another direction) on social relations. From then on, to confine oneself to the exposé of the institutions and the grounds which justified their setting up, was to stay with the ideology—to fall into the imaginary 'short cuts' which have Chinese communes rising out of the Guinean countryside.[51]

Conclusion

The ideology of the P.D.G. had played an active part in the emergence and constitution of a state bourgeoisie, thanks to its theses on the non-existence of classes combined with treating the State–Nation–People–Party as identical. It had assumed then (and still does) above all the function of preserving the relations of production, by means of solutions supposed to correspond to a socialist-type transformation.

All through these two stages, the ideology had justified constant recourse to repression and dictatorial methods by means of a system of false oppositions (society–individual, communocratism–individualism) and doubtful identities (State–Nation–People–Party, intellectual–individualist). The solutions provided by the ideology to real problems (economic growth and independence, the strengthening of classes) were not intentionally mere fantasies. They 'recognised' the existence of capitalist relations of production since the existence of classes was referred to (albeit in psychological terms), although it had been denied before, and they 'recognised' the need to evolve towards socialism. But while doing that, the solutions placed emphasis on negative behaviour (and suppressed scapegoats) but refused to analyse and transform the relations of production; they extolled and organised the production of a new man likely to transform the countryside, but refused to attack the existing social relations. Thus there arose a perpetual process of correspondence and non-correspondence between this ideology and reality. Different from the most typical variants of African socialism, even further removed from Marxism, from which it only borrows a limited vocabulary, this construction fitted in perfectly with what Althusser calls ideology:

> Ideology concerns the relationship in which men live with their world. This relationship which only appears to be conscious on condition of being unconscious seems in the same way only to be simple on condition of being complex, of not being an essential relationship but a relationship of relationships, a relationship at one degree removed. In ideology men express in fact not their relationship to their conditions of existence, but the way in which they live their relationship to their conditions of existence: which supposes a real relationship and a lived imaginary relationship. . . . In ideology, the real relationship is inevitably invested in the imaginary relationship: a relationship which expresses a wish

(conservative, conformist, reformist, revolutionary) or indeed
a hope or nostalgia, more than it describes in reality.[52]

Our analysis of the relations of production in Guinea enables
us to understand why, while borrowing from Marxism, the
official ideology is basically distinct from it,[53] and also to
understand to what extent it is thus in a better position to
contribute to the maintaining of relations of production, including doing so by means of the objective effects of obscuring issues
which it produces in the working-class and its allies.

The ideology of the P.D.G. is organised around certain major
themes which are the pre-eminence of the State, of the nation,
and independence regarding all foreign protection, and which
speak out through a system of thought which is unable vigorously
to account for the existence of classes. By virtue of this fact, this
ideology plays a *real* role in the country's economic difficulties, in
its preoccupying stagnation. The latter resides finally in a
strategy of controlled dependence (or one which would like to be
controlled) which gave rise to the reticence of foreign capital
while at the same time excluding the possibility of a self-
maintained growth (for which the political and ideological
conditions do not both exist). Far from being a veil over the face
of reality which would produce camouflage effects, the ideology
reveals itself as a social instance which has its own efficacity in the
state capitalism of Guinea, in its social reproduction.

NOTES

1. Alpha Conde, *Guinée: Albanie de l'Afrique ou néocolonie américaine*, (Ed. Git-le-Coeur 1972), p. 168.
2. Y. Benot, *Idéologies des Indépendances Africaines*, 2nd ed., (Maspéro, 1972), pp. 391, 392, 393.
3. *Ibid.*, p. 267.
4. *Ibid.*, p. 268.
5. *Ibid.*, p. 270, (our underlinings).
6. A conflict which exceeded that of 1957, during the phase of internal autonomy, between the government already headed by Sékou Touré, the unions, and the left at the heart of the Parti Démocratique de Guinée (and whose positions coincided with those of the P.A.I. which was only created in 1957).
7. Y. Benot, p. 274.
8. Let us note that the continued offensive carried on against the working-class corresponded with a reduction in its size.

9. C. Rivière, *Dynamique de la stratification sociale en Guinée*, (Librairie Champion), 1975, p. 254.
10. Asked explicitly by students at the Institut Polytechnique in 1970.
11. A. Condé, p. 93.
12. B. Charles, 'La Guinée' in A. Mabileau and J. Meyriat (eds.), *Décolonisation et régimes politiques en Afrique Noire*, (Paris: Colin, 1967).
13. *Horoya*, daily newspaper of the P.D.G., 19th November 1964.
14. Y. Benot, p. 350. Benot's remarks were written before the integration of the C.N.T.G. into the Party in 1969.
15. Sékou Touré, *La lutte du P.D.G. pour l'emancipation africaine*, (Conakry, 1960), pp. 27 ff (vol. iv of the works of the P.D.G.).
16. Quoted by I. Wallerstein, *Idéologie du P.D.G.*, *Présence Africaine*, 1st Term 1962, p. 46.
17. *Ibid.*, p. 46.
18. S. Touré, *La Révolution guinéenne et le progrès social*, (vol. vi) (Conakry, 1962), pp. 368–9.
19. S. Touré, *L'Afrique et la Revolution*, (vol. xiii).
20. S. Touré, *L'Afrique et la Révolution.*
21. C. Rivière, *Mutations Sociales en Guinée*, (Edit. Rivière, 1971), p. 406.
22. Y. Benot, 'Idéologies, Nation et structures sociales en Afrique Noire', in *Tiers-Monde*, January–June 1974, p. 149.
23. B. Charles, *Cadres guinéens et appartenances ethniques*, thesis, Sorbonne, Paris 1968.
24. S. Touré, *Défendre la Révolution*, 2nd ed., (Conakry, 1969), vol. xv, p. 146.
25. *Ibid.*, p. 149.
26. To use the expression of Benot, *Idéologies des Indépendances Africaines*, p. 346.
27. *Ibid.*, pp. 417–8, (our underlinings).
28. S. Touré, *La Révolution Culturelle*, 2nd ed., (Conakry, 1969), vol. xvii, p. 56.
29. S. Touré, *Défendre la Révolution*, p. 335.
30. L. Althusser, *Positions*, (Editions Sociales, 1976), p. 121.
31. *Ibid.*, pp. 119–20.
32. S. Touré, *Défendre la Révolution*, p. 335.
33. *Ibid.*, p. 335.
34. L. Althusser, pp. 131–2.
35. S. Touré, *Défendre la Révolution*, p. 344.
36. Y. Benot, *Idéologies des Indépendances Africaines*, p. 257.
37. See above p. oo of this translation, p. 78 of original.
38. X. Leunda, 'Les nouvelles institutions rurales en Guinée', in *Civilisations*, vols. xxiii–xxiv, nos. 1–2, Year 1973–74, (Brussels).
39. *Ibid.*, p. 172.
40. *Ibid.*, p. 173.
41. X. Leunda, 'La réforme de l'enseignement et son incidence sur l'évolution rurale en Guinée', in *Civilisations*, no. 22(2), 1972, p. 255.
42. *Ibid.*, p. 254.
43. X. Leunda, 'Les nouvelles institutions', p. 180.
44. *Ibid.*, p. 180.
45. A. Cournanel, 'Le capitalisme d'Etat en Afrique', p. 36.
46. S. Touré, 'Le Plan, cette exigence', in *l'Economiste du Tiers-Monde*, December 1973–January 1974, p. 33.
47. X. Leunda, 'Les nouvelles institutions', p. 184.
48. Which provided a way of using managerial staff originally destined for other economic functions which had been relegated to a second place by the stagnation.
49. M. Sangaré, article in in *l'Economiste du Tiers-Monde*, November–December 1974, p. 21.
50. Y. Benot, 'Idéologies, Nation et structures', p. 170.
51. This is the essential criticism we have of the articles by Leunda we have quoted.

52. L. Althusser, *Pour Marx*, (Maspero 1966), p. 240.
53. On this point we are fully in agreement with what B. Charles has written in *Décolonisation et régimes politiques en Afrique Noire*, p. 179.

Summary

The author sets out to describe the links between economic strategy, class struggle and ideology in the Republic of Guinea since Independence in 1958. Under the influence of such Marxist planners as Charles Bettelheim, priority was given during the first stage of economic strategy to growth based on national accumulation. In practice, however, only the instruments of economic autonomy (national monetary zone, state-controlled banking and trade system) were created while existing and developing capitalist relations of production remained unchanged. This strategy was officially altered in the early sixties, before the end of the Marxist inspired Three-Year Development Plan. The second stage of economic strategy, still in force today, is characterized by growing dependence on foreign capital concentrated in big mining projects and these now determine economic planning (Seven-Year Plan 1964–1971; Five-Year Plan 1973–1978). The result of the new strategy has been remarkable economic stagnation since 1967.

Such an economic situation leads to an intensified class struggle not only between working class organizations (trade unions) and the emerging bureaucratic bourgeoisie, but also between the different groups of the ruling class ('state' and 'private' bourgeoisie). The conflicts in 1964/65 and 1969/71 resulted in a victory for a small leading group of the bureaucratic bourgeoisie over the 'private' (commercial) bourgeoisie and their allies within the bureaucratic bourgeoisie. The most important instrument of this group is the unity party (PDG-Parti Démocratique de Guinée).

During its first phase (national democracy) the ideology of the PDG did not accept the existence of social classes in Africa and it was not until the 8th Party Congress in 1967 that Sekou Touré spoke of an emerging 'lumpen-bourgeoisie'. However, in PDG terms, this social class is mainly characterized by negative conduct (corruption, etc.) and not by fundamental economic interests. As a result, scapegoats are punished while the relations of production are neither analyzed nor changed. Thus, the ideology of the PDG is revealed as an efficient social instrument within the Guinean state capitalism and its social reproduction.

The role of the political party in Tanzania since the Arusha Declaration

Introduction

In the debate on the post-colonial state there has been little or no appreciation of the importance of what Althusser calls the ideological state apparatuses, such as the political party, juridical and political ideology, etc. Indeed, there would appear to be a denial that there are important ideological functions on the part of some writers. With regards to the political party, one of Alavi's main points in his influential essay on Pakistan and Bangladesh (wholly reproduced in this volume) is that in the post-colonial state the military–bureaucratic oligarchy can afford to dispense with the mediation of politicians and political parties. 'We have yet to see,' he argues, 'a clear case of unambiguous control of state power by a political party in a capitalist post-colonial state',[1] but this has not been seen in developed capitalist formations either. It would be more correct to say that the role of the political party in developed capitalist formations is not essentially to control state power—this question of the control of state power is a separate, although not unrelated, question—but to play a significant *mediatory* role within the arena of class struggles and to provide a bridge between this arena and the state.

Similar conclusions to Alavi's have been drawn by radical observers, following Fanon, regarding the political party in some African post-colonial states. Fanon observed that the political party in African states 'sinks into an extraordinary lethargy'[2] at independence. Speaking of the Tanganyika African National Union, with which this paper is concerned, Henry Mapolu argues that it is a party which is 'much talked about and revered but whose manifestations are really non-existent';[3] the Party's 'occasional pronouncements at the top . . . completely lack substance and hence initiative and creativity at the grass-root level'.[4] Statements of this kind reflect the frustrations of those populists who entertain misplaced expectations of such institutions in the context of underdeveloped capitalist formations. It is not surprising therefore that such writers find much solace and inspiration in that aspect of Fanon's observation that smacks of his populism.

But Fanon's populist language hides one of his important insights into the nature of the post-colonial state in Africa: the second aspect of his observation, which is generally ignored, is that with independence the party not only becomes lethargic, it also transforms itself into 'an administration'.[5] The apparent contradiction here shades over an important fact: the nationalist party may very well cease to have the mass–appeal it once had and certainly it ceases to be an instrument solely for mobilising support around broadly defined demands, but it becomes, in addition, an instrument of coercion, unlike parties in developed capitalist formations.

This development of the party has its basis in the social contradictions of the dominant class of the underdeveloped capitalist social formation of the type under consideration. After independence the need for the dominant petite bourgeoisie to establish firm control over all possible sources of power, so as to ensure that it strengthens its weak socio–economic base which lagged behind this class's political strength, asserts itself. In Kenya the response to this need has resulted in the state's encouragement of the 'Africanisation' of particular areas of the economy within the framework of active private capital accumulation. The response, on the other hand, in Tanzania has been the development of state capitalism officially justified by an ideology of socialism enunciated in the Arusha Declaration of 1967.

The preponderance of the state over socio–economic life which leads to a pre-emption of the activities of politics, forces the state to provide institutions whereby the rituals and the forms, if not the substance, of political life are seen to be intact. The very nature of the political party as an institution—control from above, whilst providing for a measure of active but controlled participation at various levels—lends itself readily to a class conscious of itself and acutely aware of the fact that its interests are not the same as those of other classes, particularly those of the depressed classes. Moreover, the lack of political institutions immediately appropriate to a developing capitalist state makes the party an attractive instrument for the governing faction of the petite bourgeoisie in African post-colonial states. This point requires greater elaboration than can be given here, but the main point is that it is not surprising that of the various institutions that are regarded as parts of the 'Westminster model' of government, it is the political party—significantly modified—which has found the firmest roots in the more stable post-colonial states on the African continent.

Much of what I have said here may be applicable to different African post-colonial states in varying degrees. The argument of this paper is that the function of the political party within the specificity of the Tanzanian post-colonial state, between the 1967 Declaration and the founding of Chama Cha Mapinduzi (C.C.M.) in 1977 out of the Tanganyika African National Union (T.A.N.U.) of mainland Tanzania and the Afro–Shiraz–Party (A.S.P.) of Zanzibar, is problematic and far from obvious as many radical writers would appear to think. The argument is presented in more concrete terms by demonstrating the dual role of TANU in this period as both an ideological and a repressive/coercive instrument of the state. The suggestion, therefore, is that the political party in African post-colonial states has a more crucial as well as a more extensive function than have parties in developed capitalist social formations.

The party as an ideological instrument:

By providing the regime with a legitimate base, integrating the various elements of the social formation and fostering a cohesion within the state itself, TANU performed an indispensable ideological role in the post-colonial state in Tanzania. Each of these can be treated separately.

It is said, perhaps correctly, that throughout mainland Tanzania, formerly Tanganyika, TANU was a household name;

it would appear to have been the single most well known institution in this part of the United Republic. This is hardly surprising for it was, after all, the Party under whose leadership political independence was won in 1961 and although other political parties appeared between 1954 when TANU was founded and 1965 when the Republic became, *de jure*, a one-party state, none were able to pose a serious threat to it.[6] Thus, even before the 1965 (Interim) constitution under which TANU's status was institutionalised, it was really the only viable party in Tanganyika.

The Party's leader, J. K. Nyerere, was and continues to be able to generate considerable public confidence in the Party, being himself a popular figure as indicated by his titles Mwalimu (teacher) and Baba wa Taifa (Father of the Nation), which have not been conferred by promulgation as is the more usual case in Africa. Such is his widespread influence that Nyerere himself has spoken of the dangerous repercussions this could have against the process of institutionalisation and has indicated his willingness to vacate the presidency so as not to thwart this process. To be associated with TANU was to become acceptable and to be associated with its leader was political capital for politicians, as was shown in the 1970 Election campaign.[7]

TANU was organised on a country-wide basis and penetrated all important areas of social life: at the base the Ten House Cell unit provided the Party, however inadequately, with an important wedge into local communities along household/familial patterns.[8] Individuals belonging to these social units may not have been members of the Party but they came within the purview of the leader who had responsibilities of a quasi-legal/formal nature to the unit *as a whole* and to the local Party Branch. There were Party representatives at District and Regional levels and at the centre the National Conference elected members for the National Executive Committee which in turn elected its Central Committee. In this respect TANU was no doubt different from most African political parties which started as 'movements' and later developed into parties, largely in name only; TANU however, also had a very real presence throughout the mainland.

The Party had always had in the independence period a very real monopoly of political representation. For demands to be met they had to be channelled through TANU which also absorbed discontent at various levels and was therefore in a position to control as well as to initiate demands. The Party provided a structure whereby even radicals were absorbed into the state apparatuses, thereby providing for an *apparently* more democratic structure than may be common in similar African states. The regular and periodic elections for bureaucratic posts within the Party were heatedly contested and the general elections to the National Assembly, conducted under the aegis of TANU, were not mere charades. To this extent Cliffe's 'one-party democracy' was in fact a functioning democracy as much as some two- or multi-party systems.[9]

Thus, TANU provided and reproduced a legitimate base for the regime. Its mediatory role had been fostered by the regime itself and is supported by the petite bourgeoisie, a faction of which holds formal state power. In this respect TANU's role in the political system was not qualitatively different from parties in developed social formations under capitalism. This is not to say however, that the specific forms the Party assumes in order to fulfil its task are not different from the former. To this extent also it may be said that the Tanzanian variant of the post-colonial state is similar to the state in developed capitalist societies.

Although it is a general mistake to assume that independence represented a fundamental break in the imperialist process, there were nonetheless some definite and significant changes brought by political independence in Africa. One of these was the realignment of socio–economic forces, the precise forms of which should be subject for more careful analysis than has been hitherto offered. The development of a new petite bourgeoisie alongside existing small-owners who were also able to expand, the new arrangements between this class and the various international bourgeoisies as a result of the political representation of the indigenous petite bourgeoisie necessitated the founding of integrative institutions—in other words what is usually referred to in behavioural political science as institution-building. In Tanzania TANU played this role after independence and until C.C.M. was founded, continued to do so within a developing social formation. One or two examples may serve to illustrate the point.

Firstly, TANU sought, particularly after Arusha, to 'involve' people on a broad basis within the political process. One of the main tenets of the Party which aided it in this task was the ideology that TANU is the Party of workers and peasants only; indeed, there was no major document since 1967 which did not reiterate this claim. For example, the President's paper on *Decentralization* (1972)[10] argued in no uncertain terms that 'the people' ought to be in control of affairs which affect their lives. Populist ideology pervades the paper which reads in parts: '. . . the planning and control of development in this country must be exercised at local level to a much greater extent than at present',[11] proposed Development Councils and Committees would have the responsibility 'to lead the work of direct consultation with the people, so that this decentralisation really does result in the people themselves having a say (sic) in their own affairs'.[12]

This is in sharp contrast with the view of one writer that the articulated ideology of the governing faction in Tanzania is 'characterised by bureaucratic decision-making and technocratic implementation'.[13] The populist ideology of the petite bourgeoisie became even more evident in the months building up to the Tenth Anniversary of the Arusha Declaration. This was accentuated by the much talked about merger of the ASP and TANU on the same day as the celebrations (5 February). The claim was frequently made that the new party, Chama Cha Mapinduzi (The Revolutionary Party), will accommodate only workers and peasants and will more effectively involve the people in decision-making;[14] no day passed without the government-owned *Daily News* praising the democratic nature of the then impending and now new Party.

In class society where dominant classes do not maintain their dominance only by repressive means this ideological function by the political I.S.A. is of great significance. What is important of course is not the extent to which these claims are practicalised or the extent to which they correctly reflect in social practice but simply that they are made and that they are understood to be made.

Secondly, TANU's integrative role in these years may be illustrated by its membership which not only went across class but also across tribal and racial lines. In comparison with her neighbours to the north, Tanzania's 'tribal problem' is limited and has proved manageable since the relatively underdeveloped nature of her economy did not allow for the development of a dominant tribe capable of dominating the country. This is not the same as saying that there is no tribal factor to contend with in the country; indeed, it is sometimes suggested that tribal patterns can be traced within particular institutions of state; for example, one tribe being dominant in say the administration whilst another may be dominant in the police and army and thereby reproducing colonial patterns. The point is simply that in general and comparative terms tribalism has not been a dominant factor in political life and the degree to which this continues to be true is to some extent due to TANU's integrative role both before and after Arusha.

At the political level it would appear that Tanzania, again in comparative terms, has been able to integrate individuals and perhaps even pockets of non-Africans (used in an ethnic sense) and in the extent to which this has been done the Party has played an integrative role. Thus, although in comparison to Kenya, Tanzania's path to 'development' spells doom to direct non-African participation in the economy and the reproduction of ideological institutions (such as the schools, the family, social clubs, etc.) on lines which keep racial groups effectively apart in social terms, in the political sphere there appears a measure of integration. This of course, results in giving the country a reputation for integration which apparently does not obtain in Kenya or Uganda, but it is really a situation resembling tolerance along liberal lines, which is capable of allowing what is covert to become suddenly overt. The objective basis of racism in Tanzania, as in the rest of East Africa, has not been removed as it has been argued, and the limited achievement of the Party in this respect reflects this reality.

As the only political party in the country TANU has been the best suited institution to effect this integrative role, particularly as factions of the petite bourgeoisie struggled to establish predominance over classes within the country. One of the main tenets of the petit bourgeois ideology, unity, could best be propagated and developed by and within the Party. The initial breaking-up at independence of the unity of classes which had been occasioned by the nationalist struggle frightened the governing faction which was relatively untutored in the exercise of formal power and a new consensus was sought so as to blur differences. The Arusha Declaration marked, in political terms, the most daring attempt to impose this unity from above. The new 'unity' was to be around 'socialism' which the leadership claimed to be building. The point here is that this was achieved through TANU—thus strengthening its own position vis-à-vis other ideological state apparatuses and its legitimacy also secured and reinforced.

After the Arusha Declaration therefore, TANU came to play an increasingly significant ideological role by providing cohesion within the state itself. The Declaration charged the Party with seeing to its implementation and to this end the Party's membership was to be modified so that only adherents to its principles of socialism would be accepted, whereas before all were free to join and thereby making TANU resemble a movement as much as a political party. Some see the Declaration as representing a crystalisation of Nyerere's socialism insofar as his earlier definition of socialism as 'an attitude of mind' changed or, more correctly, was added to so that socialism was understood to represent a way of planning the economy and to be concerned with development strategies. Certainly Arusha gave a more definite perspective and form to the regime's version of socialism but what is important to note at this point is that it also gave TANU a new purpose within the state institutions, a purpose which was not evident when Bienen[15] did his work and one which, although glaringly obvious, Mapolu would appear to deny.

The TANU *Mwongozo* (Guidelines, 1971)[16] which came in the wake of the military coup in Uganda and the Portuguese abortive invasion of Guinea, reiterated the responsibilities of the Party in no uncertain terms. It was seen as the only institution upon which the state and the governing elements could depend for control and mobilisation of the army and the people respectively. TANU was therefore portrayed as the guide of the people in 'all their activities'; it was to safeguard the 'African revolution' and see to the correct implementation of the Guidelines. Of particular importance was the fact that TANU was to have control over the proposed People's Militia so as to have the people braced against any attempts to disturb the course of things from within or without. Further, the Party was to play a *supervisory* role over the whole bureaucracy and important socio–economic areas such as housing, education, the economy itself, etc.

Speculation regarding what was behind this stress on the Party playing such an extensive and vital role could stretch in all directions but certainly the result was that its already strong position was further strengthened. Indeed, so much so that the political party (essentially an ideological apparatus) became overburdened by a variety of ideological tasks but more importantly, as a central yet extensive institution, the political party in Tanzania has been pushed to the point where some of its tasks are no longer adequately described as being only ideological.

The party as a coercive instrument:

The distinction between the state's ideological apparatuses and its coercive ones is really one of degree rather than of absolutes: a particular ideological apparatus will exercise a measure of repression/coercion (for example suspension) whilst a particular coercive apparatus will promote certain ideological postures (for example professionalism in the army/neutrality in the bureaucracy). One characteristic of the post-colonial state would seem to be that the clear distinction between the two sets of apparatuses in states under advanced capitalism is relatively absent, or the distinction in most cases is blurred. Sometimes the one dominates over the other as in the case of Alavi's Pakistan. In the specific instance of Tanzania, it can be said tentatively that the Party, particularly after Arusha, has come to play an increasingly ideological–cum–coercive role which goes beyond its ideological tasks. In this respect TANU's 'supremacy' which C.C.M. has inherited may be illustrated by its supervisory role over the educational ideological apparatus, its authority in the field of industrial conflict and its hegemony over potentially competing institutions.

Under capitalism the education system becomes of particular importance to the dominant class(es) because it plays the crucial role of reproducing the relations of production as well as being involved in partial reproduction of the means of production (skills, etc.). In Althusser's view[17] the educational I.S.A. under capitalism occupies the place the church occupied under feudalism. Indeed, even under backward capitalism of the type prevalent in the post-colonial society under consideration, the educational I.S.A. is of great importance although it may be doubtful whether it occupies quite the same position it does under developed capitalism, because the former type of capitalism does not require the same degree of skill, ideology is even less 'purely' bourgeois and the level of the class struggle may not warrant the same advanced ideological apparatus.[18] The most important ideological state apparatus in Tanzania therefore, would seem not to be the educational I.S.A. but the political I.S.A. in general and in particular the political party. The apparent task of TANU in this area after the Declaration was to subordinate the educational I.S.A. by eroding, but not smashing entirely, what little autonomy the educational system enjoyed as a result of being a creation of the colonial period and was therefore not entirely removed from the influence of a dying liberalism in the metropolitan country.

Undoubtedly, the main document on education since Arusha was the Party's *Education for Self-Reliance*, (1967),[19] written by Nyerere himself—the main spokesman for the Party's ideology since its founding. The main argument of the paper was that education was rather irrelevant to the needs of the country.[20] From this an attack was launched against a liberal type of education and the call for educational relevance—meaning that education must relate directly to work situations—resulted in the intervention of the Party in the educational field. For example, whereas in most post-colonial societies the state insists on 'civics' being placed prominently on the curriculum, in Tanzania the state went further and insisted on a body of political ideas being taught in the schools under the heading of 'political education'. The holding ethic in this intervention is anti-capitalist but more in a 'backward' than 'forward' direction, that is, whereas under capitalism manpower is trained largely in educational institutions rather than on the job itself, as indicated earlier, under pre-capitalist modes of production the learning/training process went hand in hand with the work process, for example, the 'apprentice' learnt from the 'master'. Justification for such a departure can therefore be supplied from a wider historical experience than the African past.

If the political aim of *Education for Self-Reliance* was to give the Party a leeway into the schools, then the *Musoma Declaration*, (1974),[21] provided for inroads into higher education. Apart from calling for universal primary education by 1977 (rather than 1989 as had previously been forecast) the Declaration made it clear that the traditional system of pupils leaving school to enter university was to cease. School graduates were now to undergo an examplary period, so to speak, in the work process before they were to be allowed to go on to the University. This would make the University, it was argued, a place for adults; again, the justification was that work and education should be more closely related. It is interesting to note that although it may well have been beneficial to bring people with a middle school education into certain jobs instead of employing university graduates, no such argument was in fact presented as justification. In view of this the facts of the situation would seem to suggest that an important aim of the N.E.C. was that a potentially vocal and possibly critical, because transitory, group of students should be in a position where the Party and the Government could effectively control it.

After Form Six the scholar must be 'ready to serve the nation that educated him to the level he has attained. The students must know this, the parents understand this and the employers acknowledge this'.[22] No doubt the new scheme would have some advantages as people were being forced to change their attitudes towards the educational ladder (rather than education itself) but the 'other gains' of the scheme reflected the deeper and more important aim of the Party: 'his [the student's] admission will also take into account his character, his attitudes, his competence at serving the masses in his work-place, and his other abilities'.[23] At different points in the document much is made of the potential student's 'competence' or 'ability' to 'serve the masses'; this 'ability' or 'competence' would be assessed by the Party leaders at the place of work. In this way the potential student's uncritical acceptance of Party rule is more or less ensured, or at any rate potential opposition is significantly minimised. Of course, there is ample allowance here for opportunism but this is hardly of moment: what is important is that the Party is strategically placed as *gateman* into the University without in fact seeming to directly infringe on the internal autonomy of the educational system.[24] This is not to say that in another step the Party might not enter more directly/overtly into the inner confines of the system.

Moreover, the Party has been active in developing its own educational facilities independently of existing institutions. The best known of these new institutions is of course Kivukoni College in Dar es Salaam which prepares various political officers. It would appear also to take in such functionaries as school teachers for refresher courses. Law graduates from the University of Dar es Salaam are also obliged to do three months internship at the College, thus three of their six months internship period is spent being ideologically prepared by the Party.

What is involved here is not merely a process of 'development' conceived in a general and vague sense, more significantly it is a process of institutionalising means whereby effective control over areas which could possibly serve as rallying points for factions of the petite bourgeoisie. This may also have the effect of blocking-off any possible alliance between factions of the petite bourgeoisie and the submerged classes. In this struggle the necessity to subdue the one ideological state apparatus to another involves a measure of coercion (as opposed to persuasion/ideological factors), particularly in regards to those institutions which enjoyed a modicum of autonomy in the past.

The Party's coercive role is best seen in the area of industrial and related conflict. As an institution it intervenes both indirectly and directly in this area. It operates through the National Union of Tanganyika Workers (NUTA), (since early 1978 the name of the Union has been changed to the Union of Tanzania Workers), the only and official union in the country and which is supervised by the Party. The Secretary-General is usually at the same time the Minister of Labour and in both capacities he is appointed by the President of the United Republic. This body was set up after the army mutiny of 1964 replacing the Tanganyika Federation of Labour (T.F.L.) a voluntary body which had supported the struggle for independence but after this became a thorn in the flesh of the new TANU Government since they ostensibly represented opposing sides in industrial conflict.[25] The establishment of NUTA was to provide the Government with a controlling mechanism over potentially organised workers but this act did not effectively silence them.[26] The early 1970s witnessed attempts by the workers to exploit anomalies in the official structure to good effect and although these have since been 'remedied' by the state the events showed that there is no way of ultimately silencing class protest. Nonetheless, by controlling the only organised channel for expression the regime has been able to effect an institution for control of no insignificant importance. Without going into the various ramifications of this institution suffice it to say that it comes directly under the aegis of the Party.

But TANU ensured a direct presence at the workplace also. After Arusha the Party became active in establishing branches at these points, plus representation on the various controlling committees/councils whose functions are essentially to gain the cooperation of the workers and thereby ensure high productivity. Thus, apart from its representatives and the work of NUTA, TANU had a definite role to play within the workplace. In this capacity it presented itself as 'honest broker', a mediator. Yet, in this same capacity the Party had the responsibility of applying drastic measures in the interest of the nation/people, such as recommending the retirement of workers or calling in the police or militia (of which it is in charge) to restore order' in the workplace. With respect to ujamaa villages, for which the Party had sole responsibility, it is part of its function to authorise the militia to impose remedies to disputes which hold up production. Dumont's advice has been taken seriously: he argued that the Party 'must be involved in all the measures indispensable to development, *especially when they are unpopular*' (his emphasis).[27]

Since in Tanzania there has been, since Arusha, only workers and peasants (President Nyerere's 1976 speech at Ibadan [reproduced in this volume] has somewhat qualified and corrected this view)—all others were exploiters by virtue of being unemployed—then it followed that the interests of management and workers are identical. Job Lusinde, a prominent member of the Government, speaking at a conference of National Development Corporation Group Managers in 1970, puts it thus:

> Managers are no longer owners of these enterprises [nationalised industries] nor are they representatives of private owners. These enterprises are owned by the public who include the workers of the enterprises themselves.[28]

One need not look far to see the utility of a populist ideology which stresses the importance of unity, of 'oneness'. Thus in the strike situations it falls upon the Party of workers and peasants to impose a solution and when it comes to clearing Dar es Salaam of its 'exploiters' (the unemployed) it is also the Party which does this by calling upon the police and the militia.[29]

For all this however, the Party had difficulties in practically establishing its 'supremacy'. Msekwa, himself of longstanding prominence in the Party and now Secretary-General of C.C.M., has pointed out that at headquarters TANU 'was poorly staffed and for that reason the National Executive Council [hereafter N.E.C.] did not have the kind of servicing machinery that would assist it in its decision-making process'[30] in the mid-sixties. H. Bienen too, who has written the only full-scale (but now dated and quite inadequate) work on the Party, noted that at the time of writing in 1965 the administrative staff at Headquarters was extremely poor—so much so that the N.E.C. was not able to keep effective check on Regional Secretaries. He concluded therefore that at that time TANU did 'not have the instruments of coercion or the internal cohesion to enforce its views'.[31]

The process of bureaucratisation which developed rapidly after Arusha does not seem to have immediately affected TANU. In 1972, after the *Mwongozo*, Mwansasu noted that the Party's central office had only eight departments—administration, ujamaa villages, information and research, cultural and social affairs, political education, accounts, Tan-Zam construction and Youth—and only fifty-one establishment officers of which ten posts were vacant. All the departments, apart from Youth, had only eight officers each. In view of this Mwansasu observed that: 'This raises the question of whether the Headquarters, as constituted, can effectively exercise the organisational leadership of the masses and their institutions as well as act as the watchdog over them.'[32] For example, there were only eight education officers to see to the implementation of the policy of *Education for Self Reliance*. Another important example in this respect, is that in the formation of the 1969 *Five Year Plan* the Party could not play an active part—'the nature of the Party was much too limited to allow it to participate in a work of this nature' as Svendsen admitted.[33] Initiation of public policy was therefore left to other institutions.

Party 'supremacy'

Party 'supremacy' over the bureaucracy would *appear* therefore, at least until recently, to be of a very dubious nature; Mwansasu doubted even whether the Party was able to act as a sort of 'shadow government' effectively. But the answer to this question must be sought not only in terms of a process of bureaucratisation within TANU but also in terms of its penetration into the bureaucracy. For example, in 1965 some senior civil servants were shifted to TANU's headquarters and it would appear that particularly after Arusha, in Msekwa's words, the 'entire Civil Service machinery was put at the disposal of the N.E.C. for the purpose of collecting information or preparing position papers, as well as for implementing the decisions made'.[34] In this way, it would appear that the Party has been able to remain relatively unbureaucratised whilst strengthening itself within the various institutions of state. For example, it has been the practice since the mutiny of 1964 to control the army by allowing military men, like civil servants, to participate in politics at certain levels, but more importantly perhaps by establishing TANU branches within the barracks. The extent to which this process really does represent a genuine penetration of the bureaucracy by the Party, or alternatively, the extent to which it is really a case of the Party being throttled by the bureaucracy, (in which case the problem would be just as interesting) remain matters for empirical investigation. But it would appear that TANU was earnest in establishing itself as a controlling institution over the others as is borne out not only by its penetration of the administration and other institutions but also by its own internal periodic modifications. It is to be seen what important effect the merger of TANU and ASP will have upon this process in the near future.

As an ideological state apparatus, TANU's functions passed beyond its essential tasks and to a significant degree can be termed coercive also. As an institution the Party has proved of considerable utility to the governing faction in the country. What is called for therefore, is not denial of this fact—a denial based partly on, it would seem, ultimately overstressing problems *internal* to the Party and which may be resolved given certain conditions—but the formulation of theoretical tools sufficiently adequate to explain a dynamic situation.

In the process of the establishment of the hegemony of a faction of the petite bourgeoisie the Party came to assume control over a number of would-be pressure groups and therefore potentially alternative points of organised political power. Apart from NUTA, there are the Party's Youth League and the women's union (Umoja wa Wanawake wa Tanzania). These organisations have also changed their names since early 1978. In this way all alternative platforms for voicing political opinions are effectively controlled and criticism, friendly or not, must take place under the umbrella of the Party.

Also, the 1965 Constitution which made TANU the only political party in the land was more than a mere act of institutionalisation—it also effectively barred any other party from emerging in the political arena. The 'supremacy' of the Party, in fact, dates from then, with the Constitution declaring that: 'All political activity in Tanzania, other than that of the organs of State . . . shall be conducted by or under the auspices of the Party.'[35] But the story did not end there. The N.E.C. meeting at Musoma in November 1974, received a resolution from the Central Committee to issue to the Government a directive to the effect that TANU should become supreme also in matters of state.[36] During the course of the debate and reports in the *Daily News* it became clear that there were those who felt that the 1965 Constitution treated matters too vaguely. Supremacy, it seemed to these people, could be taken to mean supremacy in matters such as the organisation of public meetings etc., which apparently did not amount to much. When therefore, the 1965 Constitution was amended in June 1975, the relevant additional clause read thus: 'The functions of all the organs of State of the United Republic shall be performed under the auspices of the Party'.[37] This did not leave room for speculation.

Yet in reality this was similar to the constitutional recognition of 1965 of what had already been taking place, particularly after the Declaration in 1967. In other words, the N.E.C. of the Party had been functioning steadily in such a way as to erode the influence and power of the legislature, the National Assembly. The 1964 *Presidential Commission on the Setting-up of a One Party State*,[38] considered the idea of abolishing the legislature and rejected it although even then it was quite clear that the legislature was not playing an indispensable role in the political system *inside* the country. Its role effectively had been pre-empted by the N.E.C. which was itself about the same size as the legislature and, it was alleged, the N.E.C. was a more democratic body; besides, the legislature was entirely filled by TANU members. But although no visible value could be seen in the retention of this body, this is true only as regards the country's *internal*, not *external*, politics: the National Assembly continues to have utility for the regime because such formalism matters to international partners who place some value on such institutions, and particularly in the 1960s it was important to be seen to have a popularly elected body.

Party 'supremacy' is therefore not a new development but the maturation of a process. The President of the Republic is also the President of the Party and although he could have tilted the balance in the direction of the National Assembly, Nyerere has always taken particularly important policy papers/proposals to the N.E.C. rather than to the Assembly. This was the case with the *Arusha Declaration* itself, the *Mwongozo, Education for Self-Reliance*, the *Musoma Declaration*, the matter of enshrining Party supremacy, and many other important issues affecting the Government, areas of particular conflict/tension and the nation as a whole. In this respect, it is possible to speak of *the N.E.C. having become a legislative body* for some time now: it makes effective use of directives, takes part in the formation of public policy, provides a forum for debate; indeed, it would appear to be the only effective debating forum. On the other hand the National Assembly does not participate in any noteworthy way in the total process of decision-making nor is it called upon to offer critical comments on what *has been decided* at the N.E.C.; its task is restricted to rubber-stamping decisions taken elsewhere because it is still, in legal terms, the body responsible for effecting legislation of a certain type. The M.P.'s duty in this situation is not primarily to represent the views of his constituents (even in theory) but to asist in the implementation of policies. In this sense therefore, the *de facto* Parliament of Tanzania is the N.E.C. of the Party.

Msekwa, now Secretary-General of C.C.M., accounts for this by arguing that this is the case because Nyerere is the chairman of the N.E.C. and his popularity has helped to win this body its prestige and influence whereas in contrast, the Speaker of the

Assembly is unknown to the public. This suggestion may be pointing in an important direction of which Msekwa is unaware: it may well be that the degree of institutionalisation for which Tanzania is noted in Africa is less than we have come to believe and that personalism is stronger than we would care to contemplate.

Conclusion: Party or executive 'supremacy'?

This leads to an important point with respect to the post-colonial state in Tanzania: from the foregoing it would appear that the system in Tanzania differs in some significant ways from other African post-colonial states. The Party not only plays an important ideological but also an important coercive role in the system and is therefore more important than parties in developed capitalist countries (barring fascist ones). But the function of the party does not explain the Party itself in much the same way as the Tanzanian bureaucracy or any other institution does not explain itself. The correct point of departure for a correct analysis of the Party in Tanzania lies elsewhere and poses the important question of what in fact stands behind Party supremacy in this particular instance.

The answer to this leads back to a more general problem in the debate on the post-colonial state. If the interventionist state corresponds to the monopoly phase of capitalism in advanced capitalist social formation, then undoubtedly in the under-developed capitalist formations imperialism at its post-colonial juncture engenders the development of an extremely strong executive which predominates over all other institutions of state. At the present juncture of monopoly capitalism it may well be the case that in advanced capitalist countries one of the effects of the internationalisation of capital is the decomposition (cf. the U.K., Spain, etc.) of the nation state which played such a vital role in the development of capital,[39] but in post-colonial societies the centrality of the state and its increasingly important regulatory role in the economy forces the need for a vital all-embracing centralism. Both 'pull' factors have their historical ramifications. The phenomenon of presidentialism is therefore not an isolated instance in the African post-colonial state; it is not merely the institutionalisation of the would-be Weberian charismatic figure, it in fact represents the predominance of the executive arm of the state under imperialism. Just as Parliamentary predominance may have corresponded to a particular phase of the capitalist state so may the predominance of the executive represent another phase in the same process.[40] In this respect too the post-colonial state is really not that far removed from the state in advanced capitalist countries. This is not to belittle however, the far-reaching effects of the facts that post-colonial societies in some instances missed out on particular pre-capitalist formations and particular phases of capitalism itself and are, after all, dependencies in more than an economic sense.

There is no doubt that it is the executive which is supreme in Tanzania as in other African post-colonial states of a similar type. The Party's supremacy therefore, represents in effect the power of the presidency. TANU's success has been the success of the executive in presenting itself in democratic yet powerful terms to elements of the petite bourgeoisie and the submerged classes and in absorbing significant elements of these classes into a machinery which reproduces the much needed legitimacy of a regime. Some important questions arise from these considerations: firstly, why has the governing faction of the petite bourgeoisie chosen or has been forced to extend, in effect, the arm of the executive power throughout the country in the way it has done;[41] secondly, the specific links between economy and polity which forces the latter to take certain directions, which in turn rebound on the former needs to be established in precise terms with respect to Tanzania, taking into account the objective and specific function of ideology; thirdly, as indicated earlier, it is important to arrive at an understanding of the different phases of party political systems which corresponds to the different phases of the political system with respect to the post-colonial state. This may help to form part of the beginning of a fruitful investigation.

NOTES

1. Hamza Alavi, 'The state in Post-Colonial Societies: Pakistan and Bangladesh', *New Left Review*, no. 74, July/August 1972, p. 63 (see p. 43 this volume—ed.).
2. Franz Fanon, *The Wretched of the Earth*, (Penguin, 1965), p. 137.
3. H. Mapolu, 'The Organization and Participation of Workers in Tanzania', in H. Mapolu (ed.), *Workers and Management*, (Tanzania Publishing House, 1976), p. 205.

4. *Ibid.*

5. Fanon, p. 137.

6. See for example, M. H. Kaniki, 'TANU: The Party of Independence and National Consolidation', in G. Ruhumbika (ed.), *Towards Ujamaa: Twenty Years of TANU: Twenty Years of TANU Leadership*, (East African Literature Bureau, 1974), ch. 1.

7. See for example, J. S. Saul, 'Background to the Tanzanian Election, 1970', in L. Cliffe and J. S. Saul, *Socialism in Tanzania: An Interdisciplinary Reader*, (East African Publishing House, 1973), vol. 1, pp. 277ff.

8. See H. Kjekshus (ed.), *The Party: Essays on TANU*, University of Dar es Salaam, Studies in Political Science, No. 6, (Tanzania Publishing House, 1976); also J. H. Proctor (ed.), *The Cell System of the Tanganyika African National Union*, University of Dar es Salaam, Studies in Political Science, No. 1 (Tanzania Publishing House, 1975).

9. See, L. Cliffe, 'Democracy in a One-Party State: The Tanzanian Experience', in Cliffe and Saul, pp. 241ff.

10. J. K. Nyerere, *Decentralization*, (Government Printer, 1972).

11. *Ibid.*, p. 1.

12. *Ibid.*, p. 3.

13. I. G. Shivji, *Class Struggles in Tanzania*, (Dar-es-Salaam: Tanzania Publishing House, 1975), p. 96.

14. P. Msekwa, Secretary to the Commission responsible for the Constitution, etc. of the new party and now C.C.M. Secretary-General, made this point repeatedly in the months before February.

15. H. Bienen, *TANU: Party Transformation and Economic Development*, (Princeton University Press, 1966).

16. 'Mwongozo, TANU Guidelines on Guarding, Consolidating and Advancing the Revolution of Tanzania and of Africa', published in *The African Review*, vol. 1, no. 4 (April 1972).

17. L. Althusser, 'Ideology and Ideological State Apparatus: Notes Towards an Investigation', in *Lenin and Philosophy and Other Essays*, (Monthly Review Press, 1971).

18. There is an important point, however, to be developed in this regard: the education system plays more than the usually important role in a post-colonial state such as Tanzania where the level of class developments has been very low. The faction of the petite bourgeoisie which becomes the *governing* faction after independence is predominantly of a *salaried* nature and as such they depend very much on education to justify their position, unlike the bourgeoisie in developed capitalist societies which reproduces itself mainly through inheritance of wealth. The petite bourgeoisie in the post-colonial state, such as Tanzania, reproduces itself, partly through the education system. Although this theoretical point is not broached empirical material is assembled to demonstrate this point, at least tentatively, in Marjorie Mbilinyi, 'Peasants' Education in Tanzania', paper presented at the 12th Annual Conference of the Arts and Social Sciences, University of Dar es Salaam, December, 1976.

19. J. K. Nyerere, *Ujamaa: Essays on Socialism*, (Oxford University Press, 1968/74).

20. For a more elaborate assessment of this document, see Mbilinyi, pp. 34–45.

21. 'The Musoma Declaration', *Daily News*, 7 and 8 January 1975, p. 4.

22. *Ibid.*, 8 January, p. 4.

23. *Ibid.*

24. This point could be more strongly stated: for example, some see this move as being an attempt by the bureaucracy to establish means of favourably competing with younger people leaving school/University and who, as time passes, will become more qualified than its current members.

25. See W. F. Freidland, 'Cooperation, Conflict and Conscription: TANU–TFL Relations, 1955–64', in J. Butler and A. A. Castagno (eds.), *Transition in African Politics*, (Praeger, 1967), pp. 67ff.

26. Mapolu, 'The Organization and Participation of Workers in Tanzania'.

27. Rene Dumont, *Tanzania Agriculture after the Arusha Declaration*, (National Printing Co. Ltd., Ministry of Economic Affairs and Development Planning, 1969), p. 39.

28. J. Lusinde, 'Workers' Participation in Industrial Management in Tanzania', in H. Mapolu, *Workers and Management*, p. 162.

29. Periodically the Party and Government decide to clear Dar es Salaam of 'exploiters' (the unemployed) in the fashion of the colonial state, by physically pushing them into villages from which such people came. In the latter months of 1976 the campaign to this effect resulted in a great deal of forceful activities by the Party and the Militia which the Party controls; see for example, 'Handling the Jobless Problem: The Merits of Mass Mobilization', *Sunday News*, 5 December 1976.

30. P. Msekwa, 'Towards Party Supremacy: The Changing Pattern of Relationship between the National Assembly and the National Executive Committee of TANU before and after 1965', *Independent Study for the M.A. (Political Science), 1973/74*, University of Dar es Salaam, p. 45.

31. Bienen, *TANU*, p. 190.

32. B. Mwansasu, 'Commentary on Mwongozo wa TANU, 1971', *The African Review*, vol. 1, no. 4, (April 1972), p. 26.

33. *Ibid.*, pp. 24–5.

34. Msekwa, 'Towards Party Supremacy', p. 47.

35. *Interim Constitution of Tanzania, 1965* (Government Publications Agency, 1976 ed.), p. 7.

36. See for example, 'Call to Discuss Party Supremacy: TANU is People's Watchdog', *Daily News*, 24 February 1975, p. 1; 'Constitutional Changes Necessary to Ensure Party Supremacy', *Daily News*, 1 April 1975, p. 4.

37. 'An Act to Amend the Interim Constitution of Tanzania, 1965', in *Gazette of the United Republic of Tanzania*, no. 24, vol. lvi (13 June 1975), p. 76.

38. (Dar es Salaam: Government Printers, 1965); 'Guide to the One-Party State Commission', in J. K. Nyerere: *Freedom and Unity/Uhuru na Umoja*, (Oxford University Press, 1966).

39. See N. Poulantzas, *Classes in Contemporary Capitalism*, (New Left Books, 1975), particularly pp. 78–80.

40. See N. Poulantzas, *Political Power and Social Classes*, (New Left Books, 1975), Part iv, ch. 5.

41. I pose this as a question here because it would take considerable time to elucidate and elaborate on elements of an answer which is not too important within the present context.

c) Class and the military

12 MAHMOOD MAMDANI

The aftermath of the Amin Coup in Uganda in 1971[†]

After the coup, the leadership of the bureaucratic petty bourgeoisie took refuge in Dar-es-Salaam. With a core of some 600
soldiers who had escaped at the time of the coup, and another
1,000 or so in the Sudan, training camps were established,
awaiting a suitable opportunity to make a bid for a return to
power. True to its class character, the only form of armed
opposition the bureaucratic petty bourgeoisie could consider was
that of an invasion. Its principle was not to unite with the people
and bring their interests to the fore, but to champion its own
interests and hope the people would remain passive bystanders.
It could not champion the interests of the people, for they were
objectively antagonistic to its own; neither could it arm the
people without fearing the possibility of their independent
organizational expression and thus the loss of its own leading role.
It should not be the least surprising, then, that in its hour of need
it turned, not to the people of Uganda, but to friendly ruling
classes elsewhere. Nor should it be surprising that as its
instrument it sought to train another professional mercenary
armed force and invade.

[†] From the author's *Politics and Class Formation in Uganda*, (Heinemann, 1976), pp. 302–
313.

This fact had a decisive impact on Amin's policy, in both its external and internal dimensions. In his foreign policy, in spite of close relations with Israel, Amin continued the rapprochement Obote had begun with the Sudan. A formal agreement was concluded in 1971. When their supplies from northern Uganda dried up, a section of the ex-Anyanya guerrillas joined Amin's military forces. Amin's reward was the removal of Obote's military base in the Sudan. The effect on Israeli-Ugandan relations was immediate and it formed the backdrop of the expulsion of the Israeli mission from Uganda.

But Obote's armed camps in Tanzania remained. In light of this fact, the existing factionalism within the army assumed primary significance. It was necessary that it be immediately and effectively resolved. Shortly after the coup Amin ordered a major recruitment drive for the armed forces. In three months the army more than doubled as about 10,000 men were recruited. The core of the new recruits were some 4,000 Sudanese ex-Anyanya[1] fighters, along with a sprinkling of former Zairian freedom fighters. The bulk of the remainder came from Amin's own West Nile District; 40 percent of these were Muslims.[2] In sum, the new army was primarily a *mercenary* force. The greatest care was taken to ensure that the condition of their survival was the continuation of Amin's rule.

Amin then set about methodically resolving the factional split within the army through the physical elimination of the opposing faction. Thousands of Acholi and Langi officers were systemati-cally murdered in a wave of massacres. A few escaped to Tanzania to tell the grim details.[3,4] The new order had received its birthmark, stamped in cold blood.

In the decade between independence and the coup, the contradiction between the petty bourgeoisie as a whole and Asian capital remained secondary, while the struggle within the petty bourgeoisie was resolved. In fact, the contradiction between the two factions of the petty bourgeoisie (the governing bureaucracy on the one hand and the kulaks and traders on the other) was brought out precisely by the question of *how* the state was to be used to undermine the base of the Asian commercial bourgeoisie and hence strengthen that of the petty bourgeoisie. The point was that there were two alternate methods of using state power: to create state private property[5] or to create individual private property. The method adopted would strengthen either the section of the class based within the state apparatus or that located outside of it. Objectively, then, the contradiction within the petty bourgeoisie had to be resolved before the contradiction with the commercial bourgeoisie could be dealt with. Its resolution was the coup. Then, after the state power had consolidated its coercive apparatus, the contradiction between the petty bourgeoisie and Asian capital (both the Asian petty and commercial bourgeoisies) emerged as the principal contradiction. Amin brought the·same decisive resolution to this contradiction that he had to factionalism in the army. Just as the Obote faction in the army was physically eliminated, so these two classes were physically expelled.

As we have seen, the Asian expulsion was not the first in Uganda's neocolonial history. It was preceded by that of Kenyan workers during the Obote years. The expulsion of entire classes or sections of classes, nationally based but nonnational in origin, has also been seen in countries other than Uganda. The expulsion of nonnationals, as a political event, has punctuated the period following independence in a number of African countries. Its objective basis, in the context of a dependent capitalist economy, is the failure to expand the productive forces and thus the economic base of the appropriating classes. Given a relatively stagnant economy, with little more than simple reproduction of the productive forces taking place, the secondary contradictions among the propertied classes intensify. For the working class, the crisis of accumulation of the propertied classes appears as an unemployment crisis. To make room at the top or the bottom, where there exist nonnational classes (or sections of classes) like the Kenyan workers or the Indian commercial bourgeoisie in Uganda, expulsion becomes one way of resolving the crisis of the dependent ruling class. The official ideology produced and propagated as an explanation of the event—be it racial, national chauvinist, or tribal chauvinist—should not obscure the class content and the objective basis of the expulsion as a political phenomenon.

But let us follow the events to their conclusion.[6] On June 28, 1971, the General assured the African traders that his government would do everything in its power to place the economy in their hands. On October 7, a census of the Asian population only was ordered, and every Asian was required to carry a 'green card.' On December 7, following the 'Asian census', Amin put a stamp of finality on the noncitizen status of many Asian traders by canceling the applications of over 12,000 Asians for Ugandan citizenship. At the same time, he called together a conference of 'Asian community leaders' and accused them of economic malpractice, of sabotaging government policies, and of failing to integrate into the community—by which he meant (of course) the petty bourgeoisie community. Threats to the commercial bourgeoisie, articulated in a racial form, continued. On January 5, 1972, Amin warned thirteen representatives of the Asian community that 'Uganda is not an Indian colony'. A week later he said he would like to see Ugandans owning businesses on Kampala's main street. Meanwhile, the state power attempted to use its economic apparatus against the commercial bourgeoisie. On May 9, the minister of finance was instructed to tell the Bank of Uganda to give available money to Africans and not to Asians. But Uganda was a neocolony. Commercial financing was controlled, as we shall see, by British banking capital, not by the Bank of Uganda. The process reached its culminating point on August 9 when—addressing the Annual Conference of Cooperative Societies in Uganda, a congregation of the petty bourgeoisie—Amin proclaimed that noncitizen Asians would have to leave Uganda in three months.

In the first few days after the announcement, Amin vacillated between expelling all Asians or just Asian commercial capital. Publicly, this was articulated in his indecision over whether or not to exempt professionals from the expulsion order. Another issue was legal. An expulsion confined to noncitizens would leave the bulk of big Asian capital untouched; furthermore, it might also leave this section of the Asian bourgeoisie in control of the material assets of the entire class once the process came to a conclusion. Once this was realized, the class struggle lost its veil of legality. Political actions were shorn of their legal forms and the class content lay bare for all to see. The citizen Asians, asked to queue in order to confirm the validity of their citizenship, found their passports and certificates torn up. Eventually all Asians were expelled. Neither citizen nor professional remained.

The process of expulsion highlighted the social composition of Amin's new army. Apart from the estimated 4,000 ex-Anyanya and other mercenaries, most of the 10,000 new recruits were either from West Nile or were Muslims. The Muslim Nubians in East Africa are predominantly urban; their social origin is from among the urban unemployed, living on the fringes of respectable society, partaking of the social product through either temporary employment or temporary crime. Newly recruited, these soldiers were not yet subject to a disciplined organization. While their social origin did not affect their political behavior, it did determine their social behavior. The expulsion was seized upon as an opportunity for private accumulation. Armed greed led to kidnapping, extortion, theft, and even murder.

The theft of Asian property, even at its most chaotic, followed an established pattern. Everything the Asians had to leave behind was guarded carefully by the army and police officials. Any potential looters were shot dead on sight. Amin's orders were that the Asians' property be guarded as ruthlessly as the Asians themselves were being expelled. The same material interest was at stake in both cases, for once the Asians had departed a large part of their businesses, houses, and cars would be legitimately acquired by the upper sections of the army and of the petty bourgeoisie. It was here that contradictory interests between army officials, potential members of the property-owning petty bourgeoisie, and the rank-and-file became evident. The soldiers realized that when the time came for the legal allocation of Asian property, the sun would shine only on high-ranking officials. If ordinary soldiers were to share in the spoils, their opportunity for doing so was before the Asians' departure, and to do this they had to resort to loot and plunder, unprotected by the halo of bourgeois legality.

It is tempting to see in this process an historical similarity, the reoccurrence of what Marx described as the 'primitive accumulation of capital' in England, 'a set of events written in the annals of mankind in letters of blood and fire'. The difference could be ascribed to an originality of forms: in England, embezzlement of church funds, robbery on the high seas, and the expulsion of peasants from the land; in Uganda, embezzlement of state funds, robbery on the highways, and the expulsion of the Asians.[7] But the analogy would be highly limited and formal, and thus quite misleading. Its limits are those of the Ugandan petty bourgeoisie, constrained by the historical and international context of its development. The petty bourgeoisie is not an autonomous class with effective control over the use of the nationally generated economic surplus; on the contrary, it is a dependent class, an intermediary in the exploitation of the neocolony by the centres of imperial capitalism. What it amasses is not capital, but wealth; this is not the productive accumulation of an industrialist but the unproductive riches of a merchant. Its riches are not destined to be transformed into means of production, thereby expanding the productive base of the economy; it will merely lubricate the export-import economy, at most permitting the assembly of a few luxury goods internally, thereby facilitating the metropolitan-style consumption of this intermediate class. This is not the bourgeoisie of capitalist development; it is the petty bourgeoisie of capitalist underdevelopment. Its objective constraints, the historically created international links of the neocolony, were brought into the open during the process of expulsion.

In October 1972, when Asian businesses started closing down en masse, the main streets of Kampala were lined with signs saying 'Property of Barclays Bank D.C.O.' or 'Property of Standard Bank'. Financial connections usually hidden in small print in the text of a contract or an agreement were now advertised for all to see. The fact was that the Indian commercial bourgeoisie was still a dependent class. Functionally, it lubricated the export-import economy; financially, it was heavily reliant on and subordinate to British banking capital. It was clear that unless the state moved against the British banks, the primary beneficiary of the Asian expulsion would be the British big bourgeoisie, not the Ugandan petty bourgeoisie. Thus there began the second phase of the 'economic war'. Confined to British capital, it focused on banking capital but extended to its weakest section, the plantations.

Whereas the first phase of the economic war nationalized the compradore sector (the commercial sector of the export-import economy), replacing the Asian compradore class with an African one, its second phase abrogated the primary dependence of the economy on a single metropolitan power (Britain) and diversified this dependence. The new international friends of the Amin government were the Soviet Union and France (through Libya), who were the primary suppliers of arms; Saudi Arabia and Libya, which gave small but critical grants at times of crisis, such as the time of the severe foreign-exchange shortage in the months prior to the scheduled OAU conference in Kampala; and increasingly, India and Pakistan. While Pakistani teachers and technicians have provided the necessary personnel to replace those who have departed, Indian capital (specifically, the House of Birla) is expanding its operations in the country's manufacturing sector through both investments (a jute mill) and management contracts (Birla is currently negotiating management contracts on the bulk of what used to be the Madhvani industrial empire).[8] While the internal expression of the unilateral dependence on British capital was the colonially nurtured Asian bourgeoisie, the expression of multilateralized dependence on international capitalism is the postindependence nationalist petty bourgeoisie, which is fast expanding into a commercial bourgeoisie.

But the rise of the petty bourgeoisie to the position of a commercial bourgeoisie has not been smooth. Its political weakness, evident in its inability to come to power through an independent struggle, meant its ascent to power through an armed coup. The expression of this political weakness was the strength of Amin's own individuality. In fact, the weakness of the petty bourgeoisie as a class remains necessary for the survival of Amin's power as the personalization of class rule. Amin's policy has precisely the effect of preventing the consolidation of the petty bourgeoisie, and thus its rise to the stature of a class that governs for itself.

Hence the continuation and even the institutionalization of terror in Uganda since the Asian expulsion. The petty bourgeoisie advances as a class, but not necessarily as individuals. The rule of private property is consolidated with each passing day, but there is not the same security for any particular expression of it. Businessmen survive—in fact, they prosper. But it is not rare for a businessman to be killed or his property to be appropriated.[9] The result has been a rapid erosion of Amin's own social base. The petty bourgeoisie, ardent supporters of Amin at the time of the 1971 coup and the 1972 expulsion, were delighted with his rule when it brought them the fruit of their wildest dreams, but now they suddenly find the taste turning bitter in their mouths. As its internal social base rapidly disintegrates, the state power has attempted to secure its rule by transforming its military apparatus into a nonnational mercenary force. While the core of its army is the disciplined ex-Anyanya guerrillas, the provider of arms is imperialism. Today, the Amin dictatorship is simply a dictatorship of arms.

Amin, however, is caught in an insoluble contradiction. While officially encouraged terror prevents the consolidation of a commercial bourgeoisie, it also prevents the stabilization of the economy. Price rises and commodity scarcities become a daily phenomenon. The result, increasingly, is economic retaliation by the cash-crop growing peasantry and a refusal to sell crop surpluses on the market as spiralling inflation renders paper money worthless—Uganda's version of the Soviet scissors crisis of the 1920s. Such an economic crisis could fast turn into a political crisis, for both the state power and the petty bourgeoisie. On the other hand, if the petty bourgeoisie is allowed to consolidate its base in the interests of stabilizing the economy, this will undermine the objective basis of Amin's power. Amin's dominant role is possible precisely because it is necessary—because the petty bourgeoisie is too weak to rule as a class. A consolidated commercial bourgeoisie would mean the substitution of class rule for individual rule. In such circumstances, Amin's role would diminish drastically. Far more likely, rendered unfit precisely because of his present exaggerated stature, Amin would be replaced by another individual situated much more closely within the ruling class.

But the political weakness of the petty bourgeoisie also makes another process possible: the integration of individual members of the army officer corps into the ranks of the petty bourgeoisie as its material base expands. Unlike the precoup governing bureaucracy, the army officers are not transforming themselves into a class by developing an independent economic base. Quite the contrary: members of the officer corps are being integrated into the emerging commercial bourgeoisie, and their individual interests are beginning to coincide with its class interests, even though their recent origin is the armed forces, their ethnic origin the West Nile, and their religious affiliation Islam. Amin, the very leader who made possible their new class position, now appears as the primary obstacle to consolidating this position. Given their origin in the armed forces, the resolution of this contradiction may well be another coup. Numerous attempts to assassinate Amin in the past year would seem to bear out this prediction. And yet, what is striking is the relative stability of state power in the short run. The political contradiction has been late in maturing precisely because the economic crisis has been late in developing. The aftermath of the Asian expulsion was not just a decline in export-crop production by the peasantry; just as important was a far more rapid drop in luxury import consumption. With the expulsion of the Asian commercial bourgeoisie, the primary consumer of conspicuous-consumption goods until late 1972, there was a dramatic change in the structure of consumption in the neocolony. Even though the economic base of the petty bourgeoisie has expanded, the change in its consumption habits has been relatively slow. The fall in export production has been more than matched by that in import consumption. Had it not been for the phenomenal expansion in arms imports, the economic crisis—and with it the political crisis—would have been even further delayed.

But the rule of arms has brought into being a tendency of far greater significance in the longer run. This is the intensified appropriation of the producers in the countryside. The tendency in some western regions has been toward the creation of a landless peasantry: a petty bourgeois or an army officer, with the aid of a group of soldiers, evicts small holders from their plots and encloses their land as private property. Elsewhere, a version of warlordism is becoming evident. The local army commanders, in alliance with the local cooperatives, forcibly appropriate both food and industrial crops from the peasants, consume the former and export the latter to either Kenya or Ruanda, circumventing state export agencies and hence state taxation. Under the protective umbrella of imperialism there emerges both a greedy commercial bourgeoisie with an insatiable appetite, unable to challenge imperialist appropriation but dissatisfied with the crumbs on the table, and a landless peasantry whose wretchedness is a recent historical creation. Its ranks expanding with the passage of time, this appropriated rural mass, a natural ally of the urban proletariat, becomes fertile ground for organization by a revolutionary party. Whatever the form of appropriation of the producers, rural and urban, exploitation no longer wears an alien face and its class character emerges in the open. At the same time, those who organized the workers in the years after independence, along with the exiled intelligentsia, after the failure of instant panaceas and the reckless invasions of the two years after the coup, have begun to recognize the necessity of a prolonged struggle and an organization that can sustain it. The order creates its own gravediggers, and the time of reckoning draws near.

NOTES

1. Former guerrilla rebels in southern Sudan.
2. *The Times*, London, 27 January 1971, p. 2.
3. *The Observor*, 23 December 1972; *The Guardian*, London, 19 January 1973; and Colin Legum (ed.), *Africa: Contemporary Record*, p. 3272.
4. It is extremely difficult to verify the extent of the massacres. One attempt to do so by two American journalists, Nicholas Stroh and Robert Siedle, resulted in their murder at the Mbarara barracks in July 1971. The only sources on these massacres are the few victims who have managed to escape.
5. By *private* property is here meant class property, whether the legal form is that of state ownership or individual ownership.
6. This narrative follows L. Stevens, 'Uganda Since the Coup', pp. 15–16, and was checked against the relevant issues of *Uganda Argus*. See also *East Africa Journal*, February 1972, pp. 2–5.
7. To other specifically English forms, slavery and colonial plunder, it is difficult to find even *apparent* parallels in Uganda.
8. Although Amin first attempted to get technical assistance from Germany, and later from Japan, exploratory studies showed that the machinery used in much of the manufacturing industry (such as the sugar factory at Kakira) was so dated that spare parts and technicians could only be found in the Indian subcontinent. The technical structure of Uganda industry was thus one factor compelling Amin to turn to Indian and Pakistani technicians and equipment to avert a serious drop in manufacturing production.
9. The terror, of course, is not directed only at the members of the petty bourgeoisie. Its target includes any potential class opposition to the present order, and any particular opposition to the core of the petty bourgeoisie, the Baganda petty bourgeoisie. Individual progressives of any hue (from university-based progressives to liberals like the university vice-chancellor, Mr Kalimuzo), are killed unless they flee. So are prominent members of the Baganda Catholic hierarchy, those who traditionally opposed the petty bourgeois Lukiko, from Benedicto Kiwanuka (chief justice and leader of the D.P.) to Father Kiggude (editor of the liberal Catholic paper *Munno*). Thus the ambivalent attitude of the petty bourgeoisie to official violence: the same violence that periodically terrorizes its members also eliminates its historical opposition.

13 IAN ROXBOROUGH, PHIL O'BRIEN AND JACKIE RODDICK

Background to the military overthrow of Allende, 1973 [†]

The Armed Forces as Arbiter in the Class Struggle

. . . It was Popular Unity itself which did most to bring the armed forces and their officers into politics, as an 'impartial arbiter' in the class conflict and a political weight on the side of the legal government. This increasing involvement of the military began in December 1971 with the March of Women with Empty Pots—an attempt by the Right to create the kind of detonator which had been used successfully in Brazil in 1964 to bring on a coup. In Brazil, the women and the Church together had taken to the streets claiming that 'all that was most sacred' and the very bourgeois family itself was being endangered, and the armed forces responded.

In Chile, the Right was given a nasty shock. Instead of moving to overthrow the government, the police and the armed forces moved to support Allende. The women coming into the centre of Santiago were dispersed with tear gas bombs after a violent clash between their 'guard of honour' (supplied and armed by Fatherland and Freedom, and the Christian Democrat youth brigade) and some construction workers, well before the march had reached the presidential palace. Many young men of wealthy families and right-wing sympathies were arrested during the demonstration and held incommunicado for a number of days. In the days which followed, a State of Emergency was declared in Santiago, an army general was in control of the city,

† Extract from the authors', *Chile: The State and Revolution*, (Macmillan, 1977), pp. 194–203.

and soldiers patrolled enforcing a curfew in the city's wealthiest suburb. There was even a shooting incident: a young member of Fatherland and Freedom was accosted by soldiers after curfew driving through the suburb, and refused to stop (as it turned out, his car was carrying arms). In the skirmish which followed, the soldiers shot him in the leg. The right-wing press was bitterly indignant.

The events of December marked the beginning of a new right-wing campaign against the armed forces—a campaign which centred on denouncing them as cowards, traitors, men who were weakly supporting the Marxists in government when their first and foremost duty was to defend the nation against the totalitarian threat, people who had 'sold their country' for the price of a slightly higher wage and a few extra privileges. This campaign continued throughout 1972 and 1973, reaching its culmination in May and June 1973, when officers began receiving white feathers through the post—the universal emblem of cowardice. It alternated in slightly schizophrenic fashion with demands from the Right that the military be used to 'guarantee' the government's behaviour in key conjunctures—such as the period from the bosses' strike of October 1972 to the March 1973 elections.

These right-wing attacks on the military gave the government and its different parties a sense of security. With so much venom being expended on the armed forces by the Right, it seemed unlikely that they would move practically to support their denouncers. In March 1972, the police and the armed forces came to the government's rescue again in a situation very similar to that of December. A massive 'March for Freedom' had been organized by the opposition, and the government got wind of a plot by Fatherland and Freedom to make it the occasion for a massive outbreak of violence, and establish connections with some officers to make the violence an excuse for a coup. Another State of Emergency was declared in Santiago, with a general in charge, this time lasting almost three weeks. Police raided the Fatherland and Freedom headquarters and posed for news photos a wide and frightening assemblage of weapons, and hand-lettered placards with slogans like 'Women March for Chile'. The pattern seemed to be confirmed: in case of an offensive from the Right, the forces of law and order would support the legal government. Officers were brought in to Chuquicamata to help the management, because Popular Unity was having increasing difficulty there with the miners (many of them Christian Democrats). There were already rumours that the military might be brought in to the cabinet. It was assumed that they were in favour of a programme of limited reforms. But in essence, so was the Communist Party: the call to 'consolidate the process' seemed to be one which the army and the right wing of Popular Unity might well share.

Two incidents during 1972 should have warned the government that the repressive apparatus of the State would be at best a dangerous ally. In March 1972, after the Santiago State of Emergency was over, the Right called a similar March for Freedom in Concepción. Once again, there was evidence that Fatherland and Freedom were preparing an orgy of violence. The CUT, the MIR, and most of the local party organizations (with the single exception of the Communists) planned a counter-march to attack the Fascist offensive. Permission for this second march was refused, with the president himself intervening to call it off, but the march of the opposition was allowed to proceed. In the event, there were two marches, one of the Right, one of the Left, and the police were brought in to prevent a clash.

In this situation, the police attacked the left-wing march. One student was shot and killed. Forty people were injured, including a fisherman, a MAPU* militant, who was chased by the police up into an apartment building and pushed out of the window. His back was broken and he was paralysed for life. The scale of the violence was obviously not consonant with a restraining action.

The second incident came in August, in Santiago, and it involved a MIR† stronghold, a *población* called Lo Hermida. The police wanted to search the *población* for a known ultra-leftist, not a *MIRista*, but a member of the more extreme 26th of July Movement. According to their story, they asked the *población* to hand over the man, and its leaders refused. So they came back the next morning with 400 men in plain clothes and uniforms, and went in shooting. One inhabitant was killed outright, and

---

* Movement for United Popular Action—ed.
† Movement of the Revolutionary Left—ed.

another was mortally wounded: other leaders were arrested and badly beaten up. The incident caused a great stir within Popular Unity. President Allende himself felt called upon to make a public apology to the *población*, and the Central Committees of the Socialist Party and the MIR jointly headed the funeral procession for the victims. The chief and the deputy chief of the Chilean CID were both fired (both of them were Popular Unity militants, one Socialist, one Communist).

Lo Hermida vividly illustrated not only the ferocity of the repressive apparatus even when nominally it was under left-wing control, but what was perhaps more important, a fundamental political stalemate. In the existing Chilean context of mass mobilization and radicalization, Allende could only 'protect' the foundations of the bourgeois State at the cost of systematic police repression of the masses. The whole of Allende's own strategy and that of the Communist Party led logically towards the systematic repression of 'extra-legal' forms of political action. If the police and the armed forces were to be reconciled permanently to the government, this policy had to be followed through: politically and in practice, the repressive apparatus of the State would not allow the mass movement to flout legal norms and would meet all its 'excesses' with a bitter and violent resentment. But Allende himself could not allow them to make this kind of attack on the movement; politically, a policy of systematic repression would have resulted in the coalition breaking up and, more important, in the alienation of Allende's only political base, the working class. In 1971 and 1972 police frustration was relieved by the persecution of those left-wing groups in the country without real political allies, the various super-Castroites and militarists who stood to the left of the MIR. When in 1971 one such group assassinated a previous Minister of the Interior who had ordered the armed forces in to repress a group of squatters (resulting in 12 deaths), Allende introduced a new statute making political assassination a crime punishable by death. In 1972, a similar but less extreme group was subjected to consistent torture with the excuse that they might have been plotting to assassinate the president. But these were tiny minorities within the country, without real political support. The same could not be said for the MIR, the Christian Left, the MAPU, or the Socialist Party.

Meanwhile, two critical elements in Popular Unity's policy

towards the armed forces were quickly being eroded. As shortages grew, the policy of 'buying them off' became less effective. It was still possible to keep their wages higher than they had been under previous administrations, high enough to match official figures of inflation. But it was no longer so easy for the armed forces themselves to translate this increased money into goods, for black market prices were very high, and goods supplied from official sources were becoming scarcer. The armed forces began to share the general middle class resentment of popular organizations and of the government's erosion of their privileged position as consumers. In the two months before the coup, when Allende's control over the military vanished completely, this resentment was to become overt.

At the same time, 'constitutionalism' was increasingly becoming a weapon for the Right as much as a weapon for the Left, as the class struggle grew fiercer, the opposition of parliament to Allende's programme more intransigent, and the independent action of the working class much more obvious. In 1972, there were several instances of conflict between the government and the judiciary: local judges who were also local landowners, inevitably sided with their class against peasants who were trying to take over farms which had been 'legally' expropriated. One instance in Melipilla near Santiago was so clear that the government itself felt forced to denounce it as an instance of 'class justice'. And obviously, in doing so, it was attacking the judiciary. The same kind of conflict was obvious in parliament, which Popular Unity had threatened to abolish in any case (it was to be replaced by a Popular Assembly): there the majority was clearly committed to forcing Allende to hand back all but a very small minority of the firms which had been taken over. This he could not do, not only because it would have involved an ultimate betrayal of the programme and the workers would not have accepted it, but because the bosses in many industries in which there had been intervention were committed to sabotaging production. The government was in a cleft stick. It could and did refuse to take any action to solve the basic conflict over power which was at the root of all these difficulties. But in the circumstances, even its failings, even its random gestures, were bound to be capable of interpretation as 'unconstitutional'.

In effect, all parties in Popular Unity were guilty of consistently misunderstanding the position of the military in the face of a dramatic social change. For the diagnosis of the Right was largely accurate. There was a sizeable conservative wing within the forces, as the Schneider assassination should have shown, willing in principle to plot against the government but not willing in practice to take on the mass movement. It was a question of nerve. A successful coup would require the armed forces to kill some of their own people: officers like Schneider, who were in sympathy with reforms and would not have supported a dictatorship, and men in the ranks with stronger convictions of class solidarity and perhaps even ties with Popular Unity itself. It would require a willingness to submit Chile to a rule of terror much bloodier than the battle which was then going on in Uruguay, much more vicious than the rule of torture in Brazil. Preparation of that kind of nerve in an army which had never fought a battle took time.

In retrospect 1972 might be christened Popular Unity's 'Year of Illusions'. These illusions came to a climax with the bringing of the military in to the cabinet in early November, to 'solve' the bosses' strike. During the strike, the police and the armed forces had once again patrolled the upper class streets of Santiago: confirmation from the point of view of the government, that they would support it in a crunch. When Allende named his new cabinet on 3 November, with three generals in it, including Prats, the Chief of Staff of the Armed Forces, as Minister of the Interior, he gave as his justification that 'it has been the workers on the one hand, and, on the other, the Armed Forces who have upheld the regime . . . these sectors which have been defending the Constitution and the law'. Thus both trade union leaders (two members of the CUT's* national executive) and generals belonged in a cabinet which was supposed to provide a political response to the right-wing offensive.

The prospect of military men in the cabinet caused an internal battle in the Socialist Party. Its official weekly, *Posición*, produced an editorial harshly criticising the government for taking this step and predicting that military participation would 'put brakes on the process'. There were even rumours that the Socialists had considered staying in the coalition, but leaving the cabinet. That

---

* Central Unica de Trabajadores—ed.

line was overcome, with the token gesture of a Socialist militant from the CUT being placed in the Ministry of Agriculture, as a guarantee that 'ultra-left' policies would continue, and the following edition of *Posición* carried a pointed speech by Altamirano himself lauding the military for their patriotism and declaring that their integration into the Chilean process was necessary and good. But in the event, *Posición*'s first prediction was correct: the net result of military involvement in government was to freeze the class struggle and retard the development of working-class organizations, perhaps in some areas (such as distribution) noticeably pushing it back.

MIR consistently opposed the inclusion of the generals in the cabinet. For the Communist Party, they were not a problem. For both sides, it was thought, were now looking for a 'consolidation' of the process.

At the end of November, General Prats himself gave two public interviews (one to a left-wing journal and one to a right-wing journal) which substantially strengthened the illusions of the Left about its support within the ranks of the armed forces. He claimed that being 'nationalistic and patriotic', the military were in favour of the government's stand against imperialism and the monopolies. He commented that for the armed forces, the strike of the bosses had been a revelation. 'By and large, it was a strike of professionals and businessmen. In previous governments it was the workers who struck against their employers,' he said. 'The country's workers have given an example of great social responsibility during the development of the strike movement, and their social conscience, their sense of order, and their desire to maintain production merit the respect of the armed forces.' It might be considered a slightly backhanded compliment to workers whose 'sense of order' had led to massive development of independent organizations. At the same time, Prats projected once again the picture of a military machine which was unwilling to pay the price of repressing the workers' movement. 'The day the rule of law is broken in this country,' he replied when asked about possibilities of a military coup, 'there will be a state of subversion in this country ten times worse than that which confronts Uruguay with the *Tupamaros*.' The armed forces would have to turn themselves into a specialized military police: this they were not willing to do.

But Prats' public stance as a reformist concealed a more fundamental reason for military participation in the cabinet, the reason which the united opposition had put forward in October in the middle of the bosses' strike, when they demanded that the military join the government to guarantee free elections in March. For the Right, and for large sections of the armed forces as well, military participation was a means of ensuring that Popular Unity would meet 'honestly' an electoral test which they hoped it would lose. From the outset of the strike, ex-President Frei had put forward the position that the coming parliamentary elections were a kind of plebiscite, a time when the nation as a whole could vote whether or not to continue with the government's programme. More optimistically, the Right were hoping that these 'free elections' would give them enough of a majority in parliament to throw Allende out legally (a hope which they seem to have shared with the USA). For one aspect of the Chilean constitution was a provision that given a two-thirds majority of both houses, parliament could impeach the president. The Right in parliament had just under the necessary two-thirds.

Prats himself was careful to keep his public statements of support for the government within the limits set by this electoral perspective. The country had voted to go forward with this programme, and as a soldier, he said, he would support them in carrying out the programme: but the country would have another chance to consider the programme in March.

Thus from 2 November 1972 to 4 March 1973, the military remained in the cabinet, while the country divided ever more clearly into two distinct and bitterly opposed camps, but neither side was able to take any action to increase its own strength. In the end, Popular Unity and its supportors took 44.33 per cent of the vote: enough actually to increase the government's support in parliament, though not to give it the majority. The Christian Democrats were shocked, once again: they had won the 'plebiscite', but with a much lower percentage of the vote than would have been expected on normal electoral predictions of voting strength of Chile's different parties, and they suddenly faced the prospect that by the time of the presidential elections Popular Unity and its supporters might gain a clear majority of the vote.

The Armed Forces Prepare For War

After the elections, Allende once again asked the commanders-in-chief of the armed forces to join the cabinet. This time he had strong opposition from the Popular Unity coalition itself, which temporarily felt strong enough to do without a military prop. But at the same time, the commanders-in-chief were growing much tougher: they proposed apparently four conditions which Allende could not accept. It was the first clear sign that the military were moving into opposition: as one admiral put it to a cocktail party in the wealthiest suburb in Santiago, it was now a matter of waiting for the politicians to discredit themselves completely.

At the same time, the armed forces began to take initiatives on their own to deal with potential threats from the working class. Using the Law for the Control of Arms, which the opposition majority in parliament had passed, giving them the right to conduct all searches for illegal weapons, they began to raid factories and other likely caches for the Left. At first these raids were few and far between. They picked up speed very rapidly after the troops themselves put down an abortive coup on 29 June, at the cost of some of their own men's lives and the lives of twenty-two spectators. The searches seem to have had three objectives.

Obviously, the military were genuinely looking for arms in some places, convinced that the Left was arming itself systematically with help from Cuba and Communist countries in Europe—a belief which had been carefully fostered for a year and a half by the right-wing press. But the officers were also trying out their soldiers: trying them out to see if they would take this confrontation with their class brothers, as a whole, and to identify the individuals who were reluctant to engage in such actions and could be picked off as possible infiltrators from Popular Unity or the MIR. Furthermore, quite clearly, they were trying to terrorize the working class and force it into retreat.

The working class refused to be terrorized: instead, it turned to the government, calling for a 'firm hand' against the Fascists on strike and against what were popularly supposed to be a minority of officers in favour of a coup. Its courage in the face of this kind of terrorization may well have made the repression that much more ferocious, as it encouraged the officers to fear for their own lives.

It is clear that, for some time, the officers had been conducting a kind of propaganda campaign of their own inside the armed forces, a campaign designed to vilify the government and all the parties inside and outside Popular Unity, and to convince the common soldier that if he did not act against the workers, the workers would murder him in his bed. In August, officers in the navy were openly discussing preparations for a coup. Serving sailors and subofficials in Valparaíso and Talcahuano who objected publicly to these preparations, tried to organize themselves to oppose them, and tried to get information to left-wing public figures like Senator Altamirano, were arrested for 'subversion' and submitted to a barrage of tortures to get them to implicate the three major left-wing figures in the 'crime' of preparing an armed uprising: Altamirano of the Socialist Party, Garretón of the MAPU, and Miguel Enríquez of the MIR.

The incidents in Valparaíso and Talcahuano were to be President Allende's most inglorious hour. At first, he himself denounced the 43 men who were under arrest as 'ultra-lefts' who had been preparing an armed uprising, and supported the navy. When evidence began to accumulate that the only crime of these men of the ranks was their public opposition to a coup, he kept silent. When the navy itself moved to charge the three left-wing political leaders with subversion, as well as the sailors, he still kept silent. The 'People's Government' was completely unable to support people in the ranks of the armed forces who were trying to preserve it against the officers' preparations for a coup—it was left to the different parties involved, the Socialists and the MAPU and MIR, to denounce the tortures and lies and bring as much public pressure as possible to bear on the navy to let them go. In the end, Allende refused to give public support even to Popular Unity's own Political Committee, when it brought out an official statement condemning the actions of the navy and the charges laid against Altamirano and Garretón. He thought it was tactically wrong.

There could be no clearer instance of the bankruptcy of 'constitutionalism'. On a key issue of power within the armed forces, whether it should lie with the ranks who supported the Left or the officers who were preparing a coup, Allende gave his tacit support to the officers, and he did so at just the time when the threat of action by the armed forces to overthrow him was at its height, and his need to rely on the common soldiers' class consciousness was greatest. The arrests in Valparaíso and Talcahuano were a clear indication that Allende's policy was madness. On 11 September, the armed forces intervened, united, to defend their officers' own class privileges and the bourgeois order on which those privileges were based.

FOUR:

Third Worldism

Introductory note

There is currently a growing awareness on the part of leaders of third-world states that much of their problems are not merely national or unique but are common and that these may be tackled jointly. In the mid '70s the influence that the OPEC members were ostensibly able to exercise impressed third-world leaders, many of whom have since tried to follow suit by founding joint primary producers' associations so as to bargain as a bloc with the more developed countries, from whom they purchase industrial goods, in the hope of securing a better deal. For example, the forum provided by UNCTAD has been recently dramatically utilised by third-world leaders to challenge the dominance of the industrialised nations in international trade. New forums have been founded—both inside and outside the U.N.—such as the bauxite producers' association, to secure better bargaining positions with trading partners.

This new and developing 'third worldism' or third-world solidarity at the level of states is giving rise to a strong opposition to imperialist domination in trade but also to closer trading and cooperative relations between themselves so as to offset the established patterns of trade, etc. The more developed of the third world countries sometimes stand to gain from this new situation. For example, although Indian industry depends on outmoded technology she is now able to successfully compete with the advanced technology of the West and Japan in Africa where the backward capitalist structures do not require hyper-modern but adequate technology. The promotion of regionalism in the Caribbean by Jamaica which left and thereby ruined the Federation of the West Indies in 1961, augers well for Jamaican manufacturers who are in search of alternative markets for their produce.

This form of cooperation not only reflects the fact that the third world is not an undifferentiated mass, it also represents a response to the increasing concentration of capital in developed capitalism. For example, the growth of the E.E.C., particularly the fact of British membership, has meant many third-world countries have had to search for new trading partners as their hitherto guaranteed markets were lost. The resulting formation of African, Pacific and Caribbean states to negotiate with the

E.E.C. is an example of the growing solidarity between third-world states.

Another aspect of this solidarity has been the resurgence of valuable material and moral support for wars of liberation. In the early days of the nationalist struggle in Africa and Asia, leaders were often aware of each others' struggles but national independence has tended to erode the solidarity of the 1930–60s. Currently, there is widespread recognition of the struggle of the Palestinian people against zionism. The fight against apartheid in South Africa and the struggle to dislodge the minority regimes in the region are gaining wider support, particularly after the defeat of Portuguese colonialism in Africa and U.S. imperialism in Indo-China the struggle against which had brought many forces together.

Furthermore, the crisis within capitalism itself is not only opening wider the contradictions within developed capitalist formations—between monopoly capital and the working-classes, the state and workers, etc.—but is also effecting the radicalisation of many third-world leaders, as prices of their countries' products fall on the world market whilst the prices of industrial goods rise dramatically. This radicalism is finding expression especially in the demand for a 'new economic order' and the call for greater autonomy of politically independent states. These are the themes of President Julius K. Nyerere of Tanzania (Essay 14) one of the leading proponents of the new order, and who has always adopted a gradualist approach to change.

These points are stressed in different ways in the selections in this section. Samir Amin (Essay 15), a leading radical third worldist, stressed the need for support of UNCTAD IV before it met in Nairobi in 1976. He argues that UNCTAD IV 'is our only hope for achieving real progress in the task of changing the international economic order' and recognises that the 'basic prerequisite for such change is unity'.

It may be noted that, as some commentators have variously argued, the demand for a new economic order which allows greater participation in the production of manufactured goods by third-world countries is a progressive one but in the interest of the capitalists from the developed countries where labour costs are rising.

Michael Manley, Prime Minister of Jamaica since 1972,

emphasises the hitherto suppressed fact that Jamaica and the Caribbean are within the third world (Essay 16). Under his leadership therefore Jamaican foreign policy has been to give both moral and material support to the liberation struggles in Latin America and Southern Africa. Manley has also been one of the most articulate third-world leaders calling for a new international economic order and he played a prominent part in the setting up of the bauxite producers' association. Manley's stress on third-world solidarity must be seen however as part of the wider move by Caribbean countries, notably Cuba and Guyana, to widen their perspective of the world beyond the U.S., Canada, the U.K. and the U.S.S.R., their traditional trading partners.

The final say is that of Samora Machel, President of Mozambique and FRELIMO, regarding the liberation struggle in Southern Africa—South Africa, Namibia and Zimbabwe. One of the leaders of the Front Line States (of Tanzania, Zambia, Angola, Mozambique and Botswana) Machel is also the man who led his people to triumph against the Portuguese. His words are not taken lightly by those involved in the struggle.

14 J. K. NYERERE

The process of liberation[†]

I am honoured to have this opportunity to address the Convocation of Ibadan University. In an endeavour to express my appreciation I propose to put before you for discussion some ideas about Liberation—its meaning, and its implications for all of us.

In the 1950s, there was a widespread but unspoken assumption in Africa that freedom from colonial rule would bring with it, almost automatically, the solution to all the ills our compatriots, our country, and our continent, were suffering from. We spoke and acted as if, given only the opportunity of self-government, we would quickly create utopias in Africa, and peace throughout Africa.

Most of Africa is now free from colonial rule. And all of Africa has been awakened out of these dreams! All independent African states are still desperately poor and undeveloped. To a very large number of Africa's people, independence has brought no change in economic conditions, and very little—if any—social change. Progress is very slow when considered in the light of what we know to be possible for life on earth. And injustice—even tyranny—is rampant in a continent whose peoples demanded independence as a remedy for those same evils.

Looking back over the fifteen years or so of Africa's extending independence, and in the full knowledge of our limited successes and many failures during that time, I know that we were right in our united demand for freedom from colonial rule. I know that we are right to support the demand for political freedom which is

† Address given by President Nyerere of Tanzania to the Convocation of Ibadan University, Nigeria on November 17, 1976, from the Tanzanian daily, *The Daily News*, Nov. 18, 1976, p. 4.

still being made by the peoples of Southern Africa, without being deflected by considerations of what might come after. Our mistake was not in our demand for freedom; it was in the assumption that freedom—real freedom—would necessarily and with little trouble follow liberation from alien rule.

To liberate means to set free; to set free from something which inhibits action or thought. Liberation is therefore not an absolute, but a relative, condition. It is relative to a previous experience, to conditions elsewhere, and also to what could be. A shackled man can liberate his arms from bondage while his legs are still bound; he can achieve physical freedom while still being mentally unfree.

Liberation is a historical process. It is not a single action which can be completed and have that completion celebrated annually. And for Africa, liberation has four aspects or stages: first is freedom from colonialism and racialist minority rule; second is freedom from external economic domination; third is freedom from poverty and from injustice and oppression imposed upon Africans by Africans. And fourth is mental freedom—an end to the mental subjugation which makes Africans look upon other peoples or other nations as inherently superior, and their experiences as being automatically transferable to Africa's needs and aspirations.

These different stages are not always and necessarily stages in time. Mental liberation in particular, can for some individuals precede all types of political and economic liberation. But mental liberation is a personal, and individual, achievement. And for most of us, it grows out of active participation in the liberation struggle of our society, our nation, and our continent, rather than preceding these things. It is therefore the social and community aspects of liberation which I shall be emphasizing today.

Liberation from Colonialism and Racism

The foundation of all other kinds of liberation for Africa is political freedom from external rule, and from racialist minority rule. Despite all the horrors that we have seen in independent Africa, I still assert that it is better to be ruled oppressively within a free nation, than to be part of a colonial empire, however mild its rule may be. For colonialism implies the inferiority of the colonised; acceptance of it means an automatic limit to self-respect. Further, a people who do not rule themselves have no power to control their own economic progress, or to fight against other inequalities or injustices within their own community. They are not full members of the world community of mankind, because they are prevented from acting as they determine and therefore from being responsible to their fellow-men for what they do. For the community as for the individual, self determination is both a moral and a spiritual necessity; in order to *be*, we have to *be responsible*—even, and perhaps especially, for our mistakes.

Within Tanzania, and in other independent states of Africa, I have frequently spoken with some scorn of 'flag independence'. But I am able to do this because we have it,—we are independent and sovereign nation-states. Political independence is not enough. But whether or not the journey towards real freedom for the citizens of that country is pursued immediately, no progress towards total liberation is possible until political independence has been achieved.

It must be clear, however, that colonialism is not an obstacle for Tanzania, or Nigeria, only when they are themselves suffering under colonial rule. Our nation states are artificial creations, carved out of the body of Africa. Each is linked—ethnically, economically, and geographically—with all its neighbours. External political domination is therefore of importance to the whole of Africa as long as it survives anywhere in this continent. All of us have a responsibility to give support to those who, by fighting in their own country, are in the front line.

This was true in the case of the Portuguese colonies, it is still true about the struggle for political freedom in Zimbabwe and Namibia. Only the peoples of those countries can fight for their freedom; people have always to free themselves if their freedom is to be real. But no African state is secure in its independence, and no African can rest secure in his own status as a free citizen of the world while any Africans are held in colonial subjection.

These same principles apply to the situation in South Africa. For South Africa is now, since the defeat of Hitler's Germany, the only state in the world which officially endorses and propagates the doctrine that men of one race have the right to govern, to oppress, and to exploit, men of other races, simply because of their race.

In saying these things I am not saying anything which is new—particularly to the people of Nigeria. All the Peoples of Africa, including those of the whole of Southern Africa, want their independence. They want it both as an end, and as a means to an end. That end is true liberation. The People of Africa are determined upon independence in order to use it for their own greater liberation.

Liberation from neo-colonialism

For once it is attained, political power has to be used, and used aggressively, if it is to be followed by an improvement in the day to day lives of the mass of the people. That is the lesson of the last fifteen or sixteen years. It has to be used aggressively not against other peoples of Africa, or against any particular external power, but against the next obstacle to liberation—neo-colonialism.

The reality of neo-colonialism quickly becomes obvious to a new African government which tries to act on economic matters in the interests of national development, and for the betterment of its own masses. For such a government immediately discovers that it inherited the power to make laws, to direct the civil service, to treat with foreign governments, and so on, but that it did not inherit effective power over economic developments in its own country. Indeed, it often discovers that there is no such thing as a national economy at all! Indeed, there exist in its land various economic activities which are owned by people outside its jurisdiction, which are directed at external needs, and which are run in the interests of external economic powers. Further, the Government's ability to secure positive action in these fields does not stem from its legal supremacy; it depends entirely upon its ability to convince the effective decision-makers that their own interests will be served by what the Government wishes to have done.

This is a very serious matter. For it means that if deliberate countervailing action is not taken, external economic forces determine the nature of the economy a country shall have, what investment shall be undertaken and where, and what kind of development—if any—will take place within our national borders.

Neo–colonialism is a very real, and very severe, limitation on national sovereignty. The total amount of credit and its distribution to different sectors of the economy, for example, is determined by the banking system. The persons or groups who control the Banks therefore have a very fundamental—almost a deciding—effect at two points. The first is on the level of current economic activity in a money economy; the second is on the comparative expansion of, say, peasant agriculture as against estate agriculture, or agriculture in general as against the development of local industry or trade. The local agents of foreign banks may well be willing to co-operate with the national government's priorities; but in the last resort their loyalty is, and must be, to their overseas employers. In case of dispute at the top policy level, the government will not be able to enforce its decisions. It may be able to stop things; it will not be able to start things. Matters of vital interest to our development are thus determined externally, without any consideration being given to our interests.

In economic matters, therefore, our countries are effectively, being governed by people who have only the most marginal interest in our affairs, —if any—and even that only in so far as it affects their own well-being. That, in fact, is the meaning—and the practice—of neo–colonialism. It operates under the cover of political colonialism while that continues. Its existence and meaning becomes more obvious after independence.

Neo–colonialism is thus both a reflection of our poverty, and a major factor in its continuation. Winning liberation from it has two aspects. First we have to loosen its grasp on our internal affairs. And secondly we have to deal with its effects on our international economic activities. Of course, these aspects are linked. The actions we take to get control over our internal economy may affect our external trade and may call down counter-action upon our heads. Conversely, plans we make for internal development may be undermined by quite unconnected developments in the international field—by booms and slumps in the major capitalist economies for example. Yet it is possible to make advances internally—that is to gain a large degree of internal economic control,—even while remaining relatively helpless in the international arena.

The fight against neo–colonialism, however, is a more difficult process than attaining political independence. In the modern world environment there is more political odium than glory attached to the possession of colonies. For a colonial power, the continuation of its rule over a colony therefore becomes primarily a question of how best to safeguard continued access to markets, and to raw materials, on an exploitative basis. And this exploitation is not affected by flag independence, as such. The colonial power may consequently decide to agree to political decolonisation, and it will often make this decision with the active support of powerful economic interests in its own country.

But when the people of an ex-colony demand economic independence, they are demanding an end to external exploitation. This would give no commensurate gain to the neo–colonialist forces, and even the mass of the people in the exploiting nation would be adversely affected by it if they have secured a reasonable share of the wealth gained from the exploitation of others. It is thus very clear that the demand for economic independence will meet with great resistance.

That is the first point of difficulty. The second is that it was easy to secure national unity in opposition to classical colonialism. Even those who received some benefit from our political masters did not really want to maintain the status quo. Whether they were active in the struggle for independence or not, they hoped to gain from it, using their education or other privileges as a stepping stone to political or economic leadership in the new state. But opposition to neo–colonialism will not be so unanimous. Some of our people identify their own personal interests with the existing neo–colonial situation. They are to be found among the local agents of foreign capitalists, and among the local capitalists who have developed in the shadow of large foreign capitalists, and among the local capitalists who have developed in the shadow of large foreign enterprises. Such people may feel that their wealth and status depend upon the continued dominance of the external economic powers.

And thirdly, although everyone understood that colonial status was a humiliation for the nation and its people, such recognition is not universal in relation to neo–colonialism. Indeed, there are Third World countries which accept their neo–colonial status, and even glory in it. They point to the statistics of their Gross National Product as an example of what can be gained from it—rather in the manner of a high-class prostitute glorying in her furs and jewels!

For these among other reasons, fighting neo–colonialism requires great realism. It also involves hard economic choices which have serious political implications. For example, getting greater control over our own internal economic affairs means putting emphasis on the use of our own productive and human resources—and adopting the appropriate technology. It means a deliberate orientation of development in order to build up a self-generating internal economy instead of one directed outwards. Further, it means concentrating our few resources on producing goods needed for the expansion of the economy and for the basic needs of the majority: we cannot continue allowing the private possession of wealth to determine what goods are produced or imported and therefore available in our shops.

The obvious implication of the fight against neo–colonialism is thus the development of a planned economy, including an Incomes and Wages Policy, as well as control over major investment decisions and of imports. This has nothing to do with socialism—although I speak as a socialist. Fascists also plan! The point is that in a free enterprise economy the internal production pattern, and the import pattern, are determined by the effective demands of the wealthy rather than by the national policy decisions. This is true whether national policy favours the needs of the majority and of the future, or supports some less admirable internal objective. And the wealth of the world is concentrated outside our own borders; there are rich individuals in African countries, but they are usually either remnants of past feudalism or the agents or compradors of external economic interests.

It must be clear that liberation from neo–colonialism also involves for our poor countries the deliberate rejection of Western standards of consumption both for individuals and for the society. Instead we have to establish, and to implement, economic goals more appropriate for our present and our expected level of national wealth–production. Any African country which looks at the pattern of consumption in the United States and Western

Europe, and decides to 'catch up', is bound to fail. It will not have the resources to do it. Western standards of living are based on the exploitation of the rest of the world and of their own poor people. To the extent that an African nation does succeed in introducing these consumption standards—or in maintaining them for the privileged—its success will be based on the creation of a small class of very wealthy people, who are exploiting a large class of very poor people.

Yet the self-reliance we have to aim at is not the same thing as self-sufficiency. All African states are, of necessity, involved in the world economy, and we shall continue to be involved whatever changes we succeed in making in our internal economic structure. It is therefore essential that we should also seek to weaken the forces of neo–colonialism as they operate at the level of internal exchange and finance.

Internationally the poor nations are like unskilled workers trying to sell their labour to a few employers, and like beggars trying to buy goods in competition with millionaires. An alliance of the poor nations in their dealings with the rich nations and with the trans-national Corporations, is the only way in which dependence can be converted into the normal inter-dependence of international trade. Co-operation among the poor nations— that is, trade among themselves and joint enterprises—is the only way in which they can maximise their own development in their own interests, without remaining utterly dependent upon the vagaries of fashion and technology in the developed countries. The fostering of developments in these directions is one of the tasks that our young countries have to undertake in the battle for economic liberation.

The struggle for personal freedom and justice

Although I have said that the fight against Neo–colonialism is much more difficult than that against classical Colonialism, both are directed at external forces. They are national struggles which can unify the vast majority of our people. The future Tyrant and the Democrat can work in unison against foreign rule. The existence of a number of One-Party states of Africa can be traced back to this fact. Similarly, the local capitalist, or potential capitalist, can join with a socialist in the economic liberation struggle, in the hope of replacing the foreign exploitation by his own. Thus unity simplifies and strengthens the national cause in both cases.

In the struggle for personal freedom and justice within our independent state such unity is inevitably broken. For it is an internal struggle, in which ideology or personal interest replaces nationalism as the motivating force.

Achieving internal liberation means enabling all the citizens of a state to live in conditions of human dignity, personal freedom, and justice. It necessarily involves the acceptance of human equality as the basis of all social attitudes and structures. It is therefore not an abstraction, nor an individual condition. The aim cannot be to enable each individual to do as he likes, regardless of the effect on others. For man cannot be divorced from the society in which he lives, and he certainly cannot achieve freedom in isolation. The objective of this final liberation struggle must be to secure for each individual as much personal freedom to develop himself—or herself—as is consistent with equal freedom for all other individuals.

Every economic, political, and social decision is thus relevant to this struggle for freedom. It is not the absence of legal or conventional restraints which marks its success. For personal freedom, and personal well-being do not come as an automatic by-product of individual actions,—although enlightened self-interest can be harnessed to the pursuit of social purposes. It is achieved by the deliberate joint action of people working together for their common good, on a basis of their human equality.

The internal liberation struggle involves a struggle for civil rights, both positive and negative. Freedom from political oppression, from arbitrary arrest, from baseless slander and from socially unnecessary restriction on liberty of expression, movement, and organisation, are all part of this. So too is freedom of religion and worship. But these things, by themselves, are not enough.

I am a socialist. I do not, and cannot, believe that we can leave economic questions out of account when we are considering human freedom. For the freedom to starve, to be diseased, or ignorant, is not a freedom which I am willing to accept for myself or for others. And I cannot believe that the poverty of our people was irrelevant to their struggle against colonialism.

People have to work in order to overcome poverty. But work will not end poverty for the individual or the society—if the product is extracted from the worker, either by laws, by custom, or by theft and trickery. A struggle for freedom therefore involves opposition to those local people who secure, and use for their own benefit, the natural resources of our land: laws and practices which facilitate this have to be changed. Real freedom requires a struggle against the exploitation of man by man including our own tendency to exploit others, or to acquiesce in that exploitation if we derive some benefit from it. Also it connotes a struggle against men's tendency to demand, rather than to give, service and respect.

Freedom from exploitation is an essential part of human liberation. But just as political equality and freedom is incomplete and insecure without this movement to economic equality and dignity, so the economic freedoms are insufficient on their own. True liberation requires political democracy and economic democracy. For the individual as for the nation, political freedom is incomplete without economic freedom, and vice versa.

For man in society, there is no inconsistency between these two aspects of freedom. Few people regard the prohibition on murder as a limitation on their freedom. Slavery is not accepted as necessary to the individual freedom of the potential slave-holder. It is equally absurd to think that the power to exploit another is essential to human liberty. Exploitation of one man by another is both immoral and anti-social. Human liberty is extended by its abolition not by its legalization.

The total struggle for liberation is complex

The three different aspects of liberation which I have talked about today are inter-linked. The moral case against oppression in Southern Africa has been made more difficult because of tyranny and inhumanity in free Africa. Foreign economic interests entrench themselves by co-operation with local exploiters and the use of local agents. And African nations have to survive economically and politically if the struggle for real liberation in Africa is to continue.

Compromise on the inessentials, and a scale of priorities, are unavoidable for African Governments and Peoples. Our states and organisations have very limited resources; not every injustice or example of exploitation can be fought at once. Attempting to do so can be an invitation to disaster, and to the triumph of reaction.

Further, enemies and friends in the liberation struggle cannot be indentified by their colour, their national origin, or their ideological label. There are friends of human rights, and economic justice, in the rich world and in the colonial states. There are traitors to the liberation struggle among the poor, and among the exploited.

The struggle for human liberation, in all its aspects, is thus a difficult, complex, and continuing one. There will be genuine differences of opinion about priorities, and about measures, among people who are all working for the same end. The opponents of liberation will use these differences for their own purposes. And it is difficult—if not impossible always to make the right judgement on national and international issues; indeed, only posterity can really tell which is the right judgement! Even while we act on it, we need always to remember that our decision may be wrong and to respect the humanity of those who disagree with us.

But it is imperative that the struggle for liberation should continue against colonialism and racialism, against neo–colonialism, and against oppression and exploitation within our own lands. And for this we, the immediate post-independence generation of leaders and educated citizens, have a special responsibility. For in our young states the national ethic, and the political and economic conventions, are still being formed. Each one of us has to choose the part he or she is going to play in the liberation struggle.

We can concentrate on our personal advancement and individual freedom from restraint. Or we can choose to give service to our fellow-men, and thus to ourselves as members of the society. If we choose the latter, we shall be working for social and economic justice, with emphasis on the needs of those under-privileged and deprived who now constitute the majority of our fellow-citizens. We shall be working for liberation.

15   SAMIR AMIN

UNCTAD IV and the new international economic order*†

For the past two years it has become a 'tradition' for the United Nations General Assembly to hold an extraordinary session in addition to its regular one, a practice imposed by the non-aligned members of the Group of 77. Efforts are now being made to turn these extraordinary sessions into a permanent feature of the General Assembly, for they provide a forum where the Third World can express its views. It was during these two extraordinary sessions that the themes and objectives of a new international economic order were defined and adopted through resolutions and recommendations put forward by the non-aligned group. Within the United Nations family, UNCTAD constitutes the developing countries' main weapon because the institution was set up at their own request to study the specific problems of their integration within the world system and to help create a common platform which would enable Third World countries to unite and so negotiate from a position of strength.

The political problems of the Third World were more or less formally 'solved' when most of our countries became independent in the three decades following World War II. However, this political independence was limited because it was generally unaccompanied by sufficient internal or external changes for real economic independence. The international economic system has remained basically unchanged during the past thirty years (in Africa it is fundamentally the same as during the colonial period) and economic dependence is as strong today as it has been for the past century, despite the fact that some changes have seeped

* Translated from the French.
† From *Africa Development*, vol. 1, no. 1, May 1976.

through in the international division of labour. The issue now is whether or not we are entering into a new phase in the battle for our real economic independence. Obviously, this battle presupposes not only internal political and social transformations but also international changes which in turn could facilitate or complicate those transformations.

Over the past twenty five years, the Third World has experienced a pattern of dependent development within which economic growth has merely been a by-product of expansion and growing prosperity in the economic centres of the developed world. The by-product of this prosperity was not only extremely unevenly distributed among our countries but also, within each, among the different social groups. The Third World supplied raw materials and energy in unlimited quantities and at constantly declining prices to meet the insatiable demand of the developed world without in any way considering its own short-term, let alone long-term, interests. Energy, and more specifically oil, provides the most striking example of the plunder of natural resources in underdeveloped countries to boost prosperity and growth in the already developed nations.

Dependent development

Dependent development has proved to be a total failure and the bill is a heavy one—a staggering increase in poverty and famine in Africa where land is generally plentiful, massive rural migration, chaotic urbanization, proliferating slums, permanent and growing unemployment, increasingly flagrant inequalities in income distribution and, consequently, the penetration of consumption patterns and ideologies of the dominant countries. Furthermore, this 'development', which in isolated cases has given rise to relatively high growth rates, has been extremely uneven among Third World countries. It has clearly accentuated the inequalities, in terms of wealth and development, between the nations of the Third World and, particularly in Africa, between those states which by a freak of nature are well-endowed in resources much coveted by the West—oil, copper, bauxite— and those that have, or appear to have, nothing. Even in geographically medium-sized countries this dependent development has resulted in marked regional inequalities, for it has generally polarized around the capital or, occasionally, around mining or plantation areas. It is against this background that over the past decades a number of contradictions have arisen in our countries leading to the present situation where Third World states have decided to engage in battle for a change in the international economic order.

The main issues in this important battle are well known: (a) raw materials and basic commodities, including energy; (b) industry and trade in manufactured goods; (c) the transfer of technology; (d) the international monetary system; (e) uneven development among developing countries; and (f) economic cooperation between Third World countries. These are also the main topics to be discussed at UNCTAD IV in Nairobi in May and it is to be hoped that the conference will bring forth a minimum, if not a maximum, degree of agreement so as to enable the Third World to confront the rich nations as a relatively homogeneous bloc with very precise demands. This is our only hope for achieving real progress in the task of changing the international economic order. The basic assumption here is that the prerequisite for such change is unity, a unity which given the right momentum and direction could facilitate the necessary, nay essential, internal transformations by thwarting the intentions of those in a position to exert pressure on developing countries taken in isolation.

Raw materials

As far as raw materials are concerned, the Third World has—for at least twenty years—been fobbed off with slogans about price stabilization and the need for special measures to do away with erratic price fluctuations, supposedly due to the laws of supply and demand but in reality only the result of political considerations and political pressures on the Third World. These arguments no longer hold water, which does not mean that stabilization measures have become totally useless but rather that we have become much more demanding; what *we want now is a substantial and stable increase in the price of raw materials*. Without the remarkable victory of OPEC many of us would probably still consider this demand to be wishful thinking. The success of the oil-producing countries is encouraging and clearly shows that the relative prices for raw materials, as compared with those for manufactured goods, are determined neither by inexorable 'economic laws' nor by a *Deus ex machina* in the form of supply and demand, but purely by political power relations. The oil cartel, mainly made up of American monopolies, was in a position to impose unfavourable prices on our countries. These were clearly political prices and now the oil-producing countries have retorted by imposing a different political price and one that, so far, has held good.

The same could apply to all raw materials of which we are the main suppliers as well as to a large range of strategic mining products and some agricultural commodities which, even if they appear to be less vital, are in fact equally strategic because of their strict inelasticity within the consumption patterns of the rich countries. Yet it is an established fact that the price paid to our producers for all those commodities is extremely low, whereas the prices paid by the consumer at the other end have kept up with the pace of initially creeping and subsequently runaway inflation. The result is that the producer did not benefit from this economic situation because his income did not rise and neither did that of the state since it could not raise the level of indirect taxes on these commodities. This clearly shows that the prices *are* political and only we can reverse the trend by imposing other political prices which correspond to different international power relations.

The time has come not merely to produce precise technical studies on each of these commodities but also to make concrete proposals for producer agreements and price indexing. That should be one of the main objectives of the Nairobi conference.

There is, however, another and more fundamental issue than prices, namely control over the exploitation of natural resources. With independence, the Third World generally inherited economic and commercial structures whereby multinational corporations were in control of most of its resources. The situation has changed, albeit unevenly, both with regard to the countries concerned and the commodities involved, through a series of legal measures such as nationalization, control of foreign trade, marketing, etc. In a large number of Third World countries, especially in Africa, concessions for the exploitation of natural resources were granted in a shameless manner by the colonial administration. Royalties were a matter of mere formality—let it not be forgotten that gun-boat diplomacy was never an empty threat. In some countries many of these agreements have now been revised and in others governments have gone one step further either by becoming majority sharehlders in such companies or by completely nationalizing their assets, with or without compensation. However, it has now become clear that the legal ownership of a company does not guarantee control and that at best, nationalization is an instrument which must be strengthened by the formulation of long-term policies for developing natural resources. However, in so far as we are integrated in an international trade system, we have certain financial needs and must therefore continue to export. These financial needs should be defined in accordance with our prospects and potential for internal development. In the long term, we must take measures to protect our natural resources and preserve them for our own use. Up to now, the system has functioned as if we were automatically obliged to satisfy the demand of the developed countries and spontaneously adjust to their needs. We have been compelled to supply, without any restrictions whatsoever, unlimited quantities of commodities through the exploitation of our natural resources, our subsoil and our soil.

Here again, the discrepancy between the developing and the developed world is striking. Not one country among us could force Canada, for instance, to supply wood or to exploit its timber resources at any rate other than that decided upon by Canada itself. No Third World nation is in a position to compel the United States to supply wheat in any quantities or at any rate other than that determined by the American administration. No one could force Poland to exploit its coal more intensively and to export it to those of us who need it. These countries are considered to possess full sovereignty and are able to decide for themselves whether or not to develop, to export or to preserve any of their own natural resources. But in the case of our states, every time we even mention slowing down exploitation of our resources, we hear cries of 'embargo!', 'unilateral decision!' accompanied by the usual threats. When the oil-producing countries, very modestly, spoke of an embargo or of limiting production, these threats became even more vehement than when the question of nationalizing the oilfields was raised. In a number of cases such nationalization measures have been accompanied by agreements entered into with multinational corporations not only to determine prices but also—and even more important for the developed centres—to guarantee supplies at a given rate. This, in effect, constitutes an attack on our sovereignty, which is not just legal but also political, for in no way is the sovereignty of developed countries similarly restricted. The Nairobi conference should, therefore, consider the establishment of export ceilings for each commodity or group of commodities. This would set the stage for the battle to win control over the exploitation of our natural resources to suit our medium- and long-term needs.

Industry and the transfer of technology

The second issue concerns industry, which I will link to the transfer of technology. Over the past twenty five years, the Third World as a whole has achieved industrialization rates, however uneven, which in the eyes of the most optimistic proponents of the system could appear truly remarkable. The average growth rate for the Third World, and even for Africa, is higher than the rate of industrial growth in the developed world. Thus, by mechanically projecting this trend into the future, the optimists are claiming that we shall be able to catch up with the developed countries as far as industrial output is concerned. A projection of between 2 and 3 per cent annual industrial growth over a period of twenty, thirty or fifty years could produce any required result, at least on paper.

It has now become clear that this import-substitution industrialization model, despite its high growth rates for some countries, cannot be prolonged indefinitely because it has produced and intensified an increasingly unequal internal income distribution and demand structure which has now reached its ceiling. Many Latin American countries have long since reached this ceiling which explains their present dramatic plight. Few African countries have as yet attained this level, with the possible exception of Egypt, but in view of the small size of

African markets and the very low level of industrialization—with no more than a few tens of thousands employed in industry—we are approaching this point.

In addition, external dependence is reinforced by import-substitution industrialization, both because of the consumption pattern on which it is based, the increasingly unequal income distribution it generates and the high degree of technological dependence which in turn is linked to the consumption pattern. Certain needs must be satisfied—and I am not referring to the needs of the masses—in such a way as to ensure that the goods produced are more or less competitive with similar imported goods. Such an industrialization model has increased not only moral and intellectual but also financial dependence through the transfer of technology. A small part of this process is revealed through the payment of royalties for patents, registered trade marks, etc. But that is only really the tip of the iceberg. What lies hidden underneath in the form of unequal prices for the cost of technology and capital goods (to serve this technology) is quite staggering. Very instructive studies have been carried out on this precise point, particularly by the Lima Group in Latin America. With the possible increase in the prices of raw materials (likely to be highly uneven since the strategic importance of commodities varies), some countries will find themselves in a better financial situation, as is the case for the oil-producing countries at present. This will enable them to think in terms of a further stage of industrialization, but because of technological dependence the spontaneous response of the system is to establish outward-looking export industries to supply the developed countries.

This is indeed in accordance with the conventional view of development. The line of reasoning is as follows: 'We have a cheap production factor available, namely labour (and some-times other cheap factors too, such as raw materials) and we could therefore sell these factors cheaply to the developed world by producing industrial goods for them.' This is nothing more or less than selling our labour cheaply in the form of consumer goods which, if they were to be produced in the developed countries would cost ten to twenty times more in wages even though productivity is the same in both cases. However, even this battle is far from being won, for the developed countries feel sufficiently sure of themselves to demand that we not only sell our labour cheaply but in addition subsidize these industries; in other words, make the peasants and the whole of our population pay to subsidize those poor consumers in the rich countries!

An alternative model of industrialization can be put forward, i.e. industrialization for ourselves, based primarily on the satisfaction of domestic needs and, as a matter of priority, the needs of the masses both at national level and at the level of groups of developing countries. This represents a different strategy for industrialization, one that does not rely mainly on the transfer of technology but on the development of a self-reliant capacity for technological research geared towards meeting the needs of the mass of the people of our countries.

The international monetary system

The crisis in the system of the international division of labour first appeared in the sixties as a crisis in the international monetary system. The post-war prosperity of the west had been built on the hegemony of the dollar, which was the monetary symbol of the economic and political domination of the United States over the western world as a whole and over our countries as western dependencies. This hegemony was first threatened by internal transformations within the developed world itself through a crisis in the American balance of payments, the accumulation of dollar reserves in Europe and Japan, the growing external debts of the United States, which for its creditors was becoming an increasingly bad debt, and finally, the *de facto*, followed by the *de jure*, devaluation of the dollar. The result was utter confusion and a gradual deterioration in the Bretton Woods system of multi-lateral transfers.

The trend, therefore, is towards isolating monetary systems from the international system. Even during the 'great boom', the Third World never really participated in the international monetary system whose virtues (the 'advantages' of unlimited transferability, the relative stability of exchange rates, the liberalization of trade, etc.) were extolled by one and all. The reason is the structural imbalances in the system, caused by our dependence on and over exploitation by the developed world. In these circumstances, we could only draw marginal 'benefits' from the system and it is unfortunate that in the present state of confusion some of us still believe in the need for re-establishing the international monetary system at any cost, for it is thought to be a good thing in itself because of those publicized virtues. In the struggle for establishing a new international monetary order, the Third World only occupies a passenger seat. It is true that every country officially has one vote within the United Nations system, but the situation is quite different in such organizations as the International Monetary Fund, where the richest countries have pride of place with a voting quota proportional to their wealth and 'importance' within the world system. The struggle was, and will no doubt continue to be waged between the United States, Japan and Europe with the Third World being manipulated rather than actively participating. Committees, like the Committee of 20, have been convened by one or other of the protagonists to suit any changes in their tactics or strategy, only to be forgotten immediately afterwards. What is important is whether concurrently with this battle which certainly is not ours the Third World can evolve a different strategy for strengthening its monetary and financial relations. This, I believe, would carry greater weight whenever decisions are taken within the international system.

Less developed countries

The situation of the less developed countries provides a further illustration of uneven development as a result of the dependent development strategy practised over the past thirty years. There is nothing mysterious about that situation, it is totally within the logic of the system. However, those responsible for promoting dependent development are now using its consequences as an argument to divide the Third World. Crocodile tears are being shed about the so-called 'Fourth World' whose peoples are said to be the victims, not of the dominant international system, but of those countries 'lucky' enough to have 'benefited' from a higher degree of integration within the international system.

There are evidently conflicts of national interest and they will persist for a long time to come even among developing countries; the crucial point now is to make sure that these conflicts are resolved among ourselves, through agreements and negotiations that would enable us to present a common front *vis-à-vis* the developed nations and not allow these secondary contradictions to override the primary contradiction between us and the developed world. If we fail in this we shall allow ourselves to be manipulated for the benefit of those who dominate us all.

Economic cooperation within the Third World

If the outcome of the Nairobi conference is agreement, or at least some measure of progress, on the issue of economic cooperation, it will be definite proof that UNCTAD has struck a new path. If not, we shall have every reason to be pessimistic, because it will mean that the new international economic order for which we are fighting would only be an empty shell, pure window dressing. The result would be a series of compromises and minor concessions, with the Third World further divided and the process of uneven development more accentuated.

Much remains to be done, for the current conventional approach to economic cooperation is based on the establishment of common markets; because of cultural and ideological alienation, we are trying to imitate structures created in other regions for a very definite purpose, i.e. the furtherance of independent developed capitalism. Our problems are fundamentally different and we must learn to plan together, to think in terms of complementarity in order to arrive at agreements and mutual concessions for the self-reliant development of our countries.

Conclusions

The outcome of the battle for a new international economic order is uncertain. The most innocuous and yet probable end result is that the whole question will be reduced to a series of minor compromises. There is cause for concern at the almost universal approval of the principle of a new international economic order and we may well suspect that the issue has been emptied of all substance. Efforts to shift the debate and concentrate on a few aspects only, such as the recycling of the financial resources of the oil-exporting countries, are highly suspect for they suggest that the industrialized countries are trying to take back with one hand what they have conceded with the other.

This battle for the new international economic order must not be used as an alibi for failing to deal with internal development problems. Development is above all a national issue, a problem of transforming domestic social, economic and political structures. Foreign relations merely reflect internal structures, but they can be used either to reinforce negative aspects or to bring about positive changes. Priority must therefore be given to our own self-reliant development at a national level and to collective self-reliance and collective autonomy within the Third World. With a policy of national and collective self-reliant development, the Third World would be in a better bargaining position and more likely to obtain real changes at the international level, whether on prices for raw materials, control over production or any other issue.

This battle will not be an easy one. It will become even more difficult in the next few years and already 1976 promises to be a year of deepening world economic crisis. This crisis is already grave and has been marked in the United States and Europe by unemployment on a scale unknown since the thirties, combined with slackening growth at a time of galloping inflation. Inflation was slowed down in 1975 because of world-scale deflationist policies in the developed countries, but a reversal of the trend is planned for 1976 in an attempt to reduce unemployment. The United States, Great Britain, Germany, Italy and other countries are due to hold elections and one can therefore expect a recrudescence of runaway inflation this year. The developed countries are planning to shift the main burden of this inflation onto the Third World by, among other things, recovering part of the benefits obtained by the oil producers and by accelerating the deterioration in the relative prices of all raw materials; but above all they will try, through the International Energy Agency, to break OPEC and to bring down the price of oil from 10 to 12 dollars to the floor price of 7 to 8 dollars in accordance with American policy.

The attempt to force the developing countries to bear the brunt of the crisis will have violent repercussions. A Dakar

newspaper recently reported that a 'great power' had threatened
to reduce its aid to Senegal because, allegedly, Senegal had voted
too often against its policy at the United Nations. Such crude and
direct language had been used rarely in the past but is likely to be
heard more often in future. Is there not a direct link between our
battle and the financial crisis of the United Nations? It is no secret
that this crisis arose as a result of the response of certain developed
countries to the growing majority which the Third World, the
non-aligned, represented at the United Nations General Assembly. There was never any talk of financial crisis in the United
Nations when it was still a political instrument of the great
powers. Things are rather different today and the United Nations
could well become a forum, however modest, where the voice of
the majority of mankind may be heard. Hence the threat to cut
the purse strings! The financial crisis will provide a pretext for
increasing attacks against those in the Third World who are
trying to turn the United Nations into an instrument capable of
serving its peoples. This, then, is the time above all when priority
must be given to the Third World and, particularly for us
Africans, to African unity and Afro-Arab unity.

16 MICHAEL MANLEY

The Caribbean and the Third World[†]

Foreign policy begins with the perception of self-interest. In the metropolitan countries foreign policy is regarded as an automatic and critical element in government strategy. The combination of size, economic power and sheer experience which are a part of the situation of a metropolitan nation leaves its people in no doubt as to the importance and relevance of this aspect of government. This comprehension is harder to come by in the case of a newly independent territory particularly if that territory lacks either size or major economic significance or both.

In any event the reality of the colonial experience is likely to have left in its wake a failure to appreciate that a country's relations with the rest of the world can be as important to its development as the relationship between the various parts of itself within its own territorial boundaries.

In the case of a country like Jamaica we find all three disabilities (geographical, economic and perceptional) present to an unusual degree. Jamaica is small. Apart from its bauxite industry its disappearance from the world scene would create scarcely a ripple on the total surface of the world's economic relationships. Finally, our experience with colonialism went on for so long as to create a near paralysis of judgement in the area of external relationships. As a consequence it has taken Jamaica quite a period of time in the immediate post-independence period to begin to appreciate all that is involved in its external relations. Long habituated to trade with Great Britain, the

† From the author's, *The Politics of Change: A Jamaican Testament*, (Audré Deutsch, 1974), ch. 3.

271

United States and Canada, the average Jamaican even at the start of the decade of the 1970s found it difficult to comprehend the possibility of a relationship between Jamaica and the rest of the world. This is so despite the fact that communist Russia has long been our best customer for pimento and despite the fact that we recognised communist Yugoslavia shortly after independence. These were disconnected, one might almost say disembodied, events which seemed to hang suspended in the midst of a general assumption that the real world began in Miami from whence it proceeded due north to Canada swinging vaguely eastwards through Newfoundland but ending irrevocably at a line that might be drawn between London and Edinburgh.

It is obviously important for Jamaica to retain its friendship with this part of the world and if possible to extend and deepen its economic relations with the United States, Canada and Great Britain. However, the perpetuation of dependence upon these three relationships is inimical to Jamaica's long-term interests and is only favoured by those who remain frozen in the postures of yesterday.

Jamaica is a part of the Third World. By the Third World one means that entire range of countries, mainly tropical, that were the scene of the great colonial explosion which reached its crescendo in the latter part of the nineteenth and the first part of the twentieth centuries. All of these territories stretching as they do through the Caribbean, Africa, India and the Near and Far East were used as sources of raw materials and primary agricultural products destined for the great manufacturing centres which were mainly concentrated in Europe. After the Second World War a reverse political process commenced led by India and quickly to be followed in the Caribbean, Africa and the rest of the colonial world. In short order all the former colonies had attained political independence. However, without exception, these territories entered upon political independence suffering from enormous economic disabilities.

We live in a world of instant communication. This ensures that, in a manner never experienced by mankind before, both standards of living and the ideas that attach to them experienced in one part of the world become part of the consciousness and, thus, the immediate aspirations of everyone else in the world. As a consequence, implicit in the popular support for political independence is the notion that independence should confer upon the newly liberated people the economic benefits and standards enjoyed by their former colonial masters. However, the basic economic equations which were left behind as the colonial tide receded made these popular aspirations impossible of early satisfaction. As is now well understood, all the newly independent territories have found themselves trapped in an economic dilemma. Their trade is established in traditional patterns with the metropolitan powers. In these patterns, the former colonies supply the basic materials which attract the smallest share of the 'value added' of the total economic process. These are exported to our metropolitan partners and in return we import the manufactured goods and the products of heavy industry which represent the lion's share of the 'value added' of the total process. To begin with there is this disequilibrium between what the former colonies have to offer and what our metropolitan partners supply. To make matters worse the prices of raw materials and primary agricultural products show an historic tendency to instability around general levels that do not tend to rise. On the other hand, the prices of manufactured goods in world trade tend to be consistent within a pattern of steady increases. As a consequence, and as is well documented, it takes more and more tons of Jamaican sugar to purchase an American or British tractor as the years pass. Hence, the terms of trade which are inherently against us to begin with, tend to move increasingly against us.

Finally, the former colonial territories entered upon their independence desperately short of capital and of the means to accumulate capital for themselves at a rate consistent with the consumer standards which their people had come to expect. As a result, it is vital that these territories should be able to attract overseas capital. However, we find ourselves once again in a dilemma because the price of money and hence the terms on which capital is available moves steadily to our disadvantage. So all these territories share a common dilemma of high expectations, disadvantageous trade and insufficient capital which it is increasingly expensive to attract.

A country like Jamaica cannot begin to formulate a foreign policy until it understands its place in relation to this general world problem. Since the Second World War Jamaica has sought to solve its problems by assuming, as a constant of policy, that the United States, Canada and Great Britain represented the total horizon of our opportunities. Hence it was felt that insofar as there was a foreign policy at all, it consisted of seeking favours from these countries in the form of economic aid and special price supports for certain products like sugar, bananas and citrus. The combination of this foreign policy together with a certain view of economic strategy, . . ., had brought us by the 1970s to the totally unsatisfactory situation which we sought to analyze.

Where results are the opposite of intentions it behoves a man to re-examine his strategies. Let us therefore begin by taking a fresh look at a foreign policy for a country like Jamaica.

The first thing that we have to appreciate is that in economic terms size is increasingly a pre-condition of survival in the world. Hence a first thrust of foreign policy for a small country must be to seek to become part of a larger economic region which provides a larger basic market together with greater opportunities for economic specialisation. Once this is grasped it is not too difficult to move to the second leg of a foreign policy which flows from the recognition of the common dilemma of the Third World.

In Jamaica's case the break-up in 1961 of the abortive West Indian Federation created a general ambivalence towards regionalism even in its economic form. It is *not* the purpose of this book [Manley's] to debate the issue of political Federation which is closed for the time being. It *is* the purpose of this book, however, to point out that the emotional consequence of the political trauma of 1961 must never be allowed to cloud our judgement of contemporary reality. It is vital to Jamaica's future that we should play our part in the creation of a Caribbean Common Market[1]. This involves many steps and considerable technical adaptation but the objective must be clear and must be of an eventual scope to include all the countries of the Caribbean regardless of their ethnic, linguistic or political characteristics. Indeed, in the broadest sweep of history, economic regionalism must be seen as extending to include all the countries of Central and Latin America which embrace the Caribbean. Guyana and Belize represent geographical out-posts and are historical pioneers of this concept. Belize, Guatemala, Honduras, El Salvador,

Nicaragua, Costa Rica, Panama, Colombia, Venezuela, Guyana, Surinam, French Guiana and Brazil all form a natural economic region bounded by Barbados to the east and stretching up through Cuba, the Bahamas to Bermuda to the north. Geography and a shared colonial history combine with the characteristics of Third World underdevelopment to create a region that is just beginning to awaken to the fact that it shares a common, manifest destiny. This grouping contains the resources, the diversity and the scale of potential market to make it one of the viable and exciting development areas of the world. Furthermore, if its people can summon the historical vision and political common sense to move beyond the apparent ideological differences within the region, they could demonstrate to the rest of the world a new approach to the question of foreign investment. The Caribbean contains capital exporting countries like Venezuela as well as a number of nations which must still seek to import foreign capital and technology. However, all the countries of the region have suffered from exploitation at the hands of foreign capital and are, therefore, well placed to learn the lessons of history and to evolve new relationships in which the movement of capital is responsive to the needs and national objectives of both the exporting and the host countries.

The challenge of the future is to shake off the shackles of yesterday's assumptions which have delivered us into a separatist trap. The logic of tomorrow's possibilities unfolds in the larger context of regional co-operation and economic integration. This is so for precisely the same reasons that make it logical for the countries of Europe, after two thousand years of conflict, to form an economic block now. It is so for the same reasons that connect the respective economic accomplishments of America and Russia to their sheer size.

The perception that leads one to the conclusion that economic regionalism is a logical pre-condition of accelerated national development must now be applied to the world situation. It is one of the tragedies of the post-colonial period of all those countries which we now loosely describe as the Third World, that they have permitted themselves the luxury of ideological distraction. Quarrelling constantly about political matters, they have been woefully slow to appreciate their common economic dilemma and the importance that attaches to the development of a global

Third World economic strategy. Since every Third World country is faced with the same dilemma in its dealings with the metropolitan world it follows that Third World countries need to develop a unified response to these problems. Here it is my belief that one must begin with the principle of self-reliance. Consequently the first element of a Third World strategy must be the exploration of every single possibility of trade as between Third World countries. Every act of trade within the Third World reduces the general dependence upon metropolitan economic power. This is a largely unexplored area of considerable potential. But it is an area that will only be explored if Third World countries have the will and the determination to bring together their collective expertise to the study of trading possibilities between themselves.

Second, it is critical that the Third World should create its own institutions for savings and development. In addition we must develop policies of investment in projects that reflect Third World priorities. It is also important that Third World countries begin to exchange information about technology since, as we discussed in relation to economic planning, their own technological discoveries are often more likely to be relevant to each other's problems than the discoveries of more advanced nations. Thus beginning with Caribbean regionalism, a Jamaican foreign policy must be Third World in its economic orientation.

Finally, a foreign policy must recognise that we must, to a certain extent, continue to import capital and know-how from the metropolitan world. Despite the greatest application of internal, regional and Third World self-reliance this will continue to be so for some time. However, this must involve an 'open' foreign policy as distinct from the 'closed' policy of the past which only envisaged relations with our traditional partners. In this way our capital can be sought from a variety of sources and on a wide range of terms. This is an important insurance against foreign domination which is far more likely where the sources of foreign capital are concentrated in one quarter.

Of course, implied in the idea of Third World trade and indeed in the whole concept of an 'open' foreign policy is the matter of trading with countries whose ideologies and political systems differ from one's own. Because of the sheer inexperience of the world which is produced by colonialism there are many Jamaicans who imagine that an exchange of goods in trade involves a rubbing-off of political taint. Obviously this is nonsense. Trading with communist countries, for example, does not import communist ideology into Jamaica nor for that matter does trade with Spain import Spanish fascism. All countries that are involved in trade do so from the posture of their own political systems and it is a betrayal of national self-interest to fail to seek out in the world at large those points of advantage to one's own economy. However, a distinction must be drawn at this point. One may refuse to trade with a particular country not because exchange might imply the transmission of a taint, but to exert diplomatic pressure. Hence, Jamaica does not trade with South Africa, Rhodesia or Portugal as a protest against apartheid, political repression and colonialism. In each case the policy involves the rights of a subject people and is, therefore, an appropriate target for international sanctions.

As I have indicated, trade between Third World countries is to be desired in itself because it reduces the incidence of something else that is working to our disadvantage. But even in our relationships with the metropolitan world it is fatal to believe that one's self-interest can be successfully pursued in one limited arena. There have been times in history for example, when America, Canada and Great Britain between them represented a disproportionate percentage of the world's economic power. These were the great capital exporting nations. And so our dependence upon them in the past may have been supported by a temporary historical logic. Today, however, the situation has changed. The United States and Great Britain both suffer from currencies that are under heavy pressure in the period of the 1970s and are no longer basically capital-exporting countries. On the other hand, there are countries in Europe and half-way across the world there is Japan which are the capital-exporting countries of today. A foreign policy that ignores this fact is unnecessarily limited with respect to its available options.

Obviously, if one needs to import capital and technology one must search in the areas where there is the disposition to export these commodities. In the context of an open foreign policy these options are available. Where the foreign policy is closed one may not even notice the new arena of opportunity.

Naturally, changes in foreign policy in a country like Jamaica are yet another example of things that disturb the collective unconscious in its uneasy slumber. But these things must be faced. The old way is disturbed so that the path to new opportunities may be opened. In all this Jamaica has, it is my firm conviction, a historic mission to fulfil. Our present circumstances place us firmly in the Third World. Our historical conditioning has fashioned us an essentially tough-minded and pragmatic mould. Surely, therefore, we are capable of the emotional adaptation to a Third World commitment to a new world order. I am equally confident that we are sufficiently adept, by experience, in the ways of the economic world to bring a cool pragmatism to bear upon Third World passions so that these may be guided into a constructive pattern of economic action and co-operation without which the dream of those who were dispossessed can never be brought to fulfilment.

In another context when we talk of an open foreign policy we are seeking to establish the fact that the entire world is the stage upon which a country, however small, pursues this perception of self-interest. Nor does one have to conclude that self-interest is either an immoral or an amoral phenomenon. National self-interest for example, leads no wise man into war. War has often been the resort of fools like Mussolini or knaves like Hitler. They shared a common fate. And even successful wars of aggression set in train forces that undo the temporary advantage that they may confer. The only wars that are morally justified in history are those dedicated to national liberation where it is clear that no other method can succeed. Therefore a policy of enlightened self-interest will commend to any intelligently-led nation the conclusion that peace is in every man's interest in the end. Hence every country, and Third World countries even more so, has a tremendous investment in the success of the United Nations. But even as a supporter of the United Nations, it is also important that our foreign policy reflect a clear adherence to principle and the expression of those principles in the councils of the United Nations. Very often international problems are so tangled as to render the detection of a principle extremely difficult. The commitment, however, must be there. One can illustrate the difficulty by two examples, one of which represents a case of obvious clarity and the other a case of perplexing difficulty.

On the one hand a country like Jamaica must be totally

dedicated to the active support of all those measures that can lead to the overthrow of the apartheid regime in South Africa, the Smith regime in Rhodesia and the Portuguese tyranny in Angola and Mozambique. In other words, where wars of liberation for the purpose of establishing national freedom are being fought, the objective of freedom legitimises them and commands our unswerving support.

On the other hand, if we take the case of terrorism we see a completely different picture. If terrorism is defined in a manner that includes African wars of liberation it is very difficult to see how one can oppose it. However, terrorism in the sense of hijacking planes, the slaughter at the Munich Olympics and indeed all acts that seek to involve innocent third parties as a means of applying pressure to an enemy represent outrages against humanity which are intolerable. The problem is how to distinguish the legitimate from the rest. One might retort that there is no situation in which violence can be justified at all. I am instinctively passivist and intellectually a part of the non-violent tradition of Gandhi and Martin Luther King. However, where one is faced with a tyranny like that of South Africa, one is forced to concede that there is not the remotest possibility that non-violent methods would lead to either the overthrow of that regime or even its substantial modification.

Can one, therefore, say that the black African does not have the moral right to resort to arms in the pursuit of freedom? And which metropolitan nation would dare to deny this right? The commitment must be to principle but tempered with a cautious recognition that many of the issues of international politics bristle with difficulty. In fact, it is the very complexity of these problems and the tensions that they create in the world that makes it so imperative that the United Nations itself survive and increase in influence and strength in the world. Hence a foreign policy must include a concern for everything that affects peace in the world which in turn implies a constant vigilance about international relations generally.

A relevant foreign policy for Jamaica might, then, be summarized as involving a positive commitment to Caribbean economic regionalism; the search for a common Third World economic strategy; support for the United Nations; unswerving commitment to the right of self-determination for small countries; support for policies that seek to express a commitment to international morality as distinct from cold assessments of self-interest in the context of world power politics; and an 'open' concept in which Jamaica seeks to maintain its traditional friendships while reaching out for the widest possible creative contacts in the economic and cultural field[2].

Within the framework of such a broad policy one has got to consider the problem of the multi-national corporation which, as we pointed out earlier, represents the most recent and complex expression of the problem of foreign capital in international affairs. A multi-national corporation is, of course, a single company which operates different aspects of a total industrial process in different parts of the world. For example, in the case of the aluminium industry, you can find a single company with headquarters, say, in the United States of America which may mine bauxite in Jamaica, Surinam, Australia, parts of Africa and the United States itself. Its alumina operations may be conducted in any or all of these countries. Its aluminium smelting will be sited predominantly in the United States but it may have smelters in one or two other countries. The extrusion and fabricating processes will again certainly be heavily concentrated in the United States but there may also be plants in some of the countries where one or more of the other operations take place; or it may have fabricating operations in some completely different country. Thus, with our decision-making process concentrated in one country like the United States of America, such a corporation will operate important aspects of its total business in a number of other countries.

As a consequence of this diversification of activity, the multinational corporation is peculiarly insensitive to social and political control because no one segment of its business is concentrated in a sufficiently large measure within one area of political jurisdiction. Political decisions in relation to its operations tend to have very slight impact on its total economic operation and can, therefore, be far more readily ignored than would be the case if the whole or a large part of its operations fell within the focus of a single political jurisdiction. Of course, its headquarters are always located in the metropolitan power of origin, but that is precisely where there is least likely to be exerted the kind of political pressure in the realm of policy that would be likely to be consistent with the needs and interest of some far away, developing nation. Hence, its greatest point of vulnerability is also that point where it is least likely to be subject to social pressure. On the other hand, it is in the small developing countries, where its operations may have a substantial impact on the welfare of the particular nation and where, therefore, there is the greatest need for social and political control, that it is least vulnerable to pressure and the hardest to control.

It is not possible to conceive of an answer to the multinational corporation outside of the context of international political co-operation. Interestingly enough, the workers movement, in its dealings with the multi-national corporation, has long since recognised the importance of co-operation. Realising that single unions trying to tackle one limb of the multi-national 'animal' would be up against disproportionate bargaining power, the international trade union movement embarked sometime ago on a studied policy of international union co-operation so that it could begin to match the bargaining power which, in the case of the multi-national corporation, can only be measured in international terms. Equally, Third World nations faced with this problem are going to discover that their most effective response to this phenomenon lies in practical co-operation between governments that are involved. The world has already seen a striking example of what can be accomplished at this level in the operations of OPEC. Through international action, oil producing countries have had a striking success in terms of prices for crude oil and in the area of internationally accepted levels of taxation and profit sharing in their dealings with the oil companies. Sources of primary ore such as bauxite and other metals are going to have to travel the same route if they hope for a similar success. Of course, there are difficulties inherent in the situation which are not easy to overcome. For example, bauxite exporting countries will be substantially affected in their struggle by Australian attitudes now that Australia has arrived on the aluminium scene as a major source of bauxite ore. Obviously, Australian co-operation would enormously facilitate progress since it would represent a significant addition to the bargaining power of the group. But even if particular countries will not co-operate, the rest must take up the challenge because a start has to be made somewhere.

It must also be understood that this problem cannot be seen exclusively in terms of prices for basic ore. Effective policies in relation to multi-national corporations have got to take into account the entire range of processes that go to make up the total industry and must consciously seek to secure that secondary and tertiary processes are located within the Third World alongside the basic mining processes which are the first stage of a particular industrial process. Policies should also be evolved aimed at securing a reasonable measure of contribution by multi-national corporations to the development of vital infrastructure.

In short, the presence of the basic minerals which are needed for the metropolitan industrial process should be used by the Third World as a whole, as a means to securing a basic contribution to the development of wealth. In addition, these resources should be used as the spring-board for the planned development of the entire complex of industries which are associated with the basic resource. Finally, resource development must be associated with the creation of the infrastructure which is needed to support the sophisticated economic linkages that are involved. Furthermore, this kind of approach should not be pursued apologetically as if one were seeking metropolitan favours. Rather, it should be seen in the same clear-eyed, businesslike way as the metropolitan economic interests view Third World resources. The metropolitan operation is un-sentimental and explicitly designed to obtain the most ore at the least possible cost – and without apology. Equally, we must plan to secure that we trade the least ore for the most benefit and must realise that in this context, benefit has a number of sophisticated ramifications and does not end with ore prices and royalties alone.

To succeed, a policy in relation to basic resources requires the rapid development of a considerable expertise to ensure that Third World countries really understand the capital, market, technological, transport and other implications of the various industries that are involved. Coupled with expertise, there must be Third World unity if policies of this kind are to succeed. Obviously, unless one Third World country happens to be in a very powerful position as a supplier of a particular raw material, it will find that it is in danger of being isolated when it attempts to bargain alone. If the Third World as a whole, however, establishes a policy of industrial groupings evolving joint policies and maintaining joint pressure within the context of general Third World political support, bargaining power will be enormously enhanced and progress facilitated. Once again, it is important that this kind of Third World initiative should not founder on any ideological rocks. The nationalisation of particular assets is only one aspect of a possible total strategy. At a given point of time some countries may wish to pursue this particular aspect to further their own national interest and others may not. What is important is that the Third World should not fracture its capacity for a generally unified strategy on account of particular differences in this regard.

One of the practical issues with which Third World countries must grapple in the immediate future is how to create permanent institutions that are capable of formulating specific proposals in these areas such as the relationship with multi-national corporations, questions of trade, exchange of technological information and development finance. The great problem is that the Third World has so far proven itself stronger in the realm of ideology and rhetoric than in formulating specific programmes of action. It is to this latter exercise that we are now summoned by our circumstances.

And it is here precisely that the Caribbean can make a tremendous contribution to the Third World and, indeed, that Jamaica can make a tremendous contribution to the Caribbean and, through its natural region, to the larger community. Caribbean man, if one may be forgiven the term, is the product of almost unique historical forces. The element of total transplanting together with an equally total absence of an historically indigenous population yet all joined in the bitter equation of colonialism, has created a people who are not quite like any other. If we could discover the key to self-confidence, we would find that our true strengths outweigh our weaknesses and that these strengths are not necessarily in over supply in the postcolonial world. It would be true to say that the Jamaican citizen is not naturally at home in the world of ideas and that political ideas are no exception. He is, on the other hand, a person of enormous adaptability and blessed with a rugged, humorous pragmatism which gives him a remarkable capacity for resilient survival. I choose the word 'resilient' because it imports a sense of readiness for progress. There are people in history who have responded to suffering with such bitterness that they succumb to a kind of smouldering anger which makes them destructive in outlook. There are also people who invest ideas with such passion that they become hysterically incapable of constructive action. In this regard, the world looks askance while the Irish wage a hot and brutal war ostensibly around an issue that should surely be *passé* by now. But somehow it is difficult to imagine a Jamaican reducing himself to progressive impotence in the name of a sectarian squabble. Somehow, he would cool the religious passion with humorous insight and leave his energies free to cope with the more practical exigencies of providing for his family. Hence, compared with many others the Jamaican personality may be less likely to trigger a heroic novel but is more likely to be involved in an economic miracle.

Beginning with his natural gifts of resilience and pragmatism, Caribbean man has demonstrated formidable prowess in the field of economic adaptation and political action. Colonialism left him with the negative legacies of an uncertain sense of identity, uneasiness in the world of ideas and an often unattractive appetite for conspicuous consumption. But it also left him with positive strength in the areas of political and economic action and in the mastery of the professions. The Caribbean, therefore, can serve as a bridge between the more extreme forces of the developed and the developing world. The role involves a constant summons to economic co-operation amongst developing nations. Equally, it involves the development of a persuasive diplomacy from growing strength aimed at the great economic powers. This policy must seek co-operation in the construction of a new world economic order based upon the concept of equity in the distribution of the world's wealth.

Sharing the situation and the experience of the former colonial peoples yet adept in the ways of the colonisers, the Caribbean can contribute greatly to the capacity of the Third World to translate ideas into action and to the possibility that the metropolitan world will modify traditional courses of action by the acceptance of new ideas.

Sooner or later the entire world must face this challenge of a new world order. Whole generations are emerging in both the metropolitan and the Third World that have been conditioned by the incessant preachings about international brotherhood, peace and goodwill. Increasingly the power brokers whose propaganda machines churn out this message of love while pursuing national self-interest with the most studied cynicism, are under critical scrutiny. Just as the forces of education are creating a man who will no longer accept the cruel simplicities of economic authority, so too is this same man increasingly questioning the credibility of the world power establishments. The process by which cynicism in the use of power in international affairs is modified is slow and painful; but slowly and surely progress can be observed. It may be that one cannot always attribute progress to enlightenment. Often, what appears to be progress is merely the discovery that the crude pursuit of self-interest can be self-defeating. But even if the lessons are learned in a negative way, a slow process of modification is taking place nevertheless. Furthermore, it is probable that metropolitan conduct will respond more quickly in the face of Third World . unity where that unity expresses itself in practical action and is the beneficiary of calm and lucid articulation in the councils of the world. The Caribbean can make a significant contribution to both sides of the equation and can, in the process, help to accelerate the positive circumstances of its own progress.

NOTES

1. The Treaty establishing the Caribbean Common Market was signed at Chaguaramas, Port of Spain, Trinidad, on 4th July 1973. The date, which is the anniversary of the birthday of the Jamaican National Hero, the late Right Excellent Norman Washington Manley, was chosen as a tribute to his contribution to Caribbean Regionalism. The location was chosen as a similar tribute to the Prime Minister of Trinidad and Tobago, Doctor the Right Honourable Eric Williams.

   Signing were Barbados, Trinidad and Tobago, Guyana and Jamaica. The author signed on behalf of Jamaica.
2. For a full examination of Jamaica's position in relation to Caribbean Regionalism, see 'Overcoming Insularity in Jamaica' by the author published in the American quarterly *Foreign Affairs* in the October edition, 1970.

17 SAMORA MACHEL

The liberation of Southern Africa and the struggle against imperialism* †

On behalf of the Mozambican People and the Government of the PRM, we warmly welcome the distinguished delegates and observers. We welcome you to Maputo, a trench in the battle between freedom and colonial oppression, on the confrontation line between democracy, human dignity and the monstrosity of racism. We welcome you to Mozambique, a border between human rights and fascism.

After the defeat of Portuguese colonialism in Mozambique, Humanity was able to extend her liberated zone to the doors of South Africa, a colonial and oppressive stronghold. This is a victory of our people's just liberation war, this is a victory of the cause of the United Nations, a victory of the action of the Committee of 24, a victory of your political and diplomatic battle for the implementation of the historical resolution 1514 (**XV**).

Freedom and Peace are indivisible, the security of Nations and human rights are inseparable, they are in the same compartment. The existence of an atmosphere of war in southern Africa, the growing tension in this region which threatens to involve the whole of humanity, is the direct result of colonialism and racism which still exist here. No country or man can remain indifferent to the Soweto massacres, to the death camps, to the beheadings and hangings in Zimbabwe and Namibia.

Confronted by the masses' continuous revolt, the colonialists and racists are striving to extend their internal conflicts to all

---

* Original in Portuguese. English text furnished by the Mozambique delegation.
† Address to the United Nations International Conference in Support of the Peoples of Zimbabwe and Namibia, held in Maputo, Mozambique, 16–21 May, 1977, from, *Decolonization*, no. 8, July, 1977.

neighbouring countries, in order to deflect attention from the essence of the conflict. We therefore witness a multiplication of subversive acts, border violations, provocations and aggression. The colonialists and racists intensify the arms race and lately try to step up into the stage of the atomic arms race.

Wishing to maintain the broad masses in a sub-human condition, so that a handful can live in a situation of incomparable privilege, the colonialists and racists are trying to provoke a generalised conflict, to transform their internal conflicts into clashes between great powers.

. . . The situation in Zimbabwe, the situation in Namibia are colonial situations. Colonialism is condemned by the whole of Humanity, by all member countries of the United Nations Organization, it constitutes the most serious form of violation of the people's right to choose their destiny, it represents the most violent form of aggression against the rights of man.

We are meeting so that together we may find the fastest and most efficient means of definitely liquidating colonialism in Zimbabwe and Namibia. We are meeting in order to find the fastest and most efficient means of totally transferring all powers of sovereignty and their exercise to the only legitimate owners of those powers: the people of Zimbabwe and Namibia. The United Nations Charter and the Resolutions which guide us are clear, our mission is to liquidate colonialism and racism. In order to find the just solutions we must clarify some fundamental points.

Over and above specific historical aspects, in Zimbabwe and Namibia we are faced with typical colonial situations. In Zimbabwe and Namibia colonial domination and oppression led the people to take up arms for their liberation. This was the only alternative left to them. The people had to choose between dying as a consequence of colonial oppression and taking up arms in order to live in freedom and dignity.

We feel it is wrong to talk of peaceful solutions when there already is war. We must realistically seek the means to put an end to the war. To put an end to a war means to eliminate the causes of the war. Practical experience has demonstrated that a colonial war can only end in one of two ways: the military defeat of the colonial forces or the colonial forces' acceptance of the people's right to their total and complete independence.

The successes of the armed struggle in Zimbabwe and

Namibia, combined with the political and diplomatic action of the international community and particularly the United Nations Organization and the Organization of African Unity have made the colonialists aware of the inevitability of their defeat in Zimbabwe and Namibia. This has created favourable conditions for a negotiated settlement of the existing wars. To be successful a negotiated settlement demands that the representations of the colonial forces fully accept the right to total and complete independence of Zimbabwe and Namibia in full territorial integrity. Some positive steps have been taken in this direction. Nevertheless important obstacles still exist.

Of late, we see with apprehension that certain forces, although declaring their acceptance of the principle of independence, are trying to annul it through guarantees to be conceded to minorities. Trying to understand the nature of these minorities, we find that we are not dealing with any national minorities. In fact what is happening is a subtle manoeuvre: to define minorities exclusively on the basis of skin colour, the minorities being presented as whites.

In almost all United Nations Member States there are citizens of the most varied ethnic origins. We find millions of citizens who belong to ethnic and racial groups different from the majority of the population. Nevertheless they are citizens like everyone else and they are not treated as a minority. The appearance in those countries of citizens of different races and colours results from the historical evolution and form the economic and social development of those countries.

In all African, Asian, Latin American countries, in all countries which have been subjected to colonial domination, settlers existed. Settlers are the direct result of colonial domination. They are foreigners, who for different reasons related to the colonial phenomenon, came to inhabit the dominated territory. They are settlers and not a national minority, they are foreigners who live in the territory. With the accession to independence of the dominated territory, some of these foreigners, some of these settlers, wishing to be integrated in the new country became national citizens. They are not a minority, they are citizens like the others, without any privileges or discrimination. This is the historical experience of all colonised countries.

We see no reason why the settlers of Rhodesia or Namibia should be treated otherwise. To do so is an attempt to preserve colonialism. To do so is to maintain in the country a category of citizens, very small in number but with sufficient power to block a decision of the vast majority of the population. To propose such a solution to a country which has just lived through the horrors and hatreds of a colonial war is to sow the seeds of a serious conflict in the first hours of independence. Our preoccupation is that all, regardless of race or colour, be citizens equal in rights and duties, citizens capable of being integrated in the community and strengthen national unity.

The experience of negotiations in all countries which were colonised is that negotiations take place between the representatives of the patriotic forces and the colonial power. The colonial power represents the interests of the settlers and the patriotic forces represent the interests of the masses.

We see in the negotiations which have been taking place both on Zimbabwe and on Namibia, a violation of this principle, a violation which has led the negotiations to failure.

In Zimbabwe the settlers refuse to be represented by the colonial power and wish to present themselves as a third force, since they cannot claim to represent the interests of the masses which they massacre and the patriotic forces which they fight. These are the settlers, whose numbers decrease daily, according to statistics, these are the settlers whose vast majority has a second nationality, who effectively behave as foreigners and, as in the experience of all colonial countries they leave the country after independence, these are the settlers who have repeatedly been responsible for the failure of all negotiations. The mistake is to regard them as the fundamental and decisive interlocutor, the mistake is to allow a tiny group of privileged foreigners the power to create obstacles to the implementations of the interests of the majority.

In Namibia we are surprised to see talks of settlers' parties and their puppets. Everybody knows who is fighting for Namibia's independence. Everybody knows who is imprisoned, deported, murdered in Namibia for demanding independence. Because the sacrifice of the black people of Namibia, the struggle of the oppressed and humiliated of Namibia forced South African colonialists to accept the principle of independence, today, the privileged whites of Namibia use their parties, which maintained colonial domination, to be represented as an interested party in the liberation of the country, when in fact they represent the force which hinders the liberation of the country. This state of affairs prevents a fruitful discussion between the patriotic forces represented by SWAPO and colonialism.

We are told that in Namibia the main stumbling block to a negotiated solution is the existence of only one nationalist movement—SWAPO—and we are told that one movement alone cannot claim to represent the interests of all the people. Simultaneously we are told that in Zimbabwe the lack of unity creates an obtacle to the discussions, the difficulty is the existence of many nationalist movements.

It would be convenient to use some logic to know the real obstacle to national independence. The only obstacle to national independence is colonialism.

The manoeuvres preventing the success of negotiated solutions to the colonial wars in Rhodesia and Namibia have been given decisive support by some Western circles and powers.

The United Nations have repeatedly denounced and condemned foreign investments in colonial territories. At Great Britain's request the United Nations' Security Council decreed sanctions against the British colony of Southern Rhodesia.

These sanctions have been fully implemented by the People's Republic of Mozambique, by the Republic of Zambia and by many other countries, with heavy sacrifices to their economy. We nevertheless see that they are openly and systematically broken by other United Nations Member States including Western members of the Security Council. Many arguments are presented in defence of these violations.

We are told that the paralysation of economic activities would be detrimental mainly to the black population. We are told that the pursuit of those economic activities in no way contributes towards the pursuit of the colonial wars. These same countries which violate sanctions, during the Second World War took drastic measures to isolate completely the fascist powers; they dealt heavy reprisals against companies which dared to trade with the fascist powers, they confiscated those companies' assets, arrested, tried and condemned those who were responsible. In the defence and in the name of freedom those countries rightly built up a legal arsenal of repression against those who dared collaborate with the fascist oppressers. If today those same countries refuse to undertake severe measures against those who collaborate to strengthen the potential of the fascists, colonialists and racists of southern Africa, it is surely because sordid interests have made them join sides with the inhuman camp against which they formerly fought.

It equally surprises us that citizens of Western countries members of the United Nations, citizens of Western countries members of the Security Council, are freely recruited as mercenaries for the rebel forces of Rhodesia. Once again the argument is in defence of liberty and the right to travel. However, we believe that in no country is the right to treason, the right to crime taken to be part of the democratic rights of citizens. The countries which allow the recruitment of mercenaries to Rhodesia, even today contain in their legislation extremely severe dispositions against citizens who commit crimes of treason and who collaborate with forces hostile to the country. The non-implementation of those principles can only mean that the fascist, racist and colonialist system has become an ally.

A special responsibility for prolonging the conflict falls upon those who supply the military means which enable the colonialists to continue with the policy of internal repression and colonial war and extend armed aggression to other countries. Although the United Nations clearly forbid the sale of weapons to southern Africa's colonialists and racists, we see a continuous reinforcement of Pretoria's and Salisbury's arsenal. We are sure that any responsible state has ample means at its disposal to prevent transactions of weapons which are contrary to its interests. Therefore the supply of weapons, the supply of patents for manufacture, the establishment of arms industries, the establishment of industries which can lead to the nuclear armament of colonial and racist régimes can only be interpreted as active support for the systems condemned by the United Nations.

The evolution of the Zimbabwe situation is favourable. The armed struggle for national liberation has inflicted serious drawbacks upon the rebel, minority régime. The patriots' victories galvanise the enthusiasm of the masses and bring about their increasing organization and mobolization to eliminate the rebels. The sanctions decreed by the United Nations and applied by many countries including the People's Republic of Mozambique have seriously affected the already shaken economy of the British colony of Southern Rhodesia. The entire international community unanimously condemns Salisbury's cruel régime, condemns its criminal policies, condemns its massacres.

The creation of the Patriotic Front constitutes a decisive step in the unity of the people, in the efficiency of their struggle. The Patriotic Front provides for the broad masses of Zimbabwe the instrument to deal increasingly heavy blows against an odious and isolated régime.

Britain's initiatives can constitute a positive factor in the liquidation of the colonial, racist system in Rhodesia, so long as these initiatives have as a sincere objective the complete independence of Zimbabwe. They will fail if they aim to legalise colonialism; they will fail if rather than a total transfer of power to the people they aim only at allowing some black puppets to have a share of colonial, racist power. They will fail if their aim is to institutionalise privileges based on skin colour, if their objective is to preserve the interests of the so-called minorities and not of the overwhelming majority.

On Namibia, the United Nations have often held debates and proposed the just way for the solution of the conflict. Resolution 385 of the Security Council taken in its whole constitutes such a platform.

The recent initiatives by the five Western members of the Security Council, if based on this context, will contribute to the acceleration of the resolution of the conflict. If, however, once again they are aimed at safeguarding interests which are alien to the people and privileges for the settlers, if they contribute to the divisions of the territory and the appearance of puppets as pretentious valid interlocutors, then the initiatives will only serve to uselessly lengthening the conflict.

The question of Walvis Bay is an artificial one, an inheritance from Anglo–German rivalries during the Berlin Conference of 1885. In Africa we respect inherited borders even if they are not just, but an attempt to include the enclave of Walvis Bay in this context is only an attempt to sabotage the independence of Namibia in its territorial whole. There are no citizens of Walvis Bay and citizens of Namibia. It is the men of Namibia, it is the sweat of Namibian workers which account for the existence of Walvis Bay: when we talk of the territorial integrity of Namibia, we logically talk of the integration of Walvis Bay.

It is with SWAPO, recognised by the United Nations and by the Organization of African Unity that the South African government must discuss the process of the transfer of its powers to Namibia.

As in the past, the People's Republic of Mozambique carries out her internationalist duty in relation to the liberation struggle of all peoples and in particular the peoples of southern Africa. She supports the armed liberation struggle of the people of Zimbabwe and Namibia. She will continue to apply full sanctions decreed by the United Nations.

Like all peace-loving countries, like all countries which have lived through the devastating experience of war we are ardent defenders of peace, we support peaceful solutions in all regions in which the conflict has not yet reached the armed stage, we try to find negotiated solutions to the existing wars. This was our experience.

When the Portuguese government recognized our right to independence, accepted a date for our independence and agreed with us on the mechanism of transferring power, it was logical and easy to establish a cease-fire and re-establish peace.

We believe peace can be re-established in Zimbabwe once there has been agreement on the mechanism leading to independence, since the colonial power has recognized the right to independence and has agreed with the patriotic forces on the ceiling date for the independence of the Territory. We believe that the people of Zimbabwe, the people in concentration camps, the men killed in the streets for not carrying a pass, the men arrested arbitrarily, the men massacred in their peaceful villages, the men who, underground and in the guerrilla war, build the independence of their country, have the right to demand immediate and complete independence. All the other territories of the former Federation of Rhodesia and Nyasaland are independent, they have all celebrated more than 10 years of independence. To demand immediate independence is not an act of extremism when independence should have taken place already more than 10 years ago, when a tiny handful of foreign rebels supported by imperialism has for almost 12 years kept the country under the most fierce, cruel and barbarous form of oppression.

Our Conference in support of the liberation struggle of Zimbabwe and Namibia must decide on measures which politically, diplomatically and materially strengthen the liberation struggle. It must adopt measures to isolate the colonial and racist régimes because by isolating them we force them to negotiate. Our Conference must aim for measures to be taken against any economic and commerical investment or collaboration with the colonial and racist régimes. It must equally propose that the international community reinforce the economic capacity of the front-line countries to enable them to better support the southern African people's liberation struggle.

. . . A luta continua.

Bibliographical note

There are some good reasons why this is a brief bibliographical note rather than a comprehensive bibliography covering the literature on developments in the third world. First, taken as a whole, the papers included in the selection already supply what amounts to a fairly extensive coverage of the available material bearing directly on the questions of politics and state. Second, the literature on the third world forms not only an impressive body but is also a rapidly growing one. To draw up a bibliography therefore, which would do justice to writings on the third world is a task which is beyond the scope of this book which seeks only to focus attention on state and politics in these regions. These factors then, suggest a highly selective bibliography which aims at supplementing the literature mentioned in the individual contributions to this volume.

An early text bearing the title 'underdevelopment' is Agarwala, A. N. and Singh, S. P. (eds.), *The Economics of Underdevelopment*, (Oxford University Press, 1958), which contains some classic statements on development from the left as well as from the mainstream of bourgeois economic thinking. Of far greater importance and influence is Baran, Paul A., *The Political Economy of Growth*, (Pelican Books, 1973), first published in 1957. In addition to the works of Amin, Samir, referred to in the contributions in this volume, his *Neo–Colonialism in West Africa*, (Penguin Books, 1973) and *Accumulation on a World Scale: A Critique of the Theory of Underdevelopment*, (Monthly Review Press, 1974), 2 vols., are of considerable importance in the radical reply to development theorists. A wealth of material is to be found in the following books which bring together some of the best statements made against development theory:

Bernstein, H. (ed.), *Underdevelopment and Development*, (Penguin Books, 1973), the second edition of which offers an excellent critical bibliography; Girvan, N., (ed.), *Dependence and Underdevelopment in the New World and the Old*, (Institute of Social and Economic Research, University of the West Indies, 1973), which gives a good coverage of the Americas as well as other regions of the 'third world'; De Kadt, E. and Williams, G., (eds.), *Sociology and Development*, (Tavistock Publications, 1974); Oxaal, I., Barnett, A., and Booth, D., (eds.), *Beyond the Sociology of Development*, (Routledge & Kegan Paul, 1975; and Gutkind, P. and Waterman, P., (eds.), *African Social Studies: A Radical Reader*, (Monthly Review Press, 1977), which, apart from giving a very generous selection of writings offers an invaluable biblio-graphical guide by Christopher Allen who also renders this service every month in the radical journal *Review of African Political Economy*.

Some of the texts which inform much of the emerging marxist critique of radical underdevelopment theories are:

Marx, K., *Capital: A Critical Analysis of Capitalist Production*, (Progress Publishers, 1974).
—, *Capital: The Process of Circulation of Capital*, (Progress Publishers, 1974).
—, *Capital: The Process of Capitalist Production as a Whole*, (Progress Publishers, 1977).
— and Engels, F., *On Colonialism*, (Progress Publishers, 1969).
Lenin, V. I., *The Development of Capitalism in Russia*, (Progress Publishers, 1974).
—, *Imperialism: The Highest Stage of Capitalism*, (Progress Publishers, 1970).

The following are also of considerable relevance:

Kemp, T., *Theories of Imperialism*, (Dobson Books Ltd, 1967).
Althusser, L., *For Marx*, (Allen Lane, 1970).
Melotti, Umberto, *Marx and the Third World*, (Macmillan Press, 1977).
Moore, Jr, Barrington, *Social Origins of Dictatorship and Democracy*, (Penguin Books, 1966).
Bettelheim, C., *The Transition to Socialist Economy*, (Harvester Press, 1975).
—, *Economic Calculation and Forms of Property*, (Routledge Direct Edition, 1976).

In any attempt to keep pace with the growing radical and marxist literature on the third world the following journals must be considered indispensable:

Review of African Political Economy, (London).

Africa Development, (Dakar).
The African Review, (Dar-es-Salaam).
Journal of Contemporary Asia, (London).
Journal of Peasant Studies, (London).
Transition, (Georgetown).

From time to time important contributions in debates on the third world are to be found in the following journals:

New Left Review, (London).
Socialist Register, (London).
Kapitalistate, (Warwick).
Journal of Development Studies, (London).

Index